MANAGING

Systems and IT Projects

Frank Tsui
Southern Polytechnic State University

JONES & BARTLETT
LEARNING

World Headquarters
Jones & Bartlett Learning
40 Tall Pine Drive
Sudbury, MA 01776
978-443-5000
info@jblearning.com
www.jblearning.com

Jones & Bartlett Learning
Canada
6339 Ormindale Way
Mississauga, Ontario L5V 1J2
Canada

Jones & Bartlett Learning
International
Barb House, Barb Mews
London W6 7PA
United Kingdom

Jones & Bartlett Learning books and products are available through most bookstores and online booksellers. To contact Jones & Bartlett Learning directly, call 800-832-0034, fax 978-443-8000, or visit our website, www.jblearning.com.

Substantial discounts on bulk quantities of Jones & Bartlett Learning publications are available to corporations, professional associations, and other qualified organizations. For details and specific discount information, contact the special sales department at Jones & Bartlett Learning via the above contact information or send an email to specialsales@jblearning.com.

Production Credits
Publisher: Cathleen Sether
Senior Acquisitions Editor: Timothy Anderson
Associate Editor: Melissa Potter
Production Director: Amy Rose
Senior Production Editor: Katherine Crighton
Production Assistant: Lindsey Jones
Senior Marketing Manager: Andrea DeFronzo
V.P., Manufacturing and Inventory Control: Therese Connell
Cover and Title Page Design: Kristin E. Parker
Composition: Northeast Compositors, Inc.
Cover Image: top © Kts/Dreamstime.com; bottom left © Madartists/Dreamstime.com; center © Madartists/Dreamstime.com; middle right © Aleksander Radovanovic/Dreamstime.com; bottom right © Alexskopje/Dreamstime.com
Printing and Binding: Malloy, Inc.
Cover Printing: Malloy, Inc.

Library of Congress Cataloging-in-Publication Data
Tsui, Frank F.
Managing systems and IT projects / Frank Tsui.
p. cm.
Includes index.
ISBN-13: 978-0-7637-9061-5 (pbk.)
ISBN-10: 0-7637-9061-3 (ibid)
1. Computer software—Development—Management. 2. Project management. I. Title.
QA76.76.D47T783 2010
005.3068'8—dc22 2010026161

6048
Printed in the United States of America
14 13 12 11 10 10 9 8 7 6 5 4 3 2 1

This book is dedicated to
Teresa, Colleen, and Nick

Preface

Large projects have been with us since the beginning of civilization. Building the Egyptian Sphinx, or the Great Wall of China, required a complex set of skills, tasks, planning, and resources. These projects were completed with tremendous determination and somewhat "unlimited" resources. The control of these projects was done with more force than one can imagine today. Nevertheless, these projects still required the management of material, people, and time. Since these undertakings were sponsored by the rulers of the time, budget was not necessarily a limiting factor.

Today, we are faced with equally large and complex projects, such as the building of jets, aircraft carriers, skyscrapers, and software systems. The issues of managing material, people, and time remain the same. In addition, we must ensure that each project is completed within a budget. As opposed to the government- or monarchy-sponsored projects, most commercial projects are based on a business model that requires that a profit be made.

In the past 40 or so years, a new industry—the software industry—has grown from programs developed by one person in a garage to systems involving hundreds and thousands of people. Accordingly, the importance and necessity of applying project management skills to software systems and IT projects is also growing. In this book, we will study the management process, some specific management tasks, and the management skills necessary to complete large and complex projects that involve software.

I have both participated in and managed a variety of business applications and systems software projects. These projects required the efforts of teams that ranged from a few to hundreds of members, with life spans lasting from months to years. Through my experience with these software development and support projects, it became clear that software project management is not the same as software engineering. Software engineering is concerned with internal and external characteristics of software and the techniques used to attain those attributes. In contrast, software project management is concerned with the activities that must be planned and performed to achieve the previously established goals of a software project. Of course, it is an advantage for software project managers to have software engineering and direct programming experience.

The general concepts of software engineering and software project management—and the differences between them—are explored in more detail in the Introduction to this text.

This book is heavily influenced by my earlier book, *Managing Software Projects*; it focuses on the management aspects of software projects and is also influenced by my own experiences with managing large, complex software projects for IBM, MARCAM, Metamor/PSINet, and River Logic. My early experiences with software development and support for RCA and Blue Cross Blue Shield Association also helped shape my thinking as a project manager.

Organization of the Book

In this text, the discussion of project management flow follows a project through four management phases: *planning, organizing, monitoring,* and *adjusting* (POMA). This four-phase process is adapted specifically to software projects—that is, the discussions and applications all center on software projects and the software industry. For example, in the discussions of personnel, recruiting, and organizational structures, the book focuses on software developers, recruiting problems associated with the software industry, and software development and support organizations.

Part One looks at software project planning (the "P" in POMA). Chapter 1 examines the project content and deliverables, highlighting the requirements the development process used to define the desired end result of the software project. Chapter 2 discusses software project task planning using a technique called the Work Breakdown Structure (WBS). The establishment of meaningful goals and measurements for software projects is outlined in Chapter 3. Chapter 4 explores the planning required for the software project resources, which include people, processes, and tools. Every project has some risks; the identification, prioritization, and mitigation of those risks related to software projects are presented in Chapter 5.

Part Two reflects on the approved project plan and focuses on organizing (the "O" in POMA) the software project. The three chapters in this part all relate to preparing and organizing the different resources needed for the project. Chapter 6 covers the recruiting of human resources and highlights several software organizational structures that are applicable to different types of tasks. Chapter 7 discusses the timing and introduction of software processes, techniques, and tools. Implementation of planned measurements and the corresponding setup effort are explained in Chapter 8.

Part Three covers the monitoring aspects (the "M" in POMA) of a software project once the project is organized and set into motion. The mechanisms and methodologies of collecting project status information are discussed in Chapter 9. Chapter 10 introduces several data analysis and evaluation techniques, such as those for correlating information, analyzing the distribution of data, and normalizing data. The gathered and evaluated information must be presented in a meaningful way to ensure effective project monitoring, so Chapter 11 highlights a variety of information representation and communication techniques, including Pareto, pie, and control charts.

Part Four emphasizes the need for adjustments (the "A" in POMA) to a software project; such adjustments are always necessary because of the impossibility of developing a perfect project plan and performing project preparation and organization flawlessly. The specific action taken will, of course, depend on the monitored project status information. Chapter 12 proposes changes in schedule, functionality, and resources as the three main adjustments to a software project. The Release Management Council, a mechanism to assist management in project control and implementation of project adjustments, is described in Chapter 13.

The final part, Part Five, examines several skills that can enhance one's performance in conducting the four POMA phases. Chapter 14 considers the most important factor in any software project: the people who make up the software project team, and their transformation from a group of individuals into a cohesive unit working toward a common goal. Chapter 15 addresses the problem of software project scope expansion, or scope creep, and considers how it may be controlled and managed. Chapter 16 offers a detailed discussion of task scheduling. These scheduling techniques are applicable to the WBS; thus this chapter is a good complement to Chapter 2. Chapter 17 covers software project estimation, which is a cornerstone of setting realistic cost and schedule goals. Chapter 18 discusses a specific project monitoring technique, Earned Value Management (EVM) method, which was initially used in government and military projects. It is now gaining popularity in many businesses and commercial sectors. Chapter 19 covers the increasingly important topic of Procurement and Acquisition of resources.

A recurring theme throughout the book is the importance of measurement. Without collection and analysis of data gleaned through measurements, it is very difficult to manage large, complex projects. The software systems industry has been slow to adopt this philosophy, but needs to before it can improve its odds of completing software projects and meeting the goals of schedule, budget, quality, functionality, performance, and customer delight.

Intended Audience and Suggested Teaching Plan

This book is written for several audiences:

- Software engineers and technical leaders who are contemplating, or who are in the process of, making career changes to software project management
- Mature undergraduate and first-year graduate students in information technology (IT) and software project management
- Non-IT management personnel who are considering a career redirection to IT and software project management

In the past, I have used draft versions of this book for both upper-level undergraduate and first-year graduate level courses in software project management. Parts One through Four and selected chapters from Part Five were used as a one-semester course. Depending on the interests and backgrounds of the students, either the set of Chapters 14 and 15 or the set of Chapters 16, 17, and 18 was included. Chapter 19 may be included with either set.

Each chapter includes several exercises to stimulate the students' thinking, as well as a Suggested Reading list. More advanced students should be encouraged to consult the resources on the reading list and explore topics that pique their interest. If term papers are assigned as part of the course requirements, the Suggested Reading lists should serve as good starting points in finding reference materials.

Acknowledgments

In putting together this book, I received direct and indirect help from numerous individuals. As a result of their generosity, many mistakes were corrected and parts of the book were greatly improved. Any remaining errors are solely my own.

The comments from my students at Southern Polytechnic State University (SPSU) were greatly appreciated. I would especially like to thank Hans Reichgelt, the Dean of the School of Computing and Software Engineering at SPSU, and Lisa Rossbacher, the president of SPSU, for providing such a supportive environment, which allowed me to carry out my writing.

I would like to thank Tim Anderson, Melissa Potter, and Lindsey Jones at Jones & Bartlett Learning for their suggestions and help.

Lastly, it was my wife, Teresa, who suggested that I should write down the lessons learned from my 30-plus years of experience in software development and project management. I would like to thank Teresa, my daughter Colleen, and my son Nicholas for their constant and unwavering encouragement.

Frank Tsui

Contents

Introduction

What Is Software Project Management?

In this book we focus on systems and IT projects that are primarily concerned with software development, evolution, and support. Software systems differ from building skyscrapers and automobiles, in that they do not require physical materials. It is a logical construction. Software systems have presented us with a surprising amount of project challenges.

Through the years, the Standish Group has been releasing, in their *Chaos* summary reports, relatively low success rates of software system and IT projects. In its 1995 report, the Standish Group estimated that 31% of the projects would fail and 53% would face cost overruns. This failure rate has improved through the years. However, in its 2009 *Chaos* summary report, the Standish Group stated that there is a recent "marked decrease" in project success rate. Only 32% of all projects succeed in delivering on time, within budget, and with completed functionalities and features. (Please see "Standish Group" in the Suggested Reading section.)

There are numerous horror stories of systems and IT projects that have failed. In the March 2005 issue of *US News & World Report*, it was reported that the FBI's "Virtual Case File" system had to be "junked" after four years of effort and a cost of $170 million. Although there were many causes, a large part of the failure was due to the software component not performing. It would be so easy to just place all the blame on the software. But one must also question how the project managers allowed so much money, effort, and time to be spent on this project before "junking" it. Where was the management control?

Several years ago, the computing systems and management community recognized the challenges presented by systems projects, which included large, complex software. At a 1968 NATO conference, the attendees coined the term, "software engineering" and started the formalization of the concept of software development. Is there something special and unique about these systems and IT projects that involve a large amount of software? Is managing the development of a software system—a nonphysical product—intrinsically different from managing the development of physical products, such as the manufacturing of automobiles? In this Introduction we will explore and delineate some key concepts related to the following:

- software project
- software engineering
- software project management process

SOFTWARE PROJECT

Software and *software projects* may not be clearly defined, in that there is no accepted "standard" set of deliverables to be produced at the end of a software project. Rather, software, in its barest form, is just code that is a set of instructions to a device, possibly a computing device, to perform a desired set of functions. These instructions may take the form of a source program or executable code. In this book, we will use the terms "code" and "program" interchangeably. All other components of a software project are designed to ensure that the code meets three criteria:

1. It executes properly as measured against the users' requirements and the developers' design.
2. It is maintainable and extensible.
3. It is easily installable and usable.

Code A set of instructions to a device, possibly a computing device, to perform a desired set of functions.

For a long time, many people considered only the code part of a software project to be important. That is, the main focus of many projects was the actual code produced; engineers were primarily interested in how quickly they could develop code and did not concern themselves with supporting the code over the longer term. Then as support activities started to become a problem, software developers began to focus on improving programs by creating software that is easily readable, understandable, and changeable. With the explosive growth of affordable PCs and other devices, it became critical that the user interface portion of the code be easily comprehensible by many different people, including those with very little technical training.

Today, the most important task of a software project is still considered to be the development of the programming aspect. Indeed, programming is typically the first course that a software engineering or computer science student takes in school.

Software Artifacts

There is, however, a growing appreciation of the need to include requirements specifications, design documents, user help texts, test cases, reference manuals, and other materials created to support the code—collectively known as *software artifacts*—as part of a broader definition of software. As the definition of software broadens, so does the interest in activities that produce these extended artifacts. Nevertheless, with the exception of requirements specification documents or user manuals, most software organizations rarely deliver elements independent of the actual code.

In this book, we will define a software artifact as the computer program itself, in source or executable form, or any entity that is produced to aid in the development of, installation of, demonstration of, training of, or maintenance of that program. Thus requirements documents, design documents, project plans, test scenarios, user guides or manuals, reference manuals, online help materials, educational and marketing materials, initialization data, and other materials developed along with the code are all considered software artifacts. Some software artifacts are developed as deliverables to the customers and end users. Others are developed only to satisfy internal needs and may never be delivered to end users.

Software artifact A unit of material, in the form of a document, presentation, or code, that is developed as a part of, or as a contribution to, the final solution to the users.

Code Versus Noncode Software Artifacts

Software artifacts may or may not be associated with a specific set of code. A key point is that these noncode artifacts are considered to be software only if a specific set of code directly related to that artifact is eventually developed.

Software A set of software artifacts that includes code.

Requirements specifications for a system are sometimes presented as the sole software deliverable. A requirements specifications document outlines the needs of the users and details the desired functional behavior of the system solution that is to satisfy the users' needs. A requirements document is often used as the sole software deliverable when a project group is preparing to solicit others for proposals of potential solutions. For example, a government organization might ask a group of "experts" to develop a set of requirements for a specific system and then use that requirements document to seek solutions from commercial vendors. Similarly, a large commercial enterprise might ask a consulting firm to develop a requirements document for a needed system, and the document would be used to solicit proposals. In both of these cases, the initial deliverable is a document that does not include code. Many people, however, still consider the requirements document to be software. Others argue that the requirements document is really part of the broader set of software deliverables and should not be considered software itself.

Should a document that only describes the requirements of a system be considered software? Does the software solution have to include code? For the purpose of the discussion here, we will consider a requirements document to be software only if it describes a system that includes code as a part of the final set of deliverables. Thus, a requirements document for a soccer field will not be considered software, but a requirements document for a soccer scoring system, which includes programs, will be considered software. This distinction allows us to narrow our domain of coverage and continue to look at the unique qualities of software.

If the plan to develop the code is later eliminated for some reason, then the requirements document by itself is *not* considered software. For example, if a person writes a book on the generic requirements or generic design of a payroll system, then that book is not considered software. The requirements document for a specific, running payroll system, however, *is* considered software. Similarly, a paper describing a B-tree algorithm is not considered software unless it describes the algorithm used by and accompanying a specific code implementation.

As noted above, an independent requirements document that describes the characteristics of a system that includes code is itself considered software. Is there anything unique about this type of requirements document? The answer is yes, in that this document must depict the desired characteristics and behavior of a nonphysical entity—the code or programs. Such a description is inherently more difficult to develop than something that describes a physical entity, which can be seen, touched, or felt and thus is more easily measured. The requirements document attempts to portray something that is abstract and logical and thus very difficult to measure. When asked about the size of a program (a nonphysical entity), the conventional response is to ask whether one wants that information in the form of lines of code, in function points, or in some other metric—there is no industry standard for this measurement. When one asks about the size of a soccer field (a physical entity), however, the answer is readily given in units of square feet or square yards, which everyone understands. This characteristic is an extremely important distinction between that which deals with code versus that which deals with physical entities that have standard metrics and are easily measurable. The significant difference is that software addresses logical entities.

SOFTWARE ENGINEERING

Software engineering includes a set of general knowledge and specific skills that are applied to the activities that are used to develop, produce, and support all types of software artifacts—not just code artifacts. Software engineers also study properties of the internal structure of software and the resulting effects of structural changes to the external attributes of the software. The knowledge and skills applied to a specific activity are known as a *method* of developing that artifact. In this case, a method is a formal procedure for producing a specific software artifact.

> **Software engineering** The art and science of developing and applying a body of knowledge and methods to the creation and support of software artifacts that will satisfy the requirements of the users. Besides functional requirements, these user and customer requirements may also include constraints such as cost, schedule, and usability.

Several different methods may be utilized to develop a particular software artifact. For example, there are many ways to design a software system. In designing a system, one may use some combination of decomposition, synthesis, and abstraction, each of which is a design method:

- *Decomposition* is the breaking down of a complex problem into smaller pieces that can be better understood and solved.
- *Synthesis* is the creation of a component from smaller pieces.
- *Abstraction* is the hiding and postponing of the details to focus on the essentials.

Similarly, there are many ways to describe the design of a system. A method that is used to design a system, such as decomposition, may not be the same method that one would use to describe that design, such as the Unified Modeling Language (UML). UML is a modeling language for software that was put forward by James Rumbaugh, Ivar Jacobson, and Grady Booch of Rational Software, which was recently acquired by IBM.

Unified Modeling Language (UML) A set of graphical languages used to model a system; it provides a set of notations for depicting the objects, relationships, and rules of a system.

In some instances, the designing method and the describing method may be the same and are both part of a larger family of methods. A family of methods, such as the object-oriented (OO) methodology, may be quite complex and require multiple submethods. These complex methods may take years to master. Sometimes a method or a portion of a method may be borrowed from some other discipline. In generating a test scenario matrix, for example, we often utilize Boolean algebra to logically combine certain test cases with the Boolean OR or AND operators. Similarly, in designing user interfaces, we often seek guidance from psychology and cognitive science. For example, the flow of the application, as represented by the depth and number of screens, often reflects considerations related to the end user's productivity. In addition, certain icons are easily recognizable, whereas others are more cryptic. Thus, software engineering is a multidisciplinary field that borrows many methods from other established disciplines.

Software Process and Methodology

The sequencing and ordering of the activities that are used to develop specific software artifacts are another important aspect of software engineering. The definition of the sequence or order of the activities, along with the entrance and the exit criteria of these activities, is considered the software development process.

Several well-known software development processes exist, such as the waterfall process and the spiral process. The waterfall process was first depicted by Winston Royce in 1970. It models a set of software development activities in the form of a cascading waterfall, where the first activity, such as the requirements-gathering activity, is at the top. When this activity is completed, the next activity is started. Each activity is performed sequentially until the last activity is completed. Barry Boehm introduced the spiral process in 1988 with the intention of reducing project risks. The spiral process takes every activity through four phases: planning, setting goals and alternatives, evaluation of alternatives, and developing activities. For example, a requirements specification activity will go through all four phases, starting with planning for the requirements specification. The descriptions of such processes are often at such a generic or high level as to make them broadly—but not easily—applicable.

Software engineering as a discipline is still relatively young compared to other engineering disciplines. Both the process descriptions and the descriptions of the specific methods utilized in the activities of producing the software artifacts are still being developed. Currently, various forms of incremental and agile processes are being developed and used. In fact, the software engineering process has not reached a level of maturity that is comparable to the maturity of processes in other engineering disciplines, such as chemical engineering. In a chemical engineering process, every ingredient is well defined; every procedural step is well defined in terms of temperature, action, and length of time; and every outcome is well defined.

Besides the purely technical aspects of process and methods, many other environmental and human parameters go into a process. A key factor in the success of a software process, for example, is the person who is conducting the activities within the process. Software projects are heavily dependent on people. A well-trained and motivated person can bring a very different result than an ill-trained and unhappy person. These environmental and organizational parameters vary widely among software projects.

A software development or support process is often treated as a guideline; often the organization can modify and adapt it as needed. The specific adaptations made by different organizations have been quite mixed and can be unpredictable. Because of this unpredictability, many organizations choose not to adopt any process. Instead, they practice and concentrate on the limited set of methods related to low-level design, coding, and debugging activities. For small projects that require only two or three people for six months or less, developing software under the guidance of a heroic leader without a well-defined process may sometimes work. For any large, complex project, however, experience shows that some form of process must be defined, related, and practiced by the complete organization. Also, if the organization is focusing on certain design attributes and properties, such as ease of use, then specific methods such as the user interface (UI) design method must be rigorously defined to satisfy the ease of use attribute. We not only need to have well-defined methods and processes, but these defined methods and processes must also be enforced by the organization. What we do not yet have is a set of "prescriptive" processes for developing different types of software.

Components of Software Engineering

Figure I.1 is a software engineering diagram that depicts three interrelated subjects:

- Process and methodologies
- Desired internal product structure and properties
- Desired external product properties

In software engineering we are interested not only in studying the various methodologies and processes, but also in applying them to produce the desired product internal structure and properties, which in turn will provide the required external product properties. The software engineering diagram in Figure I.1 does not enforce any particular sequence; instead, it simply shows the interrelationships among the components.

Software Product Life Cycle

Software engineering also encompasses the notion of a software product life cycle, which is closely related to the idea of a software process. Software is viewed as a logical entity that evolves through various stages, taking on different artifact forms.

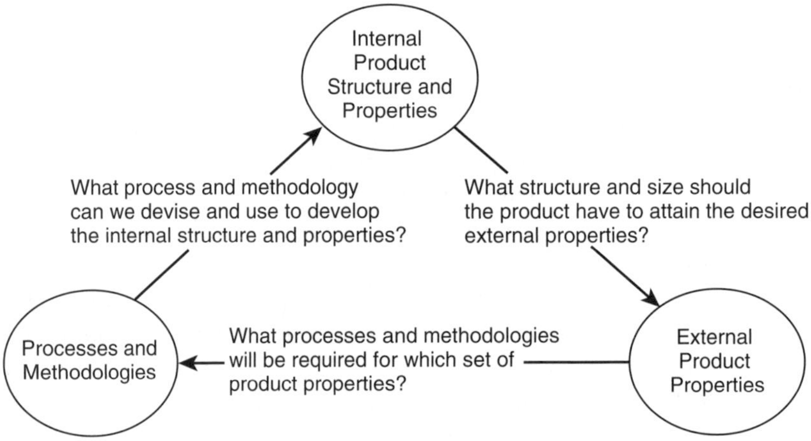

Figure I.1 Software engineering

Initially, software is just a concept stated in the form of customer needs and desires. This "wish list" evolves into a requirements specifications document as the project moves through the requirements solicitation and analysis phase of the process. Next, the software is transformed into different levels of design, depending on the amount of design activities. The design is eventually turned into an executable solution, which includes code, documentation, database setups, and operating environment setups. Simultaneously, the software artifacts are "tested" and modified through a series of mini-transformations and corrections. The software is then installed at the customers' and users' environments as Release 1. This set of activities and transformations represents the software development life cycle.

Figure I.2 shows a time line of the software product life cycle.

Software development life cycle A set of transformations, starting with requirements, that converts each incoming software artifact into an artifact closer to the final result, until the final set of artifacts that satisfy the requirements are met.

Next, the software product moves through a support phase featuring further corrections, adjustments, and enhancements. Each subsequent release may move through another software development life cycle. Eventually, the software will enter a sunset phase and be removed from the user and support environment. The complete cycle–starting with software development, going through *n* releases of the software product, and continuing until the product is ultimately withdrawn–is called the software product life cycle. The product life may encompass one or more iterations of the software development life cycle in the form of multiple releases.

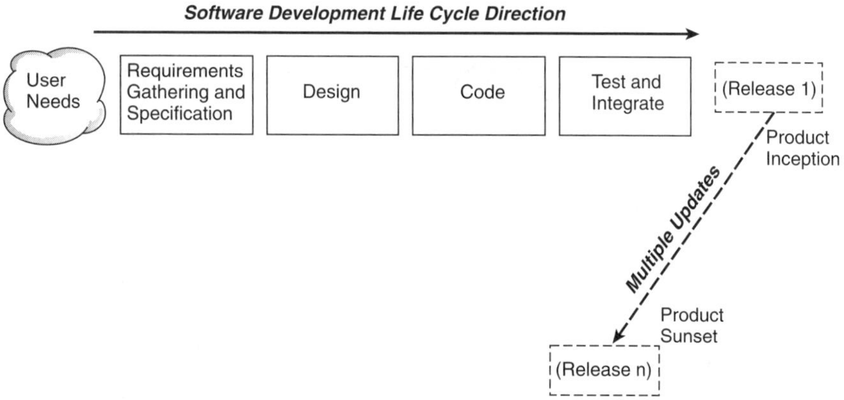

Figure I.2 Software product life cycle

Software product life cycle A period during which a software artifact is initially developed, supported, revised through multiple development life cycles, and finally unsupported and/or taken out of the market.

THE SOFTWARE PROJECT MANAGEMENT PROCESS

Software project management involves the application of good management practices to the development and support of software. By necessity, it is a multidisciplinary subject.

In terms of Figure I.1, software project management is concerned with ensuring that, for a software project, the most appropriate process and methodologies are chosen, the desired internal product structure is attained, and the external product properties are achieved. In addition, the project management constraints of schedule, budget, and resources must be met.

In terms of Figure I.2, software project management may be viewed as applying sufficient resources to ensure that the software artifacts evolve in a manner such that:

- They meet all the product functional and other requirements.
- They are developed within the cost constraints.
- They are developed within the allotted schedule.

Satisfying the product requirements, budgetary, and schedule constraints is the essence of project management. Because software projects heavily depend on the availability of human resources, software project management also requires people management.

POMA: THE PHASES OF SOFTWARE PROJECT MANAGEMENT

Software project management, much like other project management, has four major phases, called POMA:

Planning
Organizing
Monitoring
Adjusting

The POMA management process, as shown in Figure I.3, starts with the planning of tasks and moves through the remaining categories of project

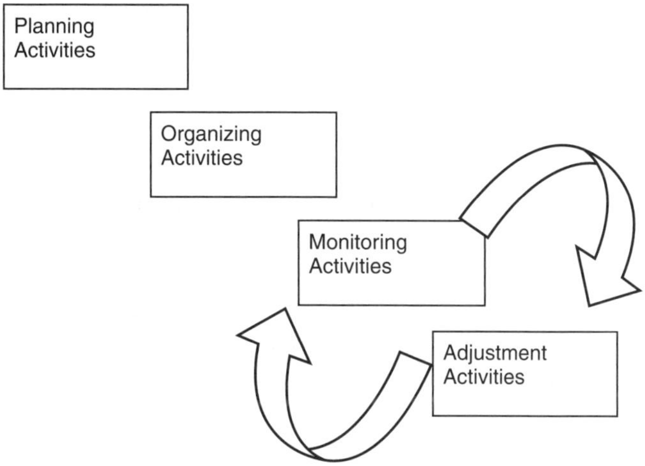

Figure I.3 The POMA management process

management activities. Unlike software engineering, which begins with a development and support process and then applies management to that process, POMA starts with management and applies software engineering's domain-specific knowledge, such as a requirements solicitation method or software measurement method, at various stages along the way. POMA models the software management life cycle much as a waterfall software process models the software development life cycle.

Note that the activities in the four process categories of POMA are not necessarily sequential. Some activities within each category may overlap, and the categories themselves may overlap. For example, the monitoring and adjustment categories are most likely to iterate. In this iteration between monitoring and adjustment, the project manager may adjust the original plan, the original organization, or both.

Planning

Software project planning consists of a set of activities that will develop a plan of attack for the project. The project plan contains the following items:

- The description of the software product in the form of software artifact contents and deliverables
- The software product attributes
- The schedule required to complete the project

- The types of and amount of resources needed to meet the project schedule
- The relevant measurements that would be used to gauge the status of the software project and to assess the final project "success"
- The risks associated with the project

Project planning includes a time-consuming and very important set of tasks that is, unfortunately, often rushed. It is much wiser to spend the appropriate time needed to develop a good plan initially than to have to make multiple and costly adjustments later. Even with a well-conceived plan, it is unusual not to encounter some conditions that require unexpected changes during the project. However, having a well-thought-out plan facilitates making project adjustments even at a much later phase.

Organizing

Software project organization seeks to construct a software development, support, and service organization based on the project plan. To build and implement the software project organization, several activities are undertaken: acquiring the various skilled individuals needed for the project, defining a process and a set of methodologies that will be utilized for the software project, obtaining a set of tools that will support the process and the methodologies, and creating a well-defined set of metrics that will be used to track and gauge the project.

A significant portion of the task of organizing activities is ensuring that all personnel brought on board are properly equipped to perform their designated tasks. This equipping of personnel includes obtaining needed tools and preparing facilities for initiation of the project, and it also includes educating the personnel in using those tools, the methodology selected, and the metrics chosen.

In addition, as part of the organizing activities, project managers need to ensure that adequate financial funding has been set aside and will be made available in a timely manner. Thus, the software project management team must either include financial management and personnel management members or have well-defined interfaces with these other organizations. Just like any organizational interface, the software project organization relies on human relationships that need to be established, nurtured, and maintained. The "people management" aspect of organizing is critically important; managers should always be cognizant of the fact that the morale of the organization affects its productivity.

Monitoring

Software project monitoring focuses on the following activities:

- Consistently and regularly collecting project status information
- Analyzing the data
- Representing and presenting the data for a defined set of reports
- Making projections and making recommendations based on the analysis of the data

Software project management, like any other project management situation, involves a heavy dosage of "people" management. Therefore, the project monitoring component must include the soft art of both physically and virtually "walking around the hallway" and tapping into day-to-day issues, concerns, and morale.

Adjusting

Adjustments and changes are a very important set of activities for software project managers. It is a rare situation in which we can develop a perfect plan and put together a perfect organization. Most of the time, we will need to make mid-course adjustments, sometimes several times. The monitoring of projects ensures that the correct adjustments can be made at a relatively early stage in the development process. In a situation that is often encountered, the design of a software artifact is found to have a high number of errors that are attributable to unclear requirements. In this situation, the software project managers might need to commission a rework on the requirements and ask for adjustments in the project schedule, resources, or content. For a software project manager to make adjustments, he or she must first recognize the need for making a change—and the risks of not doing so. Then a potential set of adjustments must be available, along with some prioritization scheme.

Unfortunately, during the course of a project many adjustments might be needed, for example, because of the loss of a skilled team member or the discovery of an unfeasible design. Adjustments and changes are often made under pressure and in uncomfortable conditions. Nevertheless, project managers must have the courage to stand up and take action. Sometimes even changes to the original plan or organizational structure are required. Later, the software project managers must continue to monitor the project after the appropriate adjustments are made. If the information from the monitoring activities dictates that further adjustments and modifications are needed, then the software project managers must make these additional changes. This potentially extensive, iterative process continues until the project is completed.

POMA at All Management Levels

All managers at different levels are involved in the four major activity categories of POMA. The difference is merely the degree to which they are involved.

Higher-level managers, including executives, tend to be more intimately involved in establishing the general plans and overall organization of the project. As a consequence, they tend to focus more on the planning and the organizing portions of POMA.

Middle managers are involved in building more specific project plans and specific organizations. They also participate in monitoring project status and help in making adjustments. These managers are the management "work horses" in that they are involved equally heavily in all four categories of project management.

Lower-level managers and project leaders perform daily project monitoring and devise instant adjustments, if they become necessary. Although these first-line managers and project leaders play important roles in higher-level planning and organizing, most of the time they focus more intently on planning and organizing just their portion of the project responsibilities. The lower-level managers therefore tend to concentrate on the monitoring and adjustment categories of POMA.

In tackling the four categories of POMA, software project managers utilize various techniques. The combination of monitoring and making adjustments is often viewed as controlling a project. The description and application of these management techniques, as they apply to software development and support for the different stages of POMA, form the heart of this book.

KEY CONCEPTS

This overview discussed three interrelated concepts: software projects, software engineering, and software project management. Following are some of the key concepts introduced:

- Software project
- Software artifacts

- Software engineering
- Software process
- Software development and software product life cycles
- Software project management
- POMA and management hierarchy

The remainder of the book will focus on the four phases of POMA–planning, organizing, monitoring, and adjusting–along with the techniques and methods needed for each phase.

EXERCISES

1. Define *software* in your own words.
2. Describe a computer program that will allow two players to play the game of tic-tac-toe without ever mentioning the word "tic-tac-toe."
3. Describe the attributes that the tic-tac-toe program described in Exercise 2 should have.
4. What is a software development life cycle and how does that differ from a software product life cycle?
5. Compare and contrast the concepts of software engineering and software project management.
6. Which level of management tends to focus more on the monitoring and adjustment phases of a software project and why?
7. Describe two situations that you believe would cause adjustments to a software project.
8. Assume that you are a software project manager and are approached by a potential customer who wants you to build a tic-tac-toe software program. Explain the planning, organizing, monitoring, and adjusting activities that you may have to go through.

SUGGESTED READING

P. F. Drucker, "They're Not Employees," *Harvard Business Review,* February 2002, 70–77.

R. S. Pressman, *Software Engineering: A Practitioner's Approach,* McGraw-Hill, 1997.

W. Royce, *Software Project Management: A Unified Framework,* Addison Wesley Longman, 1998.

I. Sommerville, *Software Engineering,* Addison-Wesley, 2001.

The Standish Group Report, *Chaos,* 1995.

The Standish Group Report, "Chaos Summary 2009," 2009.

H. Weihrich, "Management: Science, Theory, and Practice," *Software Engineering Project Management,* 2nd ed., edited by Richard H. Thayer, IEEE Computer Society, 1997, 4–13.

E. Yourdon, *Death March: The Complete Software Developer's Guide to Surviving "Mission Impossible" Projects,* Prentice Hall, 1999.

Part One

Software Project Planning (POMA)

Software project planning consists of a set of activities that set the tone for the rest of the project. If time is not taken up front and the planning of the software project is sloppy, then the software project will likely fail. Having a great plan does not ensure that no problems will arise during the course of the project, but the chance of solving the problems or recovering from damage is much better.

A TEAM EFFORT

Systems and IT projects, which include large and complex software are especially prone to marginal planning effort. This may be due to the earlier mentioned software characteristics. Software is a logical entity which is also viewed as easily modifiable and thus does not need careful planning.

The software project manager should not perform the software project planning tasks in isolation. Rather, the software project plan should be formulated with the cooperation of as many of the stakeholders as possible. The plan must also be reviewed by all stakeholders, understood by all stakeholders, and agreed to by all stakeholders.

The software project manager should be aware of–and sometimes even participate in the formulation of–the "justification" of the project, but at times the project manager may just be "told" of the justification. These justifications–such as improving customer satisfaction, improving business performance, and reducing complexity–are all very important to know and should be part of the goals and objectives as the software project plan is formulated. But there is a reason for caution here: The information technology (IT) world is full of new technology, advancements in process, and attractive concept justifications that may not be thoroughly understood. Thus, software project managers in the IT industry can easily become caught up in the emotion of the moment and embark on questionable projects.

The software project managers are responsible for thoroughly understanding the project justifications, translating them into measurable goals, and articulating them clearly in the project plan. It is only when the project managers openly include the justifications as part of the plan will these justifications be properly converted into achievable goals. The word "openly" is chosen deliberately to further emphasize the danger of having "hidden" or "obscure" justifications.

PLAN CONTENT

The content and the depth of a software project plan may differ depending on the type of software project. Ultimately, all project plans must address a set of common issues:

- What is the nature of the software project, how does it fit into the overall system, and what software artifacts are the desired deliverables?
- What is the overall schedule and the associated major project milestones?
- What are the required resources and their associated financial costs?
- What are the known risks and the areas that are still unknown?

For each of these issues, many subcategories may exist. The level of depth within each subcategory may also vary within the plan. For example, for a software development organization that is in the service business of outsourcing other organizations' software development, it may be important to delve more deeply while planning for well-organized processes, well-defined methodologies, and well-trained software engineers as part of the required resources section of the plan. At the same time, issues related to costs and schedules for a software outsourcing project may receive the same amount of emphasis as they do in other types of software projects.

In addition, the number of subcategories and the level of depth may depend on the type of plan that is required. Many times, software engineers are asked to develop an initial, quick plan solely for the purpose of developing early estimates of the project's size and scope. This plan may need to be available within days. In other situations, software engineers may be asked to develop a complex and thorough plan in response to a well-defined set of requirements set forth in a formal request for proposal (RFP). Such a plan may require weeks, and possibly months, to prepare.

One critical issue in all software projects is the management of quality. To handle this issue properly, the attribute of *quality* must first be clearly defined. Chapter 3 includes an extensive discussion of this attribute. The project plan must state the metrics to be used and the measurement methodologies to be employed to collect and analyze those software quality metrics. These and other important attributes and items need to be analyzed and stated in the form of the project's "goals." Each goal must be quantifiable or it will be difficult to track and manage. For this reason, the software project plan may need to include a section that clearly articulates the key goals of the project along with a metric for each of these goals.

LEVELS OF PLANNING

Even though there may be several levels of planning for any given project, essentially two levels of planning exist for all projects: the quick estimate and the comprehensive plan. Both of these planning tasks require some experience, and it is difficult for a new project manager to perform all the tasks by himself or herself. For example, just coming up with a reasonable list of software project risks requires some past experience.

Quick Estimate

A quick estimate often includes just the following items:

- A brief description of the problem and the project
- The deliverables needed to satisfy the project
- A high-level schedule that contains only a few major milestone dates with the associated deliverables
- A single, rolled-up resource and cost estimate
- A summary of risks and assumptions

Even for the quick estimates, there needs to be some amount of buffering since every project carries a certain level of risk. At the same time, the project plan still needs to be competitive in cost and schedule.

Comprehensive Plan

A more comprehensive plan would not only expand on the items listed in the quick estimate, but also broaden the list itself as follows:

- *Problem and Requirements:* a discussion of the customer and user problems, needs, and wishes along with characterizations of the different users.
- *Product/Project Description:* the complete scope of the project, which includes all project deliverables, a functional list, and a description of each deliverable.
- *Product/Project Attributes:* a description of the various attributes of the deliverables and the nondeliverables as they pertain to the goals of the project; these attributes must be measurable and will be used in the designing of metrics.
- *Schedule:* the sequence of tasks required to produce deliverables, along with the resources required and the relevant milestone dates.
- *Costs:* cost details given in terms of some unit, such as person-days, for each deliverable. The costs must include all other expenditures–such as those for tools, travel, training, and communications–attributed to the project.
- *Resources:* a detailed list of the people needed and the special skills that they must possess, a complete set of needed tools, any special training and ongoing information updates, and all hardware and software systems required to support the project.
- *Process and Methods:* a description of the overall process and each method to be used to accomplish the various tasks within each phase of the process. A description of the level of competency, in terms of training or years of experience, for each of the methods should be stated.
- *Risks:* a list of potential problems, with weights assigned to them based on their assessed impact and probability of occurrence. The plan should also detail actions that might help keep the risk from turning into a real problem.

Chapter 1

Project Content and Deliverables

Chapter Objectives

This chapter discusses the following concepts:

- Why requirements elicitation, analysis, specification, and agreement should be completed prior to planning
- Why software project managers must ensure that project requirements—in the form of (1) the deliverables and (2) the characterization of the needs to be satisfied by those deliverables—are available and properly prioritized
- Why software project managers should focus their energy on requirements management and let the software engineers and analysts perform the requirements development

GATHERING AND ANALYZING PROJECT REQUIREMENTS

In his study of three decades of troubled defense industry projects, D. J. Reifer has categorized the root problem of these projects as mostly software and system related. A primary cause of the problems is poor understanding of the requirments. (Please see Common Risk Patterns by Reifer in the Suggested Reading section.)

Before any project can be initiated, systems and software engineers need to identify the requirements of the project, interfaces to the project, and any other related systems or subsystems. Software requirements are the needs and the wishes of the users and the customers that may be delivered as solutions in the form of software. Gathering the requirements for a software project is one of the most difficult tasks in software engineering. In this chapter, we will not delve into the methodology used to complete individual subtasks within a set of requirements management activities, but rather will discuss strategies for managing the requirements of a project from the project management perspective.

Software requirements The needs and the wishes of the users and the customers that may be delivered as solutions in the form of software.

The software project manager needs to provide an environment conducive to proper requirements gathering and analysis. There must be ample time and suitably skilled people available to perform these tasks. The actual performance and completion of the subtasks, the mode and effectiveness of operation, and the resulting specification of the requirements are the concerns of the software project managers. This responsibility should be shared with the software engineers and analysts who are assigned to perform those tasks, though the software engineers and managers perform different roles.

Potential Pitfalls

Surprisingly, a large number of software projects are commissioned without the client or project manager fully understanding the requirements. Of course, many of them pay a high price for this neglect later. The requirements specifications are critical for the success of a project. The first step in software project management is to recognize that the requirements must be understood and agreed upon by all parties. This seemingly very simple principle is often not applied in software projects. Many requirements are generated by the software engineers themselves during development without consulting anyone. This phenomenon of increasing requirements after the requirements specification is completed is known as "scope creep" in the IT industry. Because these implemented requirements are not familiar to anyone else, the testers will not know that these features exist and should be tested, and customers may be surprised by them. Due to the lack of testing, quality issues may arise concerning the code that has been developed for the unknown and non-agreed-upon requirements. There are many causes of this unfortunate situation, and they can be attributed to both the requirements providers and the solution providers.

The following list describes some reasons why the providers (the users and the customers) of a software project fail to make clear their requirements for a given project:

- The customers and users are not fully knowledgeable about their complete needs.

- The customers and users do not know how to express all of their requirements, especially when some aspects of software project requirements are highly abstract.
- The customers and users do not remember to include everything in their set of requirements.
- The customers and users are not consistent in their presentation of the requirements.
- The customers and users take the activity for granted and therefore do not interpret it as essential.

The solution providers (the requirements receivers, such as the software engineers, business analysts, and project leaders) may also be at fault, for the following reasons:

- The software solution providers misinterpret the requirements stated by the customers and users.
- The software solution providers do not understand the requirements because the particular subject and terminology used are new to them. (Unfortunately, some software solution providers think that they are knowledgeable about every field and every discipline.)
- The software solution providers are under pressure to "make the sale" and to seize the project even without fully understanding the requirements.
- The software solution providers believe that they have a generic solution that can fit most problems within a certain category and insist that they do not need to fully analyze the requirements of the particular case at hand.

There are many more ways in which the requirements might not be fully understood, fully documented, or fully analyzed. It is the software project managers' responsibility to recognize both the potential for problems and the implications of experiencing these problems. Software project management needs to establish a process and obtain the associated resources to ensure that the project requirements gathering, analysis, and documentation activities are satisfactorily completed. This process and the arrival at a complete and mutual agreement of the requirements must be part of the project plan.

Completing the Requirements Specification as a Separate Project

Sometimes, the initial software project plan focuses on the project requirements as the sole deliverable. Indeed, the completeness, accuracy, and clarity of the requirements specification are now recognized as such significant attributes that many software projects consider the requirements gathering, analysis, and documentation activities to constitute a separate project. This set of activities is planned and managed as a separate (and often separately priced) mini-project to be completed before the main project begins.

If the requirements development activities do constitute a separate project, then the project manager must ensure that this set of activities is planned, organized, monitored, adjusted, and brought to a successful completion. Clearly, the planning of this mini-project will not be as complex as that of the complete software project, but it is no less important. The planning steps for a set of requirements gathering and analysis activities (discussed later in this chapter) can be scaled down, but the planning for a mini-project, which is just a subset of the entire project, and the planning for the total project are not dramatically different. In other words, it is still necessary to state the requirements for the requirements- gathering project, albeit not to the same degree as for the complete software project.

GENERAL REQUIREMENTS MANAGEMENT ACTIVITIES

Consider Figure 1.1, which depicts the requirements gathering, analysis, and documentation activities. Only the areas that relate to managing this process will be discussed here. An in-depth discussion of the requirements process and the details of how each task is performed may be found in the software engineering books listed at the end of this chapter. Note that prototypes are sometimes constructed to better understand the requirements. Prototyping to clarify the requirements and to explore the technical feasibility of a project is itself a project that must be properly managed or it can turn into a never-ending activity. Managing prototyping will be discussed later in this section.

> **Software prototype** A software model created to represent a user interface or a function for the purpose of better understanding the requirements and the feasibility of the proposed solution.

One key problem that often hampers requirements gathering is a shortage of (or unavailability of) knowledgeable people. Often the key users and customers are the very same people who have the least amount of time to discuss requirements with the solution providers. For this reason, a project manager should participate in several steps depicted in Figure 1.1 to ensure that these activities are completed successfully. Occasionally, project man-

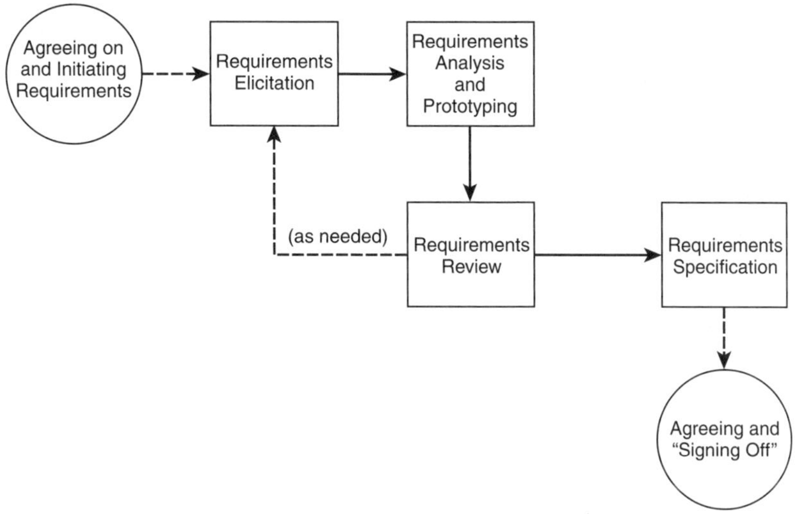

Figure 1.1 General requirements management activities

agers may need to directly intervene or even ask for upper-management assistance in order to meet the following goals:

- The initial agreement on requirements processing and the assignment of the qualified people to participate in the activities should be completed on a timely basis.
- The review of the requirements and the prototype should be conducted with a clear "end" in mind. All parties must initially agree on clear exit criteria as well.
- The final "sign-off" should be completed by all stakeholders.

Although the software project managers may sometimes need to intervene, they should allow the software engineers to actually perform the tasks depicted in Figure 1.1. The entrance and exit of each task are the points on which the project managers should focus their attention. As mentioned earlier, the reviewing of requirements statements and the prototyping efforts may potentially create a situation of never-ending modifications, extensions, and new additions to the requirements. In some cases, for example, in the absence of a clearly specified schedule, customers have asked for repeated viewing and reviewing of the user screen prototypes. Even though each review with different users may have improved the interfaces, the expended effort can greatly exceed the marginal gains made in the prototype.

To avoid this problem, clear exit criteria and the mode of operation for all activities must be defined and accepted by everyone right from the start.

In the case of prototyping, entrance criteria to that activity should also be carefully specified and fully enforced. The entrance criteria should include at least the following items:

- The availability of skilled resources
- The time frame and process for reviewing the prototype
- The overall prototype schedule
- The scope of the prototyping activity (e.g., just screens instead of fully operational programs)

The software project manager will often be asked to comment on his or her preference on the kind of prototype provided. There are two main types:

- A *rapid prototype* of the requirements that will eventually be thrown away
- *Iterative prototypes* of the requirements that may be kept as the early versions of the final product

For many managers, the notion of throwing away code seems so wasteful that it is extremely tempting to choose the iterative prototype approach. Nevertheless, one must remember that keeping the prototype carries a price. That is, the prototype code must be designed, documented, tested, controlled, and so on, just as the final code is. Thus the desired speed one can achieve in rapid prototyping is not available with iterative prototyping.

Only after the requirements are understood and analyzed can a description of the needs of the entire project be created. A list of the deliverables and a description of each deliverable are prerequisites to developing the remaining part of the software project plan. The requirements, once elicited and gathered, must be further analyzed for completeness, consistency, priority, and understandability.

TYPES OF REQUIREMENTS

The software project manager should recognize the two major types of requirements: the project deliverables and the needs satisfied by those deliverables.

Project Deliverables

The first set of requirements deals with the deliverables, the items provided to the client at the end of the project. What the project deliverables include must be clearly defined and agreed upon from the beginning. They can range from all the artifacts produced in the development of the software to only the executable object code. The following is a list of example artifacts that a software project might be asked to deliver:

- Requirements document
- Design document
- Source code
- Source message file
- Executable code
- Test scenarios
- Test cases with test data
- User guide
- Product reference manual
- Test results and quality-related data
- Process specifications
- Project plan

Each of these items must be defined in terms of its content, form, and format. For example, the requirements document could be as simple as a Microsoft Word file that is downloadable, while the user guide might consist of online HTML files that are titled separately by functional topic and made accessible through a Help icon on the toolbar. All of the artifacts must be prioritized, and a schedule for each one must be established. Resources must be assigned to develop each deliverable, and each artifact must be managed to its completion.

Note that some software enterprises, as part of their business practices, will not include certain deliverables. Source code is a primary example that many software enterprises do not deliver. There are many reasons for not wanting to deliver source code. An obvious one is related to the issue of intellectual property and the potential for the copying of the proprietary source code by others. Another source of angst is the possibility of uncontrolled, multiple modifications and extensions to the original source code made by others, which can turn the support effort into an expensive nightmare for the developer of the original deliverable.

Project Needs and Their Characterization

The second type of project requirements identifies the needs, characteristics, and constraints for which the software project must provide the solutions. This is the area on which most software engineers, rather than the project managers, would focus their energy. Clearly, the following items should be identified:

- The functions that the software must provide
- The performance and other nonfunctional constraints that the software must meet
- The business process into which the software must fit
- The interfaces that the software needs to interact with its users, and the appearance of those interfaces
- The interfaces that the software needs, to interact with other systems
- Characteristics of the data that the software solution must handle

All six of these categories describe "what" is needed. Although functional needs are commonly mentioned first in requirements gathering, the sequence in which they appear does not reflect any particular hierarchy. Indeed, their prioritization will differ by project.

An important question the software project managers will face is the decision of how to specify the requirements and how formally they should be specified. Here, we are not focusing on the technical merits of different requirements specification languages. Rather, the issue is quite nontechnical: Should the requirements be documented in the form of pseudo-English or something more formal, such as UML? This decision should normally be described and specified in the software development organization's requirements process. Because of the nature of the customers, however, a software development organization may sometimes have to revisit the decision stated in its process. Some customers are not sophisticated or trained in reading formal documents. The software project managers, in conjunction with the lead software engineers, may have to adjust the process as required.

Review and Approval of Requirements

The project manager needs to ensure that the first set of requirements (the deliverables) is clearly defined, understood, prioritized, and agreed upon by both the customer and the solution provider. To avoid potential problems and subsequent major disagreement, it is wise to have all parties formally "sign off" on the deliverables.

The same may be said about the second set of requirements (the needs and constraints). However, because the second set characterizes the details of various aspects of the project, it needs more than just a sign-off. It is strongly advisable to include a final review of the requirements specifications by the stakeholders prior to the sign-off. This requirements specifications review, if conducted, may range from somewhat formal to very formal. The software project management must determine the form of this review based on how some of the other activities in the requirements management process have fared so far. If defects were found in earlier, smaller-scale reviews or if a number of changes were made to the specifications during prototyping, then those data should be analyzed and considered in deciding how formal this final specification review should be.

INTERNAL REQUIREMENTS GENERATION AND PRIORITIZATION

Project requirements are sometimes initiated by solution providers internally. These are some of the most difficult requirements to evaluate. Oftentimes the key designer or the key marketer of an ongoing software product will make recommendations to be included for a subsequent release of software. The chief designer or architect will list a very impressive set of technical items that "must be" either modified or added. Similarly, the sales force and the marketing personnel will cite all missing functions that led to "lost sales." In the case of a multiple-release product, the customers and the support organizations will also have requirements for improvements and suggested fixes.

If there is no established procedure to help the decision-making process, a horrendous amount of energy and goodwill may be expended and perhaps wasted in the requirements development phase. It is the software project manager's responsibility to ensure that such a frustrating and languishing environment does not persist for too long.

The Prioritization Process

One potential remedy is to establish a process to handle the situation. A general prioritization procedure for both internal and external requirements is depicted in the requirements prioritization diagram shown in Figure 1.2.

The inputs from the various requirements' sources are constantly coming in to the software organization and being captured, possibly with an automated data management system or a requirements management tool such as Rational's RequisitePro or Borland's Caliber RM. The project management of the software organization must be ready to accept and respond to these requests. There needs to be both recognition of and an assignment of

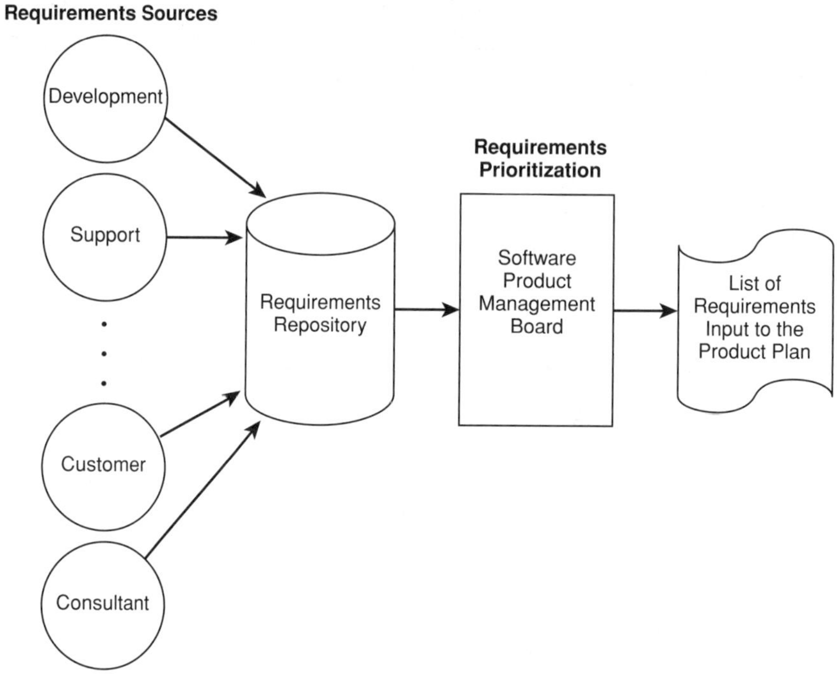

Figure 1.2 Requirements prioritization

resources to the capturing of these inputs. Furthermore, resources must be set aside for the following activities:

- Regular review of these inputs
- Analysis of the valid inputs
- Prioritization of these inputs
- Response to both the accepted ideas and the rejected ones
- Formulation of the accepted requirements subset into actual requirements for the product plan

Table 1.1 shows an example of how such a list might be organized.

Role of the Software Product Management Board

In Figure 1.2, the Software Product Management Board includes managers and leaders from various parts of the organization. This group is responsible for deciding which requirements will be included, delayed, and excluded for

Table 1.1
Requirements Prioritization List

Item#	Item description	Source	Priority	Status
Item number used to identify the item	Brief description of the item, pointing to a detailed document if necessary	Source of the request, such as the customer, internal support organization, or internal sales organization	Assigned priority of 1 through 4, where 1 is highest	Description: Accepted and included in the current product release plan, accepted for a later product release plan, or rejected

each software project. A set of candidate requirements might come from the following sources:

- Application domain area experts (such as analysts or consultants)
- The lead developer or lead architect
- User customer support personnel
- Users or customers
- Sales or marketing representatives
- Product or project managers who have authority over resources
- Strategic business planning personnel
- Trainers

Software Product Management Board A group of people chosen to assist in the determination of priorities of requirements and the grouping of requirements for product releases.

The composition and the size of this group will vary depending on the type of the software project. For a software product with a limited number of customers, the Software Product Management Board might include only two or three people. In contrast, for a complex product targeted toward millions of customers, the board might expand to 10 to 12 people. The number of people required and the length of time needed also depend on whether the software is being developed as a first release or has gone through multiple releases. For a popular, multiple-release software product such as an operating system, the organization might need to keep two or three people on the board permanently, for the purpose of managing the stream of continuous requirements.

The software project manager may pick the group members based on the potential contribution that each individual will make in the various areas that will help in the requirements prioritization decision process. Areas of interest might include some of the following:

- The project's sales, marketing, and business implications
- Its technical and architectural implications
- Its financial and resource implications
- Its implications for customer and user satisfaction, needs, and wishes
- The project's industry- and domain-specific implications

Chapter 13, which covers the Release Management Council, will also touch upon this subject, although the actual composition of a Release Management Council may be a little different than that described here. The Software Product Management Board differs from the Release Management Council in that the former is mostly concerned with product requirements and prioritization of requirements, while the latter focuses on issues related to the product release decision.

Release Management Council A group of people chosen to assist in managing the entire software project from goal setting to the final product release decision.

The managing of requirements often encountered at the review of a new software product line is similar, but slightly more complex. In this case, the sources of requirements may include a large and diverse group of people. Many times a special customer council is formulated by the software company for the purpose of gathering a basic set of requirements pertaining to solving both the fundamental problems of the represented industry and also some of the specific problems identified by the members of the customer council. In preparation for this effort, the customer council must take into account the opinions of the marketing and sales people of the organization.

The software project managers must attain the necessary financial and people resources before establishing such a council. The IT industry is full of situations in which the customer councils were abused and used as a reward for people's past good performance. In one customer council established by the author, the group initially worked very diligently. Unfortunately, as the participants became more familiar with and comfortable with one another, more socialization than real work began to take place at these meetings. Therefore, software project managers must always ensure that the participants are prepared to really work on requirements.

Once the customer council is established, the general set of requirements management activities mentioned earlier still applies. The output of the customer council becomes the input for the Software Product Management Board.

QUICK ESTIMATES AND HIGH-LEVEL REQUIREMENTS

Once the deliverables and their contents are defined and understood, the project manager and his or her team can then start on other aspects of planning activities. Sometimes project managers are pushed by the client to provide a "quick estimate" of the project's cost and schedule. In such cases, the understanding and the subsequent documentation of the deliverables may be at a high level. The question that the software project managers must ask, however, is whether this "high-level" understanding and description of the deliverables is enough to allow a rough estimation of the project's costs and schedule. Estimating the rough cost and the rough schedule carries a degree of risk. That is, the preliminary cost estimate and schedule have a high probability of changing, as does the high-level description of the deliverables. Two approaches are available to the software project managers to deal with this situation.

The first approach to handling quick estimates is to put "buffers" in the wording of the deliverables, along with buffers in the cost estimates and in the putative schedule. *Buffers* consist of extra time, money, other resources, or explanations provided to reduce potential project risks. In addition to the buffers, there must be a defined *change management process* that allows for changes in the deliverables and the associated changes in the project's cost and schedule. This change management process must be understood, concurred with, and accepted by all parties. It is the responsibility of the software project managers to ensure that change management is properly implemented throughout the life cycle of the software project. The details of the change process are discussed in a later chapter on change control and in the sections on establishment of an organization and processes for the software project in later chapters.

A second approach to handling quick estimates is to have the project manager try to convince the potential customer to turn the requirements management phase into a *separate project* and provide a quick estimate for only that phase. This approach will bind some of the risks of the quick estimate to just one phase of the software project, albeit a very important one. A separate plan for the rest of the project phases can then be established following the conclusion of the requirements management phase.

This evolutionary approach to project planning and project management, where requirements management is separated out as a different project, may be preferable for software projects in which the deliverables are nontangible information and complex (even though the media on which the deliverables reside may be physically tangible). Many experienced software project managers in software development and service organizations use this evolutionary approach of separating out the requirements phase as their standard business procedure.

Software project managers constantly wrestle with the dilemma of whether the deliverables are sufficiently understood and defined well enough for the rest of the planning activities to begin. One frequently used method to aid in this decision-making process is the review activity depicted in Figure 1.1. If the requirements are reviewed and all corrections are made, then they can be deemed "well-defined" and well-understood requirements. Furthermore, the signed-off requirements are not only well defined and understood, but also accepted as the baseline for the requirements.

It will be unusual if the baseline requirements specification is never modified. At this early stage the software project manager must often select a requirements management tool (such as one of the tools mentioned earlier) or a software configuration management tool (such as PVCS) to help in the control of and tracking of requirements changes. The project managers must be sure to consider more than just requirements management and include change management when choosing such a tool. (See Chapter 15 on change control.)

KEY CONCEPTS

Prior to actually working on the project, the project requirements need to be

- Gathered
- Analyzed
- Documented
- Reviewed
- Accepted with a sign-off

Software project managers should focus on providing the necessary resources and creating an environment that enhances the requirements development process. There are two major types of requirements:

- The list and the description of the deliverables
- The characterization of the needs and of the problem

In characterizing the needs of the problem, six areas should be covered:

- The functional needs
- The nonfunctional needs
- The business process
- The data and information structure

- The user interface
- The system interface

The establishment of the appropriate process and methodologies for requirements management and prioritization is the main function of the software project manager, but direct participation or even intervention by the project manager is sometimes required.

Software project managers must exercise care when responding to a request for a quick plan if the gathering or analysis of the requirements is not complete.

EXERCISES

1. Imagine that your software engineers arrive at the customer site and find that the "promised" users, who were key to the requirements gathering activity, are all in an emergency meeting that will last for at least one whole day. What are some of the things you, as the project manager, should do?
2. Why must there be clear entrance and exit criteria for requirements-processing activities?
3. List three reasons why software project requirements are sometimes not well-defined and understood.
4. After organizing and setting up a requirements prioritization process, your executive management (e.g., CEO or CFO) keeps submitting an "important client" request or "one more last" request. How should you, as a software project manager, handle the situation?
5. List two entrance criteria for prototyping.
6. If you choose to use iterative prototyping, what are some "costs" of which you need to be aware?
7. What are some activities in the requirements management phase that would benefit from automation and tools?
8. Discuss what you believe are the software artifacts that should be considered as the main software deliverables and explain the reasons for your choices.
9. List the six areas that the software requirements should address.
10. What is a Software Product Management Board and how necessary is it?
11. Define *software requirements* and discuss what more may be in a customer requirement list (see the software engineering definition in the Introduction).

SUGGESTED READING

M. Fowler and K. Scott, *UML Distilled: A Brief Guide to the Standard Object Modeling Language,* Addison-Wesley, 2000.

M. Jackson, *Software Requirements and Specifications,* Addison-Wesley, 1995.

D. Leffingwell and D. Widrig, *Managing Software Requirements: A Unified Approach,* Addison-Wesley, 2000.

B. Ramesh and M. Jake, "Towards Reference Model for Requirements Traceability," *IEEE Transactions on Software Engineering,* January 2002, 58–93.

D. J. Reifer, "Common Risk Patterns," Software Tech News, Vol. 12, No. 3, September 2009, 16–20.

K. Ryan and J. Karlson, "Prioritizing Software Requirements in an Industrial Setting," *Proceedings of the 19th International Conference on Software Engineering,* 1997, 564–565.

I. Sommerville and P. Sawyer, *Requirements Engineering: A Good Practice Guide,* John Wiley and Sons, 1997.

Chapter 2

Task Analysis

Chapter Objectives

This chapter discusses the following concepts:

- How the Work Breakdown Structure (WBS) is used to analyze the tasks that are needed to develop the deliverables specified in the requirements
- How effort, in the form of time and resources, should be assigned to the tasks shown in the WBS
- Why the preliminary schedule, with milestones, developed from the WBS is a key part of planning

WORK BREAKDOWN STRUCTURE

Once the requirements specification is understood and completed, the software project management team is ready to start on the Work Breakdown Structure (WBS) activity. Note that we used the term "software project management team" rather than "project manager" in describing who participates in the WBS activity. Even at this early stage of planning, the knowledge and experience of the technical systems and software engineers may be required.

> **Work Breakdown Structure (WBS)** A depiction of the project in terms of the discrete pieces of work needed to complete the project and the ordering of those pieces of work.

The WBS first looks at the macro requirements of what needs to be delivered. In other words, the initial, high level WBS considers the "big picture" and evaluates what needs to be accomplished from a high level, rather than focusing on the details. From the list of the artifacts that are required to be completed and delivered, a high-level set of tasks or work that will produce the artifacts is identified. The sequencing or the ordering of these tasks is also important and will be defined as part of the WBS.

In this early stage of planning, the software management team might have only a global understanding of the software development and support process, with details of the needed process not yet being fully defined and refined. Later, each task or work unit should be further refined into smaller units of subtasks or work units by the management team until each subtask can be performed by a single individual. At the completion of the WBS activity, the management team will have a defined set of ordered tasks for each of the deliverables. They can then use the details of the ordered tasks to formulate the initial project schedule, which includes:

- tasks
- dates
- effort

A variety of graphical tools can be used in the WBS activity, ranging from Microsoft's Visio to Smartdraw.com's Smartdraw. There are also a plethora of tools available for representing and keeping track of the schedule—for example, Primavera's TeamPlay, MinuteMan System's MinuteMan Project Management, and Microsoft's popular Project tool. Indeed, the IT industry is rife with such tools that can be used as aids in the WBS activity. But a word of caution is in order: Even though these tools are wonderful for improving management productivity, project managers should focus their attention on the information that is stored and represented by these tools, rather than "falling in love" with the tools themselves.

Steps in the WBS

The following is a list of activities that need to be performed as part of the WBS activity:

1. Examine the set of required external deliverables.
2. Identify and list the steps and tasks needed to produce the required deliverables, including any tasks for additional intermediate deliverables needed to complete the final deliverable.
3. Sequence the identified tasks required to produce the deliverable.
4. Estimate the effort required to perform each task.

5. Estimate the productivity of the resources that will be applied to the tasks.
6. Compute the time needed for each task by dividing the task effort estimates by the resource productivity estimates.
7. Lay out the time needed for each task and "label" each task with its task name and the assigned resources; this layout of sequences of tasks with their associated time and resources essentially forms the initial schedule.

Figure 2.1 graphically depicts the flow of activities involved in the WBS, ending with the formation of an initial schedule. To perform these steps, we make several key assumptions. For example, we assume that information such as process, task effort, and people productivity data are available. The management team must make estimates for each of these components using their respective techniques, some of which we will discuss in later chapters. For now, keeping in mind that we'll be making assumptions, we will demonstrate, via a software project example, how WBS is conducted.

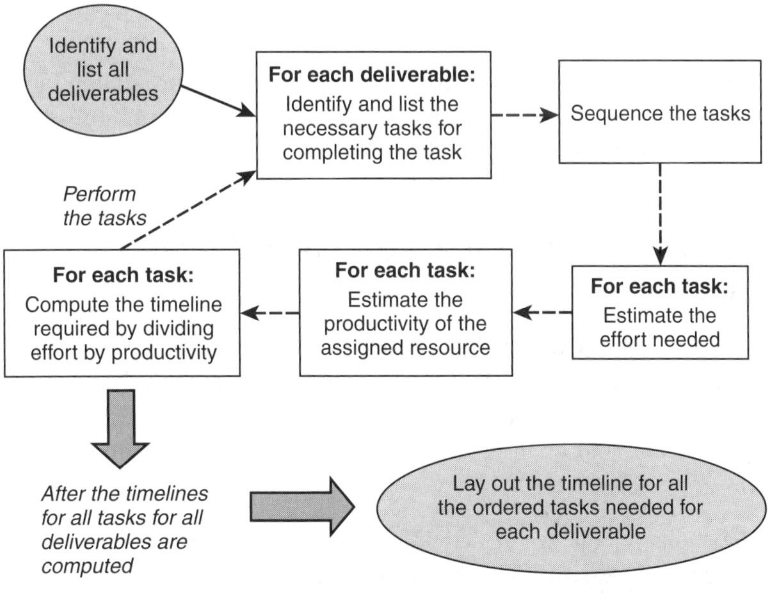

Figure 2.1 Flow of WBS to schedule

WBS IN PRACTICE: INTRODUCTION TO AN EXAMPLE

Assume that from the requirements specifications we have determined that the scope of the project is of a "small scale" and that only two software deliverables are needed:

- Deliverable 1: Executable code that is installable from a CD
- Deliverable 2: Help text, usage, and reference information that is installable from a CD

From this macro description of the deliverables, we can start planning the activities in the form of a WBS. This seemingly simple list of artifacts actually requires more planning than one might first expect. The set of activities needed for each artifact appears below. Recall that we have already completed the requirements gathering and analysis phase and, therefore, have a good idea of the software's functional and nonfunctional requirements.

Deliverable 1: Executable Code

- The activities needed to develop the executable code include requirements specification and analysis (which are already completed), design, coding, and testing.
- The activities required to make the executable code installable include—although in a simpler version—requirements specification (already completed), design, coding, and testing.

Deliverable 2: Help Text, Usage, and Reference Information

- Creating help text involves requirements specification and analysis (which is already completed), design, writing, "tucking in," and testing.
- Developing usage and reference information involves requirements specification and analysis (already completed), design, writing, "tucking in," and testing.

The choice of the set of activities and their sequencing depend on two parameters: (1) the size and complexity of both the problem and the solution, and (2) the process and methodology that the software organization has already defined, trained its people to follow, and agreed with its client to use. The existence of the client agreement is a key assumption. Sequencing the activities needed for the development of the artifacts can be a large problem for new software organizations that have neither the experience nor any of the processes defined. The front-end cost, in terms of both effort and money, of preparing an organization for any process is extensive and sometimes hard to overcome. For now, let's assume that the process is already defined and understood by most of the people in the organization. We will revisit this topic later.

WBS TASK REFINEMENT

An expansion of the WBS for the executable code deliverable, not including its installability, of this "small" project example is shown below.

Activities and Subdeliverables for Deliverable 1

We first present a list of activities, but they are not yet necessarily in the correct order:

Activity A: Designing and documenting the design using an agreed-upon notation
Activity B: Coding (in a language that is already agreed upon)
Activity C: Defining test cases and generating test scripts
Activity D: Executing test scripts
Activity E: Correcting and fixing problems found during testing
Activity F: Collecting the tested executables modules and handing them to the packaging group

Note that this expanded list includes more intermediate subdeliverables, such as the design document. The subdeliverables may be for internal consumption only and may not be delivered to the customer or the users. We include them here because these intermediate deliverables still require effort and thus need to be part of the plan.

Further refinement of just the design activity, the above Activity A, may result in a table such as Table 2.1.

To refine Activity A into these subtasks, the software project management team most likely had to spend some time analyzing and contemplating what design activities are needed for the given requirements of this "small" project (unless they had prior experience with similar projects). Once again, the software project management team might need the technical expertise and experience of the software designers if they do not possess such technical skills themselves. This refinement of tasks continues until each task can be

Table 2.1
Subtasks within the Design Activity

Tasks	Description
Task A-1	Overall application, user interface (UI), and message architecture
Task A-2	Database and relational tables design
Task A-3	Application function 1 design
Task A-4	Application function 2 design
Task A-5	Application function 3 design

assigned to a responsible person. For instance, Task A-1 might be further broken down into development of the application architecture, UI architecture, and message architecture if the software project were a larger one.

Task Sequencing and Sequence Diagram

Next, we need to examine whether any sequencing relationship exists among the subtasks. In this example, Task A-1 needs to be completed before Tasks A-3, A-4, and A-5 commence. Task A-2 may, however, be started before Task A-1 is completed because the database design does not depend on the completion of the message architecture. Depending on the tools and the methods used in the software project, the UI architecture part of Task A-1 may or may not need to be completed before Task A-2 starts. The amount of overlap between Tasks A-1 and A-2 depends on several parameters, ranging from purely technical ones to personnel availability. For initial planning purposes, we will first keep the WBS simple and force the sequencing of tasks without overlap.

Figure 2.2 graphically represents the sequence relationship for our example in a sequence diagram. The sequence diagram depicts the start-stop relationships among the various subtasks of Activity A. It may be further refined for detailed planning if any of the subtasks is too large or cannot be assigned to one responsible person.

> **Sequence diagram** A diagram that shows all the tasks required to complete an activity and the order in which those tasks must be performed, including the depiction of the tasks that may be performed in parallel.

Figure 2.2 shows that Tasks A-3, A-4, and A-5 may be performed in parallel because no ordering relationships among them are specified. Note also that there is no indication of how any task may overlap with another task. For parallel tasks, there may be total overlap, assuming that no other constraint applies. In the case of sequential tasks, neither a sequence dia-

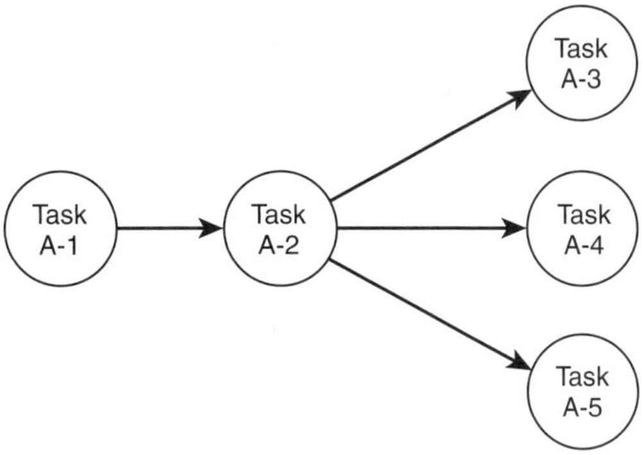

Figure 2.2 Sequence diagram (Sequence relationship of activity A subtasks)

gram nor a WBS provides a view of any potential for overlapping the tasks. This limitation can be overcome by adding the task overlapping explanation at the corner of the diagram. The only problem is that the explanation may require more space than what is available.

We will need to construct a sequence diagram for each of the remaining activities B through F that are required in developing the executable code deliverable. Similarly, for the other deliverable, Deliverable 2, we will need to create a list of activities that may then be further refined into subtasks. The sequence relationship among the subtasks needs to be established and depicted, possibly with a sequence diagram. A software management team typically uses this organization because it is an excellent way to represent the WBS.

The construction of a sequence diagram for a software project follows these steps, which are—and should be—similar to the earlier discussed construction of the WBS:

1. List the deliverables.
2. For each deliverable, list the activities that are required.
3. For each activity, list the set of subtasks that are required.
4. Further refine any of the subtasks by creating the next level of subtasks, if necessary.
5. Construct the sequence relationship of the subtasks.
6. Depict the sequence relationship with a sequence diagram.

A Word of Caution

Earlier we mentioned that there are at least two levels of any given plan: a high-level, big-picture perspective and a low-level, detailed view. Even for a high-level plan, the software project managers need to quickly put together a WBS for the deliverables. To do so, they must have some knowledge of the software development process and support activities. This software process knowledge is especially critical when it comes to the "sequencing tasks" part of the WBS. Also, the project managers need to be aware of the nonsoftware aspects of the project—in particular, hiring and team-forming tasks must precede the tasks related to the actual construction of the deliverables. These tasks that are not related to software construction must be included in the WBS, even for high-level planning. Many project planners have put themselves into a tenuous situation on day 1 because the WBS omitted a set of important tasks. These indirect tasks, which had nothing to do with the direct requirements of the deliverables, are often forgotten and never folded into the plan.

WBS TIME AND RESOURCE ASSIGNMENTS

Once we have refined the WBS to a satisfactory level, we can proceed to the next phase of task analysis. A reasonable question to ask at this point is, What would a "satisfied" level of refinement be? Unfortunately, there is no fixed answer because all projects, and the people involved in those projects, are different. However, a useful guideline is that the WBS refinement should be carried to the level where:

- Each task may be assigned to one person.
- The estimate of the task cost, stated not in terms of money but rather in terms of time required to complete it, does not extend beyond more than two or three project status meetings.

The first guideline is fairly intuitive in that having more than one person "own" a task often results in no ownership at all. Ensuring single-person accountability makes the management and tracking of the task much easier. Sometimes, however, a task is initially assigned to a team. For example, initially the requirements solicitation task may be assigned to a team of two or three requirements analysts. As the planning proceeds, each of the requirements analysts may be assigned a specific task of gathering requirements from a different user department. Thus such a task will eventually be refined into subtasks that are assignable to individual team members.

The second guideline is stated in a looser manner—it is relative to how often status meetings are conducted. Here, we assume that the project status meetings are conducted very often, possibly every day if the total software project is very small (in the range of weeks) or at weekly intervals if the total software project is large (in the range of months but less than a year). The reason for refining a task down to a level in which it will not cross more than two or three project status meetings is so that if a particular task falls behind schedule, the problem can be caught relatively early. This prevents software project managers from maintaining a wait-and-see attitude for too long.

Units of Task Measurement

Before a time estimate can be assigned to a task, the project management team must decide on the unit of measurement. If the smallest individual task can be completed in less than one working day, meaning approximately six working hours, then the task time estimates should be stated in one-hour units. If the smallest individual task requires more than a working day but less than five working days, then the unit should be half-days. For all other tasks, the unit of measurement should be days. Normally, the advice is not to extend the basic unit to a week, because the software industry has a tendency to include weekend days as part of the week. This practice of including extended work weeks as a normal week has created an assortment of problems when it is utilized for too long a period. For example, if an organization estimates that a project will take 50 weeks, a five-day work week makes for 250 days, while a seven-day work week would have 350 working days—a 100-day difference! The definition of a working day may also differ from organization to organization.

Software project managers must recognize that a software project includes the participation of all team members in many non-direct-task-related activities such as departmental meetings, telephone interruptions, or answering e-mails. This is part of the reason that the software project management team should count on only six hours of direct software project-related work per day. If the unit of measurement is a half-day, then only three hours of direct work should be expected per half-day. Clearly, some software project managers would like to lengthen the work day such that there are eight hours of direct work, with the indirect work hours being absorbed into the "extended" work-day hours of the software engineers. This practice is a dangerous one when employed for a long period of time.

There are many ways to address the issue of how to estimate the time required to complete each of the tasks required for a project. A favorite approach of software project managers is to ask the experienced software development team members who will be tagged to perform each task to estimate the time required to complete their own tasks. This approach is used for several reasons. If the person has past experience performing similar tasks, then the data from that past experience can provide a relatively good gauging factor. Also, if the people who will be responsible for the completion of the task are asked, they are more likely to take responsibility for the estimate. The term for this approach in many software projects is "bottom-up" estimating.

Another popular approach to determining how much time is required for each part of a project is to assemble a team of technical experts and have them estimate each task in terms of some common work volume unit, such as lines of code or function points for design, coding, and testing. For developing help text or message text tasks, for example, we could use a work volume stated in terms of "number of sentences." For UI-related tasks, we could use "number of fields" to assess the volume of work. Once the volume of work is estimated, an organizational productivity figure such as lines of code per hour or per day can be used to compute the estimate for the needed task completion time. This approach assumes that organizational productivity figures by type of task exist from history or from the software management team's experience. Table 2.2 is an example of possible historical information that may exist from similar, past projects in an organization.

For example, a particular task, *x*, may involve the design, implementation, and testing of 15 UI input fields. Suppose the organizational productivity of developing UI input fields from the past is *z* fields per hour. Then for this task *x*, the estimated time would be $(15/z)$ hours.

Estimating techniques, software methods, and the software development process will be covered in more detail later in this book. For our purposes here, we will simply assume that the task completion time has been estimated. Figure 2.3 shows the estimated times for the subtasks of Activity A in our ongoing example.

In Figure 2.3, there are three possible paths to the "end" state of Activity A. The longest path includes Tasks A-1, A-2, and A-3. Software project

Table 2.2
Example of Historical Information

Tasks	Possible rates
Requirements solicitation	2 interviews/person-day
Message design	15 error messages/person-day
Code implementation	2 function points/person-day; 40 lines of Java/person-day
Test generation	5 test scenarios/person-day

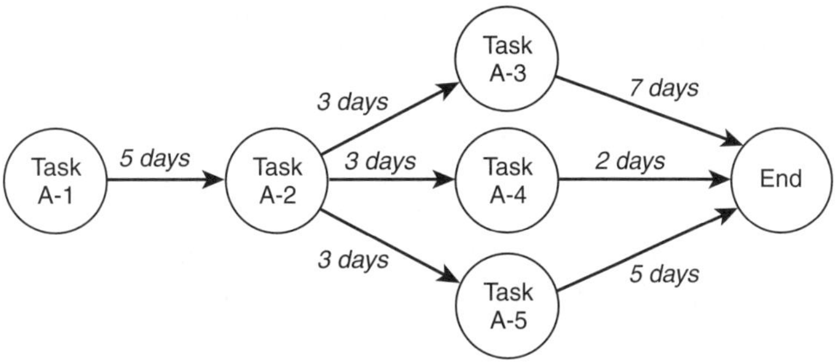

Figure 2.3 Subtasks with estimated times

managers should be aware that any slippage along this path would cause the total Activity A to miss its end date. For this reason, this longest path is known as the "critical path" for Activity A (Chapter 16) defines and explains critical paths. The other two paths, however, allow for a little slippage. Because Task A-4 takes five days less to complete than does Task A-3, it may be started later than Task A-3 or take a little longer than the estimated time. A similar case can be made for Task A-5. A more comprehensive discussion of this topic can be found in Chapter 16.

Task Estimates and Task Assignments

According to the guideline given earlier, each of the subtasks should be represented in half-day units, since the smallest task takes less than five days. In this example, we happen to have each subtask end on a day boundary, so, for simplicity, it is shown here in days.

The next step is to apply the appropriate people resources to each of the tasks in this time-estimated WBS:

1. Project management teams must first consider what skills are required to perform the subtasks. Once the skills are determined, they must seek people capable of performing these tasks.
2. The team must consider the availability of the identified skilled people.
3. The team must consider the timing of and the requirement of the identified person for another aspect of the project or another project.

These considerations must be made in conjunction with the schedule in the time-estimated WBS for the subtasks in the estimated time diagram (Figure 2.3). A few items stand out in Figure 2.3. None of the Tasks A-3, A-4, or A-5 can be started until both Tasks A-1 and A-2 are completed. Therefore, it would make sense to apply the appropriate resources to Tasks A-1 and A-2 without delay. Let us assume that Task A-1 will require a person with architectural and high-level design skills, and Task A-2 will require a person who has database skills. Most likely these individuals will be different people.

After the resources for Tasks A-1 and A-2 are accounted for, appropriate resources may be applied to Tasks A-3, A-4, and A-5. Several alternatives are possible here. If skill is not a problem, a management team may assign the same person to perform Tasks A-4 and A-5 without compromising the schedule because the estimated completion time for Task A-3 is equal to the total estimated completion time for Tasks A-4 and A-5. We may also assign the same person for Task A-1 and any of the subsequent subtasks to Task A-1. The actual assignment of the individuals will depend on the considerations listed earlier. The assignment of people may be represented via a graph or in a tabular form with bars, as shown in Table 2.3.

For this example, we chose to assign different people for each subtask. As stated earlier, Tasks A-1 and A-3 could be performed by the same person, so long as that individual possesses the appropriate skills. With today's project scheduling tools, a table like that shown in Table 2.3 can be placed into a form where the sequenced time-estimate portion can be represented in a real calendar. The schedule would then reflect a more realistic timetable, with weekends and holidays being embedded in it. A further refinement would be to consider the potential of "some" overlapping of tasks that are represented as sequential tasks, such as Tasks A-1 and A-2.

Table 2.3
Subtasks with Time Estimates and People Assignment

Subtask	Person	Sequenced time-estimate
A-1	P1	5 days
A-2	P2	3 days
A-3	P3	7 days
A-4	P4	2 days
A-5	P5	5 days

Milestones

We have taken Deliverable 1, the application's executable code, through the WBS refinement process to the point that we now have a schedule of Activity A complete with estimated time units and people assignments. At the completion of these steps for Deliverable 1, management should sponsor an activity that recognizes its team's accomplishment. The software project management needs to identify this achievement as a milestone. In general, a milestone is defined as a significant event that occurs in a project at a certain point in time.

Project milestone A significant event in a project that occurs at a specific point in time.

The labeling of a milestone gives a certain amount of priority and significance to the event. For example, management might want to label the completion of Task A-1—the application, UI, and message architecture—as a minor milestone within Activity A. Such a labeling will give a higher priority to Task A-1, relative to the other subtasks in Activity A, in the assignment of personnel resources and in the selection of a highly skilled and very dependable person. There will be more emphasis applied to milestone tasks, ensuring that the needed tools and other facilities are provided for that activity. This labeling also places more management attention on that subtask.

The completion of the Activity A, as a set of subtasks, may be labeled as a milestone as well. This is a little different than identifying the completion of a single unit of activity such as Task A-1 as a minor milestone, where a special emphasis is placed on that subtask. The labeling of Activity A completion as a milestone is intended to recognize its achievement. It does not necessarily identify Activity A as a higher priority than, say, Activity B or C. Indeed, software project management may utilize the term "milestone" for the purpose of emphasizing a particular activity, as well as for the purpose of recognizing the attainment of a significant task.

The table is now further enhanced to indicate the milestones, as shown in Table 2.4

Depending on the size of the software project, it is conceivable that one might develop a schedule depicting only the milestones. Such a schedule may be used by higher-level management, who may need to understand and track only the more significant events.

As software project management involves a heavy dosage of people management, the milestone events should not pass without some type of

Table 2.4
Subtasks with Milestones

Subtask	Person	Sequenced time-estimate
A-1	P1	5 days
A-2	P2	3 days
A-3	P3	7 days
A-4	P4	2 days
A-5	P5	5 days
		Minor Milestone; Milestone

celebration. The celebration may be anything from an informal "thank you" and a good handshake to a formal ceremony with recognition and monetary rewards for achieving a major milestone. The important thing for the software managers to remember is that the accomplishments of milestones need to be publicly recognized.

The opposite situation, where a designated milestone is "missed," also requires the software project managers' attention. Ideally, the responsible software manager will already be well aware of the high risk before a negative incident occurs and will have put an action plan in place. Nevertheless, the software manager must share the negative news, as well as the positive news, openly and candidly with his or her team. The topic of people and morale management will be discussed more in a later chapter.

WBS ITERATION AND ACCEPTANCE

There are two areas that are found to require extra care in the WBS process.

- task effort estimation
- inclusion of all relevant tasks

The estimation of any task effort requires some prior experience and is one of the least accurate and thus more risky part of WBS. In developing the schedule with WBS technique, it is important to include all tasks for the project. Often the support tasks, such as the procurement of tools, services, training or other commercially available software component, are forgotten and not included in the WBS. We will discuss procurement management in mor detail in a later chapter.

The first iteration of the WBS, the schedule, and the milestones will most likely not be the final one. This part of the plan needs to be reviewed by all stakeholders (i.e., the people who have to perform the tasks–the project team, rather than the Software Product Management Board). The problem is that, at this stage of the project, not all stakeholders may be available or on board. Nevertheless, the WBS must be reviewed, and a general agreement needs to be reached by those leaders who are already on board. Some software projects may be open enough so that customers and users are included in the review of the plan at this early stage.

In the review process, the management team should be prepared to change and adjust the plan. These reviews may be somewhat time consuming, but they achieve two important goals:

- The information in the plan is open and communicated to relevant parties.
- There is understanding and a degree of commitment to the plan.

Once there is general consensus about the WBS, the management team needs to document the date, participants, and any assumptions or circumstantial information related to the project. This provides the team with a baseline for the WBS tasks and the schedule. Modifications may be needed later, and any future changes should always be recorded and evolve from this baseline. Change control over the baseline may then be applied as discussed in Chapter 15. All plans are subject to necessary changes, but the changes need to be tracked. Again, any change needs to be managed openly.

KEY CONCEPTS

The Work Breakdown Structure (WBS) is a valuable tool for the software project managers. The process starts with the enumeration of all required deliverables and the listing of activities or tasks required to produce each of those deliverables. A sequence diagram is developed to place the tasks in some order. The sequence diagram is then enhanced to include the amount of effort and the type of resources needed, thereby converting the sequence diagram into a table that resembles a preliminary schedule.

Including milestones on the preliminary schedule is a software project management technique that will further enhance the visibility of the key tasks for the software team. These milestones may be used as a control mechanism for the overall project. Project managers must emphasize both the success of and the failure to meet these milestones.

EXERCISES

1. Create a WBS for the following:
   a. Putting together your favorite dinner dish
   b. Building a wooden picture frame
   c. Creating software that computes the average of a set of numbers and then displays the result
2. Discuss which of the three WBSs in Exercise 1 was the most challenging for you and why.
3. To what level should one refine the WBS?
4. When provided with a schedule of activities and the respective personnel assignments, what should concern you even if you know that the WBS portion is correct?
5. Why should the WBS be reviewed by others?
6. What is a project milestone, and why should it be identified?
7. Create a WBS for a software project that includes three deliverables: design document, code, and test cases. Assume that the required effort for design is 5 person-days, for coding is 15 person-days, and for test case development and testing is 7 person-days. You may make assumptions about the order and the overlapping of the activities. You may make assumptions on productivity and number of people to assign to each task. Evolve your WBS and show the project task schedule with people assignments (see Table 2.3).

SUGGESTED READING

C. F. Gray and E. W. Larson, *Project Management,* Irwin McGraw-Hill, 2000.

J. M. Nicholas, *Project Management for Business and Technology: Principles and Practice*, Prentice Hall, 2001.

S. L. Pfleeger, *Software Engineering: Theory and Practice*, Prentice Hall, 1998.

Chapter 3

Goals and Measurements

Chapter Objectives

This chapter discusses the following concepts:

- Why project and product goals should be specified during the planning phase
- Why goals should be expressed in the form of measurable attributes that have specific metrics
- How most project and product attributes require extensive analysis before an appropriate metric and corresponding measurement step can be defined

PROJECT ATTRIBUTES

After analyzing and scheduling the tasks required to develop and produce a software project's deliverables, a management team must specify the characteristics of these deliverables. This work constitutes an important component of the planning phase of project management, the first stage in the POMA process.

Preliminary Goals

It is during the planning phase that the goals for, and the measurements of, the key attributes of the product and service are determined. The management team does not start from scratch; a large portion of the product and project characterization has already been provided through the customer requirements. These functional and nonfunctional requirements are translated into preliminary goals such as the following:

- A secure system
- A fully functional system
- A high-quality system
- A user-friendly and attractive system
- A cost-efficient project
- A project that meets the schedule

The preliminary goals, as stated in these terms, are extremely difficult to achieve. Because they are not measurable, it is difficult to determine whether they have actually been reached. The planning phase is the time to recast these preliminary goals as more precise attributes, with metrics, so that the attributes are measurable, trackable, validatable, and verifiable. (These terms are defined later in this section.)

Without this recasting of the goals, one would face the issues of "what to monitor" and "how to monitor the project status" during the monitoring phase of POMA. Defining the goals in terms of attributes and pertinent metrics during the monitoring phase would be too late. As a result of not planning ahead and properly identifying the attributes and defining the metrics for those attributes, many software project managers monitor only a few obvious goals, such as the schedule. Unfortunately, more difficult-to-assess product attributes—such as ease of use, quality, and scalability—continue to receive lip service but are often not well defined and thus not actively tracked. Similarly, the project attributes dealing with efficiency, productivity, and other issues are often an after-thought for many projects, and they receive attention at a post-project analysis rather than during the project planning phase. Improved understanding and better definitions of these attributes may lead to modifications of the requirements. These modifications may in turn cause rework on the schedule. One should not be surprised that there will be multiple iterations of subtasks within the planning phase itself.

Measurable, Trackable, Validatable, and Verifiable Goals

It is important in the planning phase to first express the goals of the software project. This insistence on setting the goals during the planning phase for a software project is derived from the principles underlying the G/Q/M paradigm proposed by V. Basili and others. G/Q/M is a "systematic approach for setting project goals (tailored to specific needs) and defining them in an operational and traceable way."

G/Q/M (Goal/Question/Metric) A software metric paradigm based on identifying the goals, formulating questions about the goals in quantifiable terms, and establishing the metrics to answer the formulated questions.

A successful management team expresses project goals (G), which are characterizations of the attributes of the deliverables and of the processes, in the form of questions (Q) that are quantifiable. Then, from the specified attributes, the management team can outline and accept a set of metrics and measurements (M). An attribute must be measurable and trackable before it can be considered a meaningful attribute for a goal.

Measurable attribute An attribute for which there is a well-defined metric and a methodology for its measurement.

Tracking Keeping a record of the measurements taken on an attribute.

The notion of "measurable" is further explained later in this chapter in the section "Metrics and Measurement: An Overview." Clearly, an attribute cannot be considered trackable if it is not measurable.

Furthermore, the measurement of that attribute must be able to be validated and must be verifiable. Project goals and their measurements should be validated because the process of validation confirms that the customer requirement has been satisfied. An example would be the case in which the user's requirement asks for a response time for queries to be no more than 2 seconds. Thus the goal for the attribute called "query response time" would be set at less than 2 seconds. Certainly, one can, with some thought, construct a set of queries and then measure the response times for them. If none of the response times exceeds 2 seconds, then the customer's requirement is satisfied. Note that the goal may be validated regardless of whether the goal is actually satisfied.

Validation of goal Comparing a stated goal for an attribute with the actual measurement taken for that attribute.

The goal for an attribute and its associated measurement must be validatable. One must be able to show that the measured result matches that specified by the customer as the goal.

At the same time, the management team must verify all measurements. This effort confirms that the measurements are properly acquired and that any transformation of the raw measurements for that attribute has been performed correctly. The actual act of measurement and any computation that is performed must be traceable and demonstrable. In the preceding example of the response time attribute, the verification of the measurement for that attribute would involve ensuring that the set of activities—which includes the construction of the test cases, the running of the test cases, and the reading and recording of the clock time for each query test case—is performed properly.

Verification of measurement Ensuring that the measurement of an attribute is properly taken and recorded through repetition, tracing, or some other means.

Once the goals for the project are defined in terms of attributes that are measurable, trackable, verifiable, and validatable, it is possible to monitor the project status. The status of the project is reflected in the measurements taken on the attributes.

METRICS AND MEASUREMENTS: AN OVERVIEW

We will now take a small digression to discuss the concepts of *metric* and *measurement*. A metric is the unit that we use to characterize the attribute. A measurement is the actual act of counting, using that metric. For example, we use "hour" as a metric for the attribute "time," and we use a clock as the tool to perform the actual measurement. The reading of the clock is the measurement. In the case of measurement, the characterization of an attribute, for the purpose of project management, should be such that it ultimately results in numerically counting the metric of the attribute.

Metric The unit used to characterize an attribute.

Measurement The act of characterizing an attribute, which may involve multiple steps, utilizing the agreed-upon metric for that attribute.

It is possible to include several activities in the measurement. Suppose "elapsed time" is the attribute of interest. Then "hour" may still be the metric. To determine elapsed time, however, one would need an initial reading of the clock, a final reading of the clock, and the difference between the two readings in order to obtain the elapsed time. Thus the measurement of elapsed time as the attribute is a little more complex than the simple time attribute. In both cases, the metric remains "hour."

Aside from specifying the metrics for the deliverables, the planning team may need to define metrics for other software project-related attributes—such as productivity, team morale, tool effectiveness, and user satisfaction—that are indirectly related to the actual deliverables. These may be categorized as process attributes or as project attributes. The difference between process and project attributes is subtle and minor, and some thought is required to define them. For example, productivity may be a process attribute. We are generally interested in software development processes that offer high productivity without sacrificing product quality. At the same time, the productivity attribute of a specific project utilizing a "highly productive" process is of direct and immediate interest to that project manager. For software project managers, setting goals for these process and project attributes is as important as setting goals for the deliverables.

The schedule, the most obvious attribute for all projects, is a defined set of time goals agreed to by everyone involved; staying on schedule is an important goal that people readily understand. Both the metric and the measurement for schedules are defined in the calendar. Thus everyone appreciates the goal of meeting the project milestone dates.

The cost of the project, as an attribute, is also easy to measure because it is something that is well understood. Likewise, the cost given in terms of some currency is already a well-defined metric. The goal of meeting the estimated cost is easy to comprehend and track.

Unfortunately, aside from these two popular project attributes, most attributes and their respective goals—for example, quality, completeness of functions, and ease of use—are generally difficult to measure because we typically do not understand them well enough to define quantifiable metrics easily. Furthermore, once a numerical metric is set, the measurement process that uses that metric must be developed. Software engineers and software project managers are still working diligently to improve the measurement of software. Without a better system for metrics and measurements, activities such as tracking, verification, and validation of software attributes will continue to be more of an art than a science, and will be based on the personal experience of the various project managers.

For example, for an inexperienced organization, the project schedule is often tracked by asking for each individual's measurement. The answers from the individuals may come in a form such as "90% completed." Unfortunately, this metric of "percent completion" is not defined, nor is the measurement of how one defined and arrived at 90% completion. An inexperienced manager may interpret 90% completion as a good status and not realize that it may not mean what he or she thinks it means. For example, "90% code completion" may mean "I have coded 90% of the functions;" "I have coded 90% of the functions and these functions have passed my personal unit testing;" "I have coded 90% of the functions and these functions have gone through the formal functional test cases conducted by the test department;" or " I have coded 90% percent of the functions, these functions have gone through all the formal functional tests, and all the problems found have been corrected and retested." An experienced manager, by contrast, might first define the metric for the percent completion attribute for different tasks and then ask each individual to measure his or her schedule status by using the same metric definition and then validating his or her status against the scheduled milestone.

This type of difference in sophistication levels among organizations and managers does affect the project's end result. The Software Engineering Institute (SEI) has studied the maturity levels of many software organizations and offers its Capability Maturity Model (CMM) and Capability Maturity Model Integrated (CMMI) as guidelines for assessing software maturity levels. Interested parties should consult the article by W. S. Humphrey and the SEI website listed in the "Suggested Reading" section at the end of this chapter.

Capability Maturity Model for Software (CMM for SW) A model, defined by the Software Engineering Institute, that defines five possible levels of maturity for a software organization. The five levels are Initial, Repeatable, Defined, Managed, and Optimizing.

Capability Maturity Model Integrated (CMMI) A process assessment and improvement approach defined by the SEI. It is the follow up to the original CMM approach.

DELIVERABLE-RELATED METRICS AND MEASUREMENTS

The software project managers and the customer both need to participate in setting the goals for the deliverables. As stated earlier, much of the goal setting should have been accomplished during the requirements specification process. However, broad-statement goals such as "good-quality," "user-friendly," or "reliable" software are not sufficient; goals stated in this form cannot be measured and are difficult to validate. If the goals are immeasurable, we can never show ourselves—or our users and customers—that the goals have been met.

Let's explore some deliverable attributes that are interesting to users, customers, software developers, and software project managers alike. The following is a list of software deliverable attributes or characteristics that are often cited as important:

- Quality
- Usability
- Functional completeness
- Maintainability
- Modifiability
- Reliability
- Installability

Each of these characteristics requires some in-depth understanding and effort before a reasonable goal and metric can be designed and put into the plan. We will not cover each of these attributes here, but rather will select one to demonstrate the level of preparation and work required before a meaningful goal, metric, and measurement for that attribute can be stated. The software project managers should know the amount of effort that should be anticipated if a particular attribute is not well defined for the project and will need refining at a later stage. In general, the broader the attribute, the more time is required to break down the attribute into clear subattributes. We will demonstrate this statement by examining an example using one popular attribute, quality.

Metrics and Measurements Example I: The Quality Attribute

Quality is an attribute of the software deliverable that all software projects embrace, but it is often ill defined. Software quality may, for example, describe the amount of errors in the software. Alternatively, it may describe how well the delivered software meets all the stated application functional requirements, even if it contains errors in a nonfunctional area such as the setup function. Sometimes the quality attribute includes a performance attribute, such as response time.

For each of these alternative definitions of the quality attribute, a different metric must be defined. For example, the number of errors found would be used as a metric for one definition of quality, whereas the percentage of desired functions delivered might be a metric for a different definition of quality. One can see that it is important to clearly state and define both this attribute and its metric and then set the appropriate goal for that attribute in terms of that metric.

Assume, for the moment, that the attribute "quality" is defined and agreed upon as "the amount of known problems in the software." In this case, the metric for the attribute is the number of known problems. This assumption is nontrivial in that many discussions and arguments could have been expended to arrive at this common ground. With this definition, high quality would imply a low number of known problems, as shown in Figure 3.1.

The quality goal, therefore, would be expressed in terms of a specific number of known problems in the deliverable. Further, assume that a problem is defined to include any mistake made by the developer, regardless of whether it manifests itself as a defect during execution after delivery to the customer. This seemingly simple concept of the software quality attribute will actually require substantial planning; the number of problems can be very difficult to track and validate.

Errors Versus Defects Here we are using the terms "error" and "defect" differently than we have before, so the definitions of these terms need refinement:

- A software *error* is a mistake made by the software supplier (or developer).
- A software *defect* is the manifestation of an error during the execution of the software.

In its characterization of software quality, the management team first must choose one of these definitions to establish whether a *problem* refers to an error or a defect. Defining software quality as "a lack of known software errors" leads to one set of considerations. Alternatively, defining software quality as "a lack of known software defects" leads to a different set of considerations. For example, setting the goal for quality at "zero

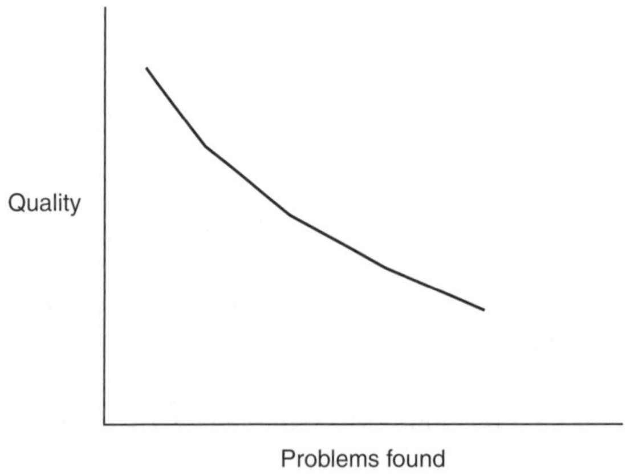

Figure 3.1 Inverse relationship of problems found versus quality

known software errors" makes the task of proving the attainment of such a goal almost impossible. We can never show that a deliverable has zero errors. Setting a goal of "zero known software defects" is a better alternative, but not by much, since the attainment of such a goal is also very difficult to show.

Note that both goals include the term "known" to qualify the types of errors and defects. For our metric and measurements, known errors and known defects are considered at specific time frames, such as at the end of testing or at the moment just prior to product release. Theoretically, more errors or defects may exist in the product, but at the specific time the product is evaluated, the product reveals only a certain number of problems. It is assumed that some set of testing methodology and process has been selected and agreed upon ahead of time, and that the attribute of quality is represented via the results of these planned testing activities. In practice, the type of testing and the use of those testing results as quality indicators are closely intertwined. The choosing and setting of methods and processes for a software project is discussed in Chapters 4 and 7.

For now, let us proceed through a series of planning steps. These steps are required when the number of software *defects* found through testing is used to determine the quality attribute.

Incremental Goals As much as one may desire to attain the goal of zero-defect software, it may not be a prudent goal in a large, commercial product environment for several reasons. First, the customer and the user may not necessarily need such a lofty goal. Second, the effort to attain zero-defect software may not be worth the cost; from a price-performance perspective, it may not be a good choice. Third, the actual measurement and analysis, or validation and verification, required to demonstrate the attainment of such a goal would likely be quite complex and costly.

Instead, the software project manager should opt for a software quality goal that is expressed in an incremental form, such as subgoals for each of the categories of software quality. The following is an example using problem severity levels. One can first identify a number of levels of defects by severity:

- *High-severity defect:* a defect that will stop the total software system and all work related to the system
- *Medium-severity defect:* a defect that will cause the loss of a function of the system, thereby preventing the user from completing his or her work as planned

- *Low-severity defect:* a defect that will cause some inconvenience and possibly require the user to perform a "workaround" to complete his or her task
- *Minor-severity defect:* a defect that will cause some misunderstanding of terminology or require a minor adjustment in the usage interpretation

Other project management teams might devise a defect categorization scheme with a different number of severity levels and different definitions of severity levels. Medium-severity in the previous list can be further refined into different types of noncatastrophic problems and thus expands the severity categorization to 5 or 6 levels. There clearly are other ways that defects can be broken down into categories that have associated subgoals. For instance, one less popular categorization of problems is based on the place at which the defects manifest themselves. With this approach, problems are categorized as either major or minor. Major problems appear on the main path of the software; the main path of the software is defined as functional options that exist only on the first screen and its immediate successor screens. All other problems are classified as minor problems.

Quantitative Subgoals Once a defect severity categorization is established, then the quality subgoals may be expressed in terms of these categories. The quality goal may be expressed in a quantitative form as follows:

- The software deliverables will contain zero known high-severity defects and zero known medium-severity defects at the time of the software release.
- The software deliverables may contain some known low-severity defects at release time, but they will all be fixed by the next maintenance update release, which will be in three to six months. (The term "some" may be changed to a more precise term such as "no more than ten.")
- The software deliverable may contain known minor-severity defects at release time, and these defects may be fixed at the convenience of the solution provider. (Again, no specific number is provided, but the team may choose to give a specific number.)

Metric Definition Given this set of subgoals, the metric for the software quality attribute would be defined for each defect type:

The number of unresolved or "open" defects by defect severity level

The Measurement Process The measurement process may be a set of weekly—or some other regular interval—tasks, including the counting, collection, and analysis of the test results. As part of the measurement process, the management team should receive regular updates on the number of defects, according to severity levels.

Reporting Format The software project management team must have a clear understanding of what needs to be tracked, in terms of defined attributes and metrics, and how these data will be presented. Table 3.1 shows an example of how the "High-severity" defects portion of a software quality evaluation would appear in a weekly quality report.

Let's take a closer look at a field-by-field description of the heading and the sample "High severity" row.

The Date field indicates the currency of the information. The Defect-type column indicates the level of severity represented by each row. The Problems-found column shows the number of defects found for that category during this reporting period, which may be by the week or by some other time interval. The Problems-closed column shows the number of problems found during this reporting period that have been fixed and retested for each of the categories during the reporting period. The Problems-still-open column gives the number of problems that have not been fixed and retested for each category during this reporting period. Thus Problems still open is calculated as Problems found minus Problems closed for that reporting period. The Accumulative-problems-still-open column shows the number of unresolved problems in each category; it includes all

Table 3.1 Weekly Quality Report

Date: (week-ending date if a weekly report)					
Defect type (by severity)	Problems found	Problems closed	Problems still open	Accumulative problems still open	Quality goal number
High severity	12	9	3	5	0 open at release
Medium severity					
Low severity					
Minor severity					

unresolved problems from earlier periods and the Still-open-problems from the current period. In this example, there were two unresolved problems left from the previous periods and three from this period, giving a total of five Accumulative-problems-still-open. Finally, the Quality-goal-number of zero shows the target for the high-severity defect level. How well the goal for the software quality attribute is attained may be validated quite easily through this kind of reporting.

The actual format of the report needs to be clear and consistent because resources will be expended in collecting and presenting the information. By forcing precision in the reporting format, the project manager ensures that the metric of the attribute of interest is defined, and that a measurement process for that attribute is in place. In the example described here, the number of defects for each severity level can be counted and collected through the various testing activities associated with the development of the software deliverable. This information can be tracked as long as the team keeps good records of the various defects found and resolved. The reports can be maintained in a database for future analysis and verification.

The information presented in the report is verifiable: We can check whether we have made the correct computations as we progress from raw numbers, such as "defects found" and "defects resolved," to derived numbers, such as "open defects" at release time. The attribute of quality can also be validated because the number of open defects can be compared with the goal number of "allowable" open defects at release time. The quality attribute of the software deliverable, through this type of planning, is formulated to be measurable, trackable, verifiable, and validatable.

As the software project progresses, the management team will need to regularly monitor the number of unresolved defects and compare it with the target goal. For any of the attributes of the software deliverable, the level of thought and planning required is similar to the degree described here for the quality attribute. In order for the organizing, monitoring, and adjusting (OMA) phases of POMA project management to operate smoothly, the goals of the project, and the measurement process of those goals, have to be considered and defined at the planning stage.

Complex Attributes

A complex attribute is an attribute whose metric definition requires a set of, or combination of, statements and definitions. In the preceding example, a set of severity levels was first defined and then metrics were defined for each severity level; from that example one can conclude that quality is a complex attribute. Usually, a complex attribute should be decomposed into several simple attributes (i.e., attributes whose metrics may be stated with a single definition) and expressed in terms of those subattributes.

Complex attribute An attribute whose metric definition requires a set of, or combination of, statements and definitions.

Simple attribute An attribute whose metric may be stated with a single definition.

Attributes of every product or project must be defined in such a manner that the metric is a specific number that may be compared and operated on arithmetically. This is a much more difficult task than it might seem at first glance. For example, the metric and measurement process for popular product attributes other than quality, such as usability and maintainability, have been carefully studied and analyzed. Nevertheless, these complex attributes still do not have standard goals, metrics, or measurements on which the software industry consistently agrees.

Consider one well-known goal for software design: "loose" coupling among software components. "Coupling" between two software components describes the interactions and the dependence of the components. Without a numerical metric for coupling, we can use only an imprecise term such as "loose." The metric for the goal of loose coupling has yet to be agreed upon, even though the attribute has been under study for nearly a quarter of a century.

Software project managers must study the work and experiences of other software projects before settling on a goal, a metric, and a measurement process for the attributes of interest in their own project. The concrete set of tasks that the project manager must perform to formulate a goal, a metric, and a measurement for an attribute that is not yet defined will depend on the specific attribute of interest. In other words, the "how" part of goal, metric, and measurement setting is determined by the particular attribute that is under evaluation. Nevertheless, the key for successful project management is to have at least the following items in the plan:

- The list of software deliverable attributes that will be measured for the project
- For each attribute, the definition of the attribute metric, stated in quantitative form
- The definition of the goal for that attribute stated in terms of that metric

- The measurement process to attain and communicate the data, stated in terms of the metric
- The exact reporting format for the information

It is also possible that multiple metrics and measurements might be needed for one complex attribute. For instance, the quality attribute that we discussed can have another metric associated with it, besides the number of problems. It would, for example, be meaningful to include a test coverage metric along with the known-defects metric. The goals for software code deliverable quality could then be stated in the following manner:

- Ninety-five percent of the executable code will be covered and executed with the planned test cases.
- The product will not contain any known high-severity defects at release time.

Complex deliverable attributes may require multiple metrics and multiple measurement methodologies. Thus, for a product attribute that is very broad, such as quality or usability, the project management team should strongly consider decomposing the attribute into a set of simpler subattributes, with metrics and goals associated with each subattribute.

PROJECT- AND PROCESS-RELATED METRICS AND MEASUREMENTS

Aside from the direct product deliverable attributes, project managers must address many project-related characteristics. We mentioned schedule and cost earlier as two primary areas that require attention. Of the two, software project managers tend to focus more attention on the schedule. Each project requires a unique set of product goals and metrics, but software project managers are often asked to describe the nature of their projects in terms of only the nondeliverable, project- and process-related attributes. The following is a list of common, nondeliverable project-related attributes:

- Schedule integrity
- Cost minimization
- Productivity
- Efficiency
- Cost-effectiveness
- Employee morale

Practically all projects must deal with the issues of schedule and cost, and it is important to clearly grasp these two attributes. The schedule integrity attribute will be discussed in some detail here.

Metrics and Measurements Example II: The Schedule Integrity Attribute

Most software project managers automatically assume that schedules must be met. *Schedule integrity,* however, is not merely "delivering the product on the release date." Just as managing the quality attribute requires substantial planning, so maintaining schedule integrity demands considerable work in terms of setting the definition, reaching general consensus, and attaining broad adoption. We do not offer a single definition for schedule integrity for the same reason that we do not offer a single definition for quality: For each project, the software project manager has the opportunity to think through and define it differently. Schedule integrity does have a commonly utilized metric, that which we use to measure time. Even so, the project manager must clearly define each of the events and the deliverables associated with every time slot in a schedule. The completion times associated with special events or deliveries are called milestones. There are major milestones and minor milestones depending on the type of event or deliverable.

The actual time metric may be specified in one of several ways. The simplest is to state one specific figure in a specific format, such as month/day/year. Another way is to provide a loosely specified time such as "end of month *x*," "middle of the month," or "end of day *z*." A third approach is to provide an interval such as "the last week of the month" or "the month of April." Some project managers use quarters as the unit, such as "the second quarter of year *x*." In all of these loosely defined intervals, it is almost inevitable that the last day of the week, of the month, or of the quarter becomes the de facto milestone date.

Once the deliverables are defined and the time schedules are specified for the milestones, the schedule integrity goal needs to be specified. For a relatively simple project whose total duration may be only one-half year, the schedule goals for the project may be stated as follows:

- The final project milestone must be met.
- All intermediate milestones must be met within two days of the scheduled time.

Such a set of schedule goals will allow the software project managers to conduct the organization, monitoring, and adjustment phases of the project. The intermediate milestones provide the software project managers with a simple monitoring mechanism that will alert them to any impending problem before the final schedule becomes hopelessly unachievable.

For an experienced company that has developed many software solutions and is managing many software projects, the goals at the organizational level for the set of projects may be stated slightly differently:

- Ninety-seven percent of projects meet the final milestone schedules.
- Ninety percent of projects meet all intermediate milestone schedules.

For a customer who is interested in only one specific project, having the schedule integrity goals stated at the organizational level, rather than at the project level, is certainly less attractive and less useful. The software project managers, therefore, may choose to have both types of goals: one for the individual project and one for the organization's long-term needs. The organizational-level goals and metric are usually more meaningful for upper and executive management.

Schedule Attribute Metric and Reporting Format The metric for the schedule is the same as that for time. The actual process of measuring time, however, needs to be further defined. For each milestone, the project manager must compare the scheduled event or deliverable time against the actual time when the event occurs or the deliverable is completed. This information must be recorded and maintained for future reference. Table 3.2 shows one possible format for a weekly schedule report.

The actual measurement is taken based on the project team's frequency of project status meetings. For a project that conducts daily status meetings, the measurements are taken daily. Likewise, projects that conduct status meetings on a monthly basis will usually take measurements on a monthly basis. Clearly, for projects that last only several weeks, the measurement

Table 3.2 Weekly Schedule Report

Milestone type and number	Description of the event or deliverable	Scheduled time (goal)	Actual time	Difference/Explanation
Major milestone 1	*Requirements prototype delivered*	*Mid-March 2003*	*3/16/2003*	*Goal met; 3/16/2003 was a Monday*

must occur more frequently than on a monthly basis, and status meetings should also be conducted more frequently.

The chart in Table 3.2 reveals whether the project milestones have been met and, if necessary, why a milestone has not been achieved. This chart, however, does not alert project managers to potential problems. For a measurement scheme that will inform the project management team about major milestones, the metric and the measurement scheme must be tied to multiple minor milestones that lead up to each major milestone. Therefore, the schedule must include an ample number of minor milestones.

Let's look at an example to illustrate the interrelationship of minor and major milestones. Let's consider a software project that has gone through the Work Breakdown Structure activity (WBS; see Chapter 2) and has all of its deliverables attached to milestone dates. Furthermore, all of its events, such as getting approval for requirements or attaining concurrency on the software design, are pegged to milestone dates. The preliminary WBS and established milestone dates are absolutely essential to the management of a schedule. If the whole project duration is defined in months, then the schedule metric should be in days, and the milestones, along with the goals, should be expressed in terms of specific dates. The metric may be scaled up to weeks if the total project duration is more than a year.

Here we assume that the example software project has a total duration of only a few months and that the WBS and the major events of this project have been worked out and set up. To keep the example simple, we will focus on only the requirements phase of this small project:

- Task 1.1: Obtain customer concurrence on requirements-gathering process.
- Task 1.2: Gather and document requirements.
- Task 1.3: Deliver requirements prototype.
- Task 1.4: Deliver requirements specification document to customer.
- Task 1.5: Review and rework requirements.

Table 3.3 shows each of these tasks, the assignment of a responsible person, and the number of units it would take for the task to be completed. The basic metric is a person-day. Every estimate that appears in Table 3.3 should be rounded upward to the next higher person-day if it is fractional. In this case, the responsible person also performs the task. In more complex situations, the responsible person may lead a team of others; the WBS would then need to be further expanded so that each task could be assigned to an individual task-performing person.

Table 3.3 Task Breakdown for Schedule Attribute Example

Task	Responsible person	Estimated person-days
1.1	P1	1 day
1.2	P2	8 days
1.3	P3	5 days
1.4	P2	4 days
1.5	P1	3 days

The project manager, together with the responsible people (P1, P2, and P3), must consider several items:

- How these tasks can be laid out in a calendar schedule form, depicting potential task overlaps
- How much buffer should be put into the estimated person-days and used to establish the milestone dates
- What the project goals should be and how they relate to the milestone dates

The planning activities described here are starting to overlap with the organizing phase of project management. Even though we may get some idea of the type of people and the talent required during the planning phase, we may not yet have a particular individual assigned to each task. In fact, the organization and assignment of specific personnel to the tasks may not be completed until the organizing phase of POMA. Thus talking to the software engineers and estimating buffers requires some guessing about the project's organization and the slotting of specific names to positions. Sometimes it is necessary to delve into the next phase to back up and better plan the current phase.

For each of the planning activities, the project manager needs to involve the other participants and consult data from past experiences with similar projects. Past experience does not always predict the future, but many past project data, such as those dealing with the adequacy of the buffers used in past projects, can prove helpful in planning the buffer allocation in the current project's schedule.

Task Overlap To assess whether any of the requirement tasks overlap, the project management team needs to look at which tasks are prerequisites of other tasks. The tasks that have a linear relationship must be carefully planned so that, if they must overlap, managing the overlap is not merely wishful thinking but is truly doable. For this example, let's assume that 20% of Task 1.3 may be started before Task 1.2 is complete, that 25% of Task 1.4 may overlap with the end of Task 1.3, and that all other tasks must not start until the previous task is completed.

When working with a visually-oriented plan and focusing on just the diagram, project managers sometimes make a mistake and overlap activities that cannot actually be conducted in parallel. The managers may not realize that they have devised a schedule that is too short, but formulating such a plan will put the project in a precarious position from the start. Managers may utilize tools that will graphically portray partial ordering. But, again, the key decision is which activities are partially ordered and which activities are totally ordered.

Buffer Size The amount of buffer to place on the initial estimate from the WBS is a project management call. Although there have been projects with more than 100% expansion of schedule, traditionally the project management team adds a 10% to 15% time buffer. The final decision depends on several criteria.

One important consideration is how adverse the customer is to schedule slippage. If the customer emphasized deadlines to the extent that he or she included a penalty clause in the contract to account for schedule integrity, then the software project manager may consider placing an extra buffer in the schedule estimates.

The project management team, together with the business development team or the sales team, also has to take the price-competitiveness aspect of the project into account in their planning. Adding a lot of buffer time to a schedule lowers the risk of missing milestone dates. However, adding too much buffer will inflate the cost, increasing the price of the project beyond that charged by competitors for similar projects. Price-competitiveness considerations must always be part of the planning.

Another consideration is how much buffering is added as each higher level of management reviews the estimate. As mentioned earlier, placing extra buffers at each level may price the project out of competitiveness.

In this example, assume that only one level of project management decides the amount of buffering—15%. The 15% buffer for this example would be equal to 21 days × 0.15 days buffer, which is 3.15 days total buffer. The 21 days is the assumed number of working days per month. We round up to the next person-day, so the buffer days will also be rounded up to four person-days. The actual schedule may show the buffer as a lump-sum number to be added to the last task of the schedule, or it may distribute the buffer across all the tasks and thus show it as part of each task. In our example, the buffer will appear as a lump-sum number added on to the last task of the schedule, Task 1.5.

Schedule Integrity Goal The schedule integrity goal of the project can now be established, given the amount of task overlap and buffer size. Within the schedule, the major milestone is the completion of the requirements review and rework–that is, the successful completion of Task 1.5. Thus a goal would be to meet this major milestone on time.

There are many ways to set subgoals for the minor milestones. The minor milestone goals should be set in such a way that if any is missed, the schedule includes enough flexibility so that the team can recover without the next minor milestone being compromised. We will call this the "immediate-recoverable" subgoal-setting method.

> **Immediate-recoverable goal setting** Setting a goal and its associated metric and measurements in such a way that if the goal is missed, there is an immediate way to recover without expending a large amount of extra resources and potentially causing other goals to be missed.

Project management teams who are particularly adverse to risky schedules often practice this approach. The project subgoal for this example, where the smallest task requires one calendar day, is set such that "at the end of any day, no task is more than one day behind." The minor milestones of completing Tasks 1.1, 1.2, 1.3, and 1.4 are further broken down into daily subgoals. The rationale behind the immediate-recoverable subgoal-setting method is that without adding resources, if every task is kept within one day of the schedule time, the task slippage may be made up over the weekend. The weekend is assumed to be two days.

Of course, this methodology may fail if the initial effort estimation is dramatically understated. It also assumes that the project will not require weekend work for a lengthy period of time. Past experience has shown that extended overtime wears people down, lowers morale, and increases the number and frequency of errors, which in turn causes more rework and additional slippage of schedule. The project manager needs to consider the disposition of the project team members and set a limit to the number of overtime weekend work hours allowed. Based on various project experiences, the author suggests this limit be no more than four consecutive weekends. In our example, the limit of four weekends allowed for working overtime will not be a problem because the whole requirements phase spans four work weeks. Furthermore, there is a 15% buffer at the end that may be used instead of overtime.

Now let's look at the schedule for this example and the related goals, shown in Figure 3.2.

The rough schedule shown in Figure 3.2 allows us to compare, on a daily basis, the schedule goals with the schedule status. A four person-day buffer appears at the end of the planned Task 1.5. The goals are to attain the major milestone—namely, completing Task 1.5 on or before Wednesday of the fifth week—and to attain all other minor task milestones within one day of the schedule, assuming the project starts on a Monday. For any week, no slippage is allowed to exceed one person-day of work within that week so that the two weekend days may be used as the immediate-recoverable time. Even if part of every weekend is used for immediate-recoverable purposes, the schedule includes only four weekends so that the chance of exhausting the team is not high.

The four person-day buffer is available for the team as well, but the project management team may decide to hold the buffer days and not use them for the immediate-recoverable weekend work. Instead, the buffer days may be saved to offset other problems, such as sickness, accidents, or family emergencies, that are not directly related to the performance of the project activities. Some management teams may choose to use part of or all of the buffer days instead of the weekend days. How a team utilizes the buffer depends on the project managers' style. More risk-adverse managers tend to save the buffer days. Some project managers are so date-driven that they not only try to save the buffer days but also attempt to squeeze in weekend days so as to beat the schedule goal, rather than use the buffer days for immediate-recovery purposes. Although it is fine to squeeze the project and try to beat the schedule, that approach should not become a standard practice. Schedule integrity addresses the issue of *meeting* the date attribute. Missing it by finishing either too late or too early is not considered good practice. Overly ambitious managers need to remember that a project completed much earlier

		Week 1							Week 2							Week 3							Week 4							Week 5		
Task	Person	M	Tu	W	Th	F	Sat	Sun	M	Tu	W	Th	F	Sat	Sun	M	Tu	W	Th	F	Sat	Sun	M	Tu	W	Th	F	Sat	Sun	M	Tu	W
1.1	P1	X																														
1.2	P2		X	X	X	X			X	X	X	X																				
1.3	P3											X	X			X	X	X														
1.4	P4																	X	X	X												
1.5	P5																						X	X	X	X						
Buffer																											Y			Y	Y	Y

Figure 3.2 Example schedule

than the expected date suggests poor planning and inadequate understanding of the capabilities of the resources.

Interrelated Attributes

Many process- and project-related attributes are intertwined. It is the relationship of these attributes that makes project management such an interesting—and potentially difficult—challenge. For example, the schedule and cost attributes are interrelated in that schedule can sometimes be significantly improved by applying more resources, which usually translates to higher costs. Conversely, cutting the budget for the project may negatively influence the schedule. It has also been the experience in the software industry that not all project schedules can be improved with more resources. Indeed, many software project schedules have been extended by the introduction of more people on the team at the wrong time, as Fred Brooks, who was the executive responsible for the IBM 360 operating system and is currently associated with the Computer Science department at the University of North Carolina, noted in his book *The Mythical Man-Month*. Brooks also stated that:

> When a task cannot be partitioned because of sequential constraints, the application of more effort has no effect on the schedule.... The bearing of a child takes nine months, no matter how many women are assigned. Many software tasks have this characteristic of sequential nature....

Adding more people when a software project is already experiencing problems will often exacerbate a schedule problem because the most knowledgeable members' focus will be diverted to teaching, coaching, and helping the new members who just came on board rather than tackling the underlying problems.

The question of when to best introduce the resources, a question that affects cost, may be further complicated by other criteria that have to be satisfied. From a software project activities perspective, resources need to be provided prior to the scheduled performance of the activities because there is usually a need for a short preparation time just before the actual performance begins. However, from a financial perspective, sometimes the resources must be held back until the beginning of the following month after the scheduled time. This tactic is employed so that the total monthly expense target, a potential financial goal, can be satisfied. Software project managers often need to work with the financial managers to ensure that both the resource needs and the monthly expense targets are satisfied.

A less discussed project attribute is employee morale. The productivity of the employees serving on the project is often closely tied to their morale, as well as their competency and other factors. A demoralized team, regardless of the reason for their low morale, will not perform as effectively as a satisfied team. The schedules, which are based on some productivity assumptions, will clearly be affected. Despite this factor's direct influence on the project's success, the job of setting the measurements for employee morale and gathering that information usually falls on the shoulders of the personnel department rather than software project managers. The software project managers, on the other hand, are responsible for setting productivity goals and measuring productivity. Tying the employee morale goal and measurements to the project productivity goal and measurements requires the coordinated efforts of both personnel and software project management members.

One example from the author's own management experience involved a situation in which a new configuration management process and tool were introduced to the software team. Initially, these changes met with a lot of resistance. Employee morale dipped, and the changes were cited as one of the causes of workers' dissatisfaction on the annual employee opinion survey. The expected productivity gains from the new configuration management process and tool did not materialize immediately, because more time was needed for the people to become educated in the new process/tool, make novice mistakes, and learn from these experiences. Over time, however, the organization's productivity shot up, people felt encouraged, and the opinion survey results became much more favorable. Missing some of the goals on employee morale provided a forum for a candid discussion of what was needed to achieve the productivity goal.

Trying to balance multiple attributes and multiple project goals can be a daunting task for software project managers, particularly those with less experience. During the monitoring phase, many attributes may show conflicting status relative to the goals. In the preceding example, bringing in a new process and tool led to declines in productivity and morale in the beginning; eventually, however, both productivity and employee morale goals were exceeded. Thus just setting the goals is not enough; the multiple goals must be prioritized. The priority of the goals may then be used to guide adjustment activities, if they later become necessary.

In software project management, as in other project management, there are many interrelationships among the product and project attributes. The following three possible attribute combinations are represented with the × symbol, which signifies that the attributes are "cross-attributes" or multiple-attributes:

- Product attribute × product attribute–for example, product quality and product functionality

- Product attribute × project attribute—for example, product functionality and project cost
- Project attribute × project attribute—for example, project schedule and project cost

Setting goals and measurements for both the product and the project requires in-depth knowledge of the various attributes and their interrelationships. During this software project planning phase, the software project managers will often need help from both peer-management and upper-management teams, as well as from technical leaders.

Because software projects are heavily people-oriented, the software project managers must pay special attention to those attributes that touch on personnel issues and study the consequences of personnel attributes as they are related to other project attributes. These "interattribute relationships" must be recognized, considered, and managed throughout all POMA phases and, indeed, throughout the entire project life cycle. Each component of software project management should not be viewed as an island unto itself. The various goals set by different people contributing to the project must not conflict with each other. For example, the goals set by the group interested in quality and the groups interested in costs or schedules or functions must all be taken into consideration when planning for the project. These interrelationships are becoming increasingly complex and are directing software project management toward a more coordinated, team-oriented management model. Note that the notions of software *project* teams and software *management* teams are similar but not necessarily the same; this topic will be discussed in more detail in Part Two of this book.

INFLUENCING DOWNSTREAM PHASES

The selection of product and project attributes that require goal setting, the definition of the metrics and measurements associated with those attributes, and the establishment of the goals for those chosen attributes form a set of activities that will dictate the tone of the later phases of the software project life cycle. The chosen attributes, goals, and measurements will be used to monitor the project and to make adjustments based on the monitored information. These goals will also influence the processes that one chooses for the project, a topic covered in Chapter 4. Similarly, the discussion of risks, covered in Chapter 5, is influenced by these goals. The risks are, in fact, related to the likelihood of not achieving the goals.

KEY CONCEPTS

The goals for a project should be defined and set during the planning phase of software project management. Many of these goals have their origins in the requirements statements. The goals must be defined in terms of either product or project attributes that have a clear metric and a measurement process. Each attribute should be defined in such a manner that it is measurable, trackable, verifiable, and validatable. Product goals may be related to the following attributes:

- Quality
- Usability
- Functional completeness
- Maintainability
- Reliability
- Modifiability
- Installability

Project goals may be related to some of the following attributes:

- Schedule integrity
- Cost-effectiveness
- Productivity
- Cost minimization
- Efficiency
- Employee morale

Complex multiple attributes and their interrelationships must also be considered by the project managers. These multiple goals must be prioritized during the planning phase to avoid the problem of conflicting status later in the monitoring and adjustment phases.

EXERCISES

1. What is the difference between a metric and a measurement?
2. What is a simple attribute, and what is a complex attribute?
3. Discuss the relationship of goal setting, product or project attributes, and measurement.
4. Define a goal for software product maintainability and an associated metric for that attribute.

5. Compare and contrast goal validation and measurement verification.
6. Define a goal for a software project attribute such as productivity. Explain how you could show that the goal is validatable and verifiable.
7. In this chapter we gave an example of goal setting for the quality attribute with different levels of defect severity. Would it be beneficial to relate these severity levels to fix-priorities? If so, discuss the implications of quality goals to setting up goals for software support goals.
8. Describe the difference between an error and a defect. Discuss how the different terms may affect the goal setting for quality.
9. Create a list of software product attributes and a list for software project attributes. Rank these in the order of how difficult you consider them to be measured; discuss the reasons for your choices.

SUGGESTED READING

V. R. Basili and D. M. Weiss, "A Methodology of Collecting Valid Software Engineering Data," *IEEE Transactions on Software Engineering,* SE 10, 1984, 728–738.

L. C. Briand, S. Morasca, and V. R. Basili, "An Operational Process for Goal-Driven Definition of Measures," *IEEE Transactions on Software Engineering,* December 2002, 1106–1125.

F. P. Brooks, Jr., *The Mythical Man-Month,* Addison-Wesley, 1975.

M. K. Daskalantonakis, "A Practical View of Software Measurement and Implementation Experience Within Motorola," *IEEE Transactions on Software Engineering,* November 1992, 998–1010.

W. S. Humphrey, "Characterizing the Software Process: A Maturity Framework," *IEEE Software,* March 1998, 73–79.

M. Shepperd and D. Ince, *Derivation and Validation of Software Metrics,* Clarendon Press, Oxford, 1993.

Software Engineering Institute (SEI), www.sei.cmu.edu, 2010.

F. Tsui and L. Brooks, "Release Management of Non-zero Defect Software," *Proceedings of the 10th International Conference on Practical Software Quality Techniques South,* March 2002.

Chapter 4

Project Resource Planning

Chapter Objectives

This chapter discusses the following concepts:

- How planning proceeds for the three main targets of software project resources planning–human resources, processes and methodologies, and tools and equipment
- How the three separate plans are pulled together into a single combined resources plan
- How resources may be outsourced and thus require the project manager to plan the human processes, tools, and equipment resources accordingly

PLANNING FOR THE THREE TYPES OF RESOURCES

Once the project deliverables, WBS, tasks, initial schedule, and goals are understood, the resources required to complete the project must be planned. The key resource for most software projects is people. Aside from personnel resources, both hardware and software packages and tools are needed. On an organizational level, processes, policies, and specific methodologies need to be available to ensure the successful completion of a software project.

These three types of resources should be considered and planned for in concert with one another. For example, the use of certain tools may potentially reduce the amount of human resources required. At the same time, there must be skilled people available to properly utilize and take advantage of that tool. Furthermore, the cost of the various resources is always a factor in the decision-making process. After the initial round of resources planning, additional iterations of planning may be necessary to adjust the resources requested based on earlier defined goals.

HUMAN RESOURCES

The number of people, the type of people with different skills, and the point at which these people need to begin working on a project all depend on the tasks that need to be performed and the goals, such as schedule, of the project.

Human resources management is concerned with the recruiting, hiring, retaining, growing, coaching, and firing of people, but software project managers will focus mostly on the recruiting effort and the timing of hiring the appropriate people during the planning stage. Recruitment and hiring proceed in two stages:

1. Based on the various tasks involved in the software project, a skills matrix is built. The number of people required for each skill category is identified, along with information on which persons, by name, are already on board.
2. Using the skills matrix, a hiring plan is developed.

The situation of outsourcing will be discussed later in this chapter. The broader issue of procurement will be taken up in a separate chapter.

Skills Matrix

Suppose that the skilled personnel listed in Table 4.1 are needed after the project software managers review the product requirements and the task analysis. For the purposes of this example, we assume that the organization is already established and has the needed processes and methodologies in place. Table 4.1 describes only the needed skills and the estimated number of those skilled resources; it does not lay out the timing at which the resources are acquired or used.

Two types of personnel are needed for any business operation: those involved in direct activities and those involved in indirect activities. Direct activities for the software project include those associated with requirements specification, design, coding, manual-writing, testing, integration, and packaging tasks that lead to a customer deliverable. Indirect activities include

Table 4.1 Skills Description of Personnel Required for the Example Software Project

Job title	Number needed	Experience/Skills
Project leader	1	Three or more years' experience in leading software project teams consisting of approximately 10 people and in successfully completing projects with a duration of approximately one year
Requirements analyst	1	Five or more years' experience in the application domain area
Designer	2	Three to five years' experience in the application domain area, two to three years' experience in the system operating environment, and two to three years' experience with the chosen application development language, database, design methodology, and design tool
Programmer	8	Two to three years' experience with the chosen application development language and development tools
Test analyst	3	Three to five years' experience in the application domain area, two to three years' testing experience, and two to three years' usage experience with the chosen test tools

those related to planning, status monitoring, staff education, and other tasks that do not lead to a customer deliverable.

Direct project activities Activities that lead to a customer deliverable. Human resources for these activities must be assigned or the customer deliverables cannot be delivered.

Indirect project activities Activities that are related to the planning, controlling, and reporting of the direct project activities. People assigned to these activities do not directly work on the customer deliverables and thus can become marginalized.

For this example, we assume that the indirect personnel are already in place and do not need to be acquired anew for this software project. Instead, only the direct software development personnel planning is considered here. Note, however, that real-world software project managers must consider both sets of people, even though their primary focus may be on the people who engage in direct activities. There will also be some preliminary thinking in terms of identifying some of the "direct" people who may remain after the project completion to perform customer support and maintenance. Mostly direct people are considered at this phase because they are engaged in the production of the customer deliverables, which require support and maintenance.

We also assume that the initial project schedule has already been established, and that the cost for each of these skilled people has been estimated. Then the human resources plan matrix for the software project must indicate the availability of the needed skills at the appropriate time, with the proper training and preparation, to perform the designated tasks. An initial skills matrix provides an early view of the number of required human resources by skill set and by time. It serves as an input to the hiring plan discussed in the next section. Table 4.2 shows an initial skills matrix for this example.

Several items stand out in this matrix. There is a fairly long period of project personnel ramp-up time before the total peak size of 12 people is reached during the eighth month. This gradual hiring pattern is quite realistic and occurs for several reasons:

- It is highly unlikely that the organization will be able to find so many good, skilled people all at once.
- New members must become acquainted with the project, and the tiered approach greatly facilitates that assimilation and education process.
- Not all tasks can be—or need to be—performed in parallel, so there is no need to ramp up fully on day 1. Having extra people on board too early is not only costly but may also cause a morale problem.

To elaborate on the final point, in times of a "super-hot" economy or a shortage of specific skills, software project managers may be forced to recruit people earlier than they are actually needed just so that these resources will be available when the project finally begins. This was the case

Table 4.2 Initial Skills Matrix

Skilled personnel	Months 1	2	3	4	5	6	7	8	9	10	11	12	13	14	...
Requirements analyst	1	1	1												
Designers			1	2	2	1									
Programmers					4	7	8	8	8	8	4	2			
Testers				1	1	1	2	3	3	3	3	3			
Project leader	1	1	1	1	1	1	1	1	1	1	1	1	1	1	1
Customer support											1	2	3	3	3
Total personnel	2	2	3	4	8	10	11	12	12	12	9	8	4	4	4

for personnel skilled in using the enterprise resources planning software package SAP from 1994 through 1996.[1] After new employees acquaint themselves with the corporate process, the software project process, and the tools, they may get bored with "education" and want to start performing using what they have just learned. If they are relegated to still more education activities, even greater boredom may set in; nonproject-related, disruptive socialization may increase; and some of the new hires may even depart the organization.

The author personally faced this situation twice at IBM and had to "invent" mini-projects just to keep the bored minds occupied. Clearly, such projects must not be just "make-work." Instead, some tasks that were not scheduled until later or do not exactly fit the team members' expertise can be moved forward. In the author's particular situation, the search for and analysis of a better test tool was used as the invented work. Even though the team ultimately did not switch tools, the employees appreciated the assignment because it enhanced their knowledge base.

Another human resources challenge that one might observe from the plan in Table 4.2 is the short peak period and the fairly rapid pace at which people leave the project. Unless the organization has many other projects that the people might join immediately after participating in this one, the project management team may face a people placement dilemma after this software project ends. Therefore, this project may be a candidate for utilizing temporary personnel, to ensure that the fast, but planned, ramp-down will not cause needless anxiety among the project team members. Personnel and economic issues are the reasons for our growing interest and emphasis in procuring resources and services.

An initial skills matrix such as the one in Table 4.2 does not show what happens to people such as the designers after they have completed their tasks. Perhaps Designer 1 will roll over to become a programmer when the design resources are reduced from month 5 to month 6. Perhaps Designer 2 will join the testing effort in month 7 after completing his or her design tasks in month 6. The names of the people joining and leaving the team, the transitioning from one role to another, and the final transitioning to the support team should be articulated in the resources plan along with the skills matrix. Also, this kind of people movement can be captured in the skills matrix if the matrix is expanded to show not just the number of each type of skilled person, but each individual, by name or by some other identifier, within that type as shown in the people hiring matrix (see Table 4.3 later in this chapter).

1. Interestingly, the shortage of SAP skills during the mid-1990s boosted the growth of outsourcing of enterprise resources planning activities.

Of course, not everyone will roll over to a new task within the same project after completing his or her assigned duties. As a consequence, there needs to be a separate plan for those individuals who will move off this project, even if some of these people are temporary employees.

Hiring Plan

Although creation of the skills matrix ought to follow development of the project task and schedule plan, project managers often need to revisit the task and schedule plan after studying the resources plan. The lead time needed for recruiting, training, and team assimilation may force them to go back and add some time to the schedule for these types of tasks, which may not have been considered during the first pass at planning and the WBS. Also, it is possible that a person with some special skill, in spite of planned recruiting lead-time, may not be found in time. In that situation, the project manager may need to revisit the project plan and get some relief in terms of schedule, functional content, or staged releases.

For estimating lead time, it would be appropriate to add an extra month (or some other appropriate period) for each person who needs to be recruited and brought on board. If three people need to be brought on board, however, that does not mean adding three months of lead time—it is still one month of lead time. The estimate of one month of lead time would depend on several factors, such as the economic environment, the company's geographical location, the type of project, and the compensation package offered to the prospective employee. During the peak of the "dot-com" boom, for example, smaller companies in the Boston and Silicon Valley areas faced the prospect of long recruiting times. At technology consulting companies such as Metamor, which at one time had a substantial presence on both U.S. coasts but did not have a broadly recognized high-tech reputation, the time required for recruiting knowledgeable technical people easily exceeded one month, even with offers of generous hiring bonuses. That situation changed as the dot-com era came to an end, however. Recruiters began calling Metamor in an effort to place some of the very experienced technical resources who were once nearly impossible to hire. Certainly, during economic downturns, the recruiting period may be as short as a few days.

In addition, if the project managers decide to hire temporary personnel to fill out the team or to use an outsourcing approach, the recruiting effort may be somewhat different. In particular, more emphasis may be placed on the employee's immediate technical skills and less emphasis may be placed on longer-term considerations related to employee retention and career development.

Table 4.3 People Hiring Matrix

Skilled personnel	Months 0	1	2	3	4	5	6	7	8	9	10	11	12	13	...
Project leader	X	1	1	1	1	1	1	1	1	1	1	1	1	1	1
Requirements analyst	X	1	1	1											
Designer 1			X	1	1	1									
Designer 2				X	1	1	1								
Programmer 1					X	1	1	1	1	1	1				
Programmer 2					X	1	1	1	1	1	1	1			
Programmer 3					X	1	1	1	1	1	1				
Programmer 4					X	1	1	1	1	1	1				
Programmer 5						D1	1	1	1	1	1	1			
Programmer 6						X	1	1	1	1	1				
Programmer 7						X	1	1	1	1	1	1	1		
Programmer 8							X	1	1	1	1	1	1		
Tester 1				X	1	1	1	1	1	1	1	1	1		
Tester 2							D2	1	1	1	1	1	1		
Tester 3								X	1	1	1	1	1		
Customer support 1										X	1	1	1	1	
Customer support 2											P1	1	1	1	
Customer support 3												X	1	1	

X = Lead time for recruiting a person from outside the project.
D1, D2 = Movement of a designer to a new role.
P1 = Movement of a programmer to a new role.

People Hiring Matrix and the Recruiting Plan

A people hiring matrix may be derived from the skills matrix as shown in Table 4.3, where X represents the "recruiting and adjustment" time. D1 represents Designer 1's preparation for moving to his or her new programming role; similarly, P1 indicates Programmer 1's preparation for moving to a customer support role.

People hiring matrix A project hiring plan shown in the form of a matrix or bar chart that indicates each specific human resource and the time period for which that person is associated with the project, including his or her recruiting and assimilation time.

Ideally, one would like to retain and move a designer and two programmers into the third customer-support role. That transition would most likely not work, however, because designers and programmers might not mind performing customer support for a very short time but probably would not tolerate it for a lengthy period. Also, the cost of customer support needs to be kept low, and it would usually be cost-prohibitive to place a higher-paid designer or programmer in this position for the long term. After these considerations are taken into account, the plan in Table 4.3 moves one programmer into the customer support role. Even then the plan should address the eventual (probably within six months) movement of this programmer out of the support role.

The people hiring plan matrix for this simple project, shown in Table 4.3, can be turned over to the company's human resources department or to a recruiting company as soon as it is established. The matrix should be accompanied by a skills description such as the one shown in Table 4.1, thereby ensuring that the right people will be brought on board. From the people hiring matrix and the skills description, a more comprehensive *recruiting plan* may be created. A recruiting plan will focus on the following items: job descriptions, job titles, number of openings to be filled, priorities in hiring, compensation and benefits packages, interviewing process and interviewing managers, internal and external avenues to solicit candidates, amount of internal hiring bonuses, range of acceptable recruiter fees, and hiring timing. The recruiting plan is described in another matrix that includes all the mentioned items listed by each open position; it should be developed by the personnel department and reviewed with the project management team. In fact, the software project managers may view personnel hiring as a mini-project within the larger project.

Later, the people hiring matrix may be used as a mechanism to monitor the hiring status; the planned recruiting and assimilation time of each person in this matrix can be compared with the actual hiring status during the downstream organizing and monitoring phases (the "O" and "M" in POMA). In other words, each X in the people hiring matrix in Table 4.3 will serve as a trigger for comparing the matrix entry against the actual hiring status.

Consider the situation in which the project leader is directly involved in the hiring of the people for the example project, including the hiring of post-development customer support personnel. Table 4.4 shows how much time the project leader may devote to recruiting.

Table 4.4 Direct Management Involvement in Recruiting

	Months involved in recruiting												
	0	1	2	3	4	5	6	7	8	9	10	11	12
Project leader	X		X	2X	4X	2X	X	X			X		X

Even though the recruiters and other human resources personnel will initially review and sort the applicants into different categories of candidates, the software project managers and project leaders still need to review the qualifications of especially attractive candidates. The software project managers and leaders will conduct the interviews and provide post-interview evaluations of these individuals. They must decide to whom to extend actual employment offers and the exact contents of the offer packages.

Sometimes, the project managers and leaders are even involved in the development and wording of recruiting brochures for some special positions. An example of a special position would be a project staff position that has responsibility for a cross-functional characteristic such as user satisfaction. This position requires a person who can interact with users and customers gregariously. At the same time, this individual must possess in-depth knowledge about opinion survey techniques, statistical analysis, the software support process, and the product so as to properly gauge customer satisfaction. The precise description of such a position will vary depending on what exactly needs to be emphasized.

As shown in Table 4.3, the project leader himself or herself is brought on board during month 0 along with the requirements analyst, but the project leader may still be involved in the recruiting of the requirements analyst.

Many people will be surprised at the amount of the project leader's time that can be consumed by the recruiting effort, as shown in Table 4.4. In that table, the number of Xs represents the number of people with whom the software manager is involved in recruiting during that month. The project leader spends time on recruiting during 9 of the 13 months shown, with the bulk of the effort coming during months 3, 4, and 5. This table should also alert project managers that they should plan for only a moderate number of other activities for the project leader during months 3, 4, and 5—especially month 4.

People As Human Capital

The preceding discussion made some major assumptions to clarify the issues: The software project planning was simplified and the availability of many support personnel was assumed. In reality, in many large projects or projects that are starting from scratch, the human resources required for the project will include a broad set of people such as technical writers, administrative support personnel, software and hardware systems support personnel, tools support personnel, and managers. These skilled people are all needed, even in our simplified example. Furthermore, the addition of 12 people to an organization, such as in the preceding example, will most likely require an increase in staffing in administrative support personnel and software-hardware desktop support personnel. Thus the human resources plan presented in the skills and people hiring matrices can serve as input not only to the project managers during their recruitment efforts, but also to the personnel responsible for planning other resources needed for the project (e.g., office space, desktop computing facilities, and communications facilities).

Unfortunately, the needed increase in human resources support in areas indirectly related to the software project is all too often forgotten. Unless *all* of the needed human resources are planned for, some problems may arise in absorbing the additional workload generated from the software project. The specific project management and other support management departments, such as the internal desktop support group and the administrative support group, will need to work together closely as one team in the planning of these indirect human resources.

After all the effort and costs that are expended in their hiring, these skilled people should be viewed as "human capital." For this reason, it makes sense for the software project managers to ensure that their workers' morale remains high and that the new employees are protected from being stolen away by other companies. Employee morale is a project attribute that should be tracked and monitored throughout the monitoring phase (the "M" in POMA). To protect against key employees leaving, companies must consider many issues ranging from basic compensation to opportunities for growth within the organization. During the planning and recruiting period, the initial offer package should be designed so as to be competitive in the marketplace, yet should be positioned in such a manner that the compensation can increase as the employee grows in experience after having been hired. Many companies establish salary and compensation ranges for each position. The best advice is to not bring people in at the top of the range; this approach ensures that the person does not have to receive a promotion to get the next raise. It is much easier to move a person up within the position ranges if that individual is brought in at the lower end of the compensation range for each position.

PROCESSES AND METHODOLOGIES

It may seem strange to some that processes and methodologies are viewed as resources. Unless the particular software project team does not need any standards and guidance on how to perform their tasks, how to coordinate activities, how to evaluate results, and so on, software processes and methodologies constitute a vital component of the resources needed for the successful completion of a software project.

In fact, the project management team already had to address the issue of processes to some degree when it formulated the list of project tasks. Depending on the assumption of which processes will be followed, the type and amount of internal artifacts that need to be developed may differ from the original assessment of processes and thus require a different set of tasks. For example, one process might include test case reviews. If so, then the project task list must include test case reviews, and the project schedule must in turn reflect the time and people required for a process that includes test case reviews. Here the term "process" means any ordered set of well-defined activities undertaken to accomplish a particular goal.

There is no single process for software development. Instead, in addition to the ordered set of defined activities that describe the defining of requirements, designing, coding, and release for a software artifact, there are processes that apply to software maintenance and to support after development and release of the product. Thus a process may be applied to the entire software project life cycle or just to a specific component of the life cycle, such as the design phase of the project. The number of tasks involved, depending on the chosen process, may differ dramatically.

> **Software development process** An ordered set of defined activities that describe the defining of requirements, designing, coding, testing, and release for a software artifact. A process may contain some subprocesses, such as the design subprocess within the software development process.

In contrast, a "methodology" is a set of rules and principles defined to accomplish a specific task. In software projects, a methodology may define a specific task such as requirements specification. A requirements specification methodology, for example, might be the specification of user scenarios utilizing the popular Use Case Diagram from the Unified Modeling Language (UML). (For more information on UML, consult the material listed in the "Suggested Reading" section at the end of this chapter.)

Software methodology A set of rules and principles defined to achieve a specific goal and to accomplish a specific task in the development or support of software.

In the project planning stage, the software project managers need to identify which processes and methodologies will be used. If they fail to do so, confusion may arise at later stages of the software project if the team members have to quickly create, find and borrow, or do without the guidance of processes and methodologies. Even worse is the situation that arises when team members disagree over which of several processes or methodologies they will use. The software project managers should ensure that the different views are heard and that some form of consensus is reached during the planning phase. They should also make sure that "methodology wars" are kept to a minimum. Many project failures have occurred when the confusion created by a lack of well-understood processes and methodologies resulted in missing schedules, poor product quality, demoralized teams, and possibly total abandonment of the project.

For example, when object-oriented methodologies were first introduced in the late 1980s and early 1990s, many projects suffered schedule delays due to a paradigm shift from the more traditional structured, waterfall process. Similar problems were observed when the inspection methodology was introduced into the software development process in the early 1970s. (Inspection methodology is the formal review step that Mike Fagan at IBM introduced into the software development process; variations of it have been in use in the IT industry for nearly 30 years.)

There are many ways for a software project to fail. The key to avoiding this fate is to ensure that a process or a methodology is well defined and understood prior to its deployment so that the chance of success is increased. This step starts with the planning phase (the "P" in POMA).

Software Project Phases

The project management team has many choices in terms of determining the overall process. In general, all software project cycles include some form of all or parts of the following phases:

- Requirements processing
- Design
- Implementation and programming
- Testing
- Product release

A software project plan must describe which of and how much of these activities are part of the specific project. Depending on the nature of the software project and the goals of the project, the processes and methodologies chosen and emphasized may differ significantly. Let's consider each of the software project phases in turn.

Requirements Process Planning

Requirements processing includes a large set of activities. To avoid subsequent confusion, a complex and large software project requires a well-defined set of requirements. It also needs a set of requirements processing activities, such as the one described in the general requirements management activities diagram in Chapter 1 (see Figure 1.1). In large, complex projects, there will most likely be modifications and changes to the established base along the way. Thus the requirements management process described in Chapter 1 needs to be expanded to include management of changes and modifications. The software project planners and managers should consider the following issues:

- Is this project already well defined or does it need extensive requirements definition?
- If there is a need for extensive requirements definition, what set of activities should be included as part of the requirements process?
- Is there a high probability of changes and modifications and, therefore, a need for a change management process?
- Is the methodology for each of the tasks or activities within the requirements process well defined and understood?

If the software project is already well defined and the requirements specifications are clearly documented, reviewed, and signed off by all parties, then no requirements process may be necessary. If not, there is a need to define how the requirements for the project will be gathered, documented, reviewed, and agreed to by all parties. If such a process already exists within the organization, then the project management team must ensure that the requirements analysts either are already experienced in using that process or can be educated in the process and its associated methodologies. In the latter case, the plan should include requirements process education as a task in the schedule. In the event that no such process or methodologies are defined within the organization but a requirements process and methodologies are needed, then the plan should account for the acquisition or creation of the process and the methodologies. The project team must then be educated on the newly defined or acquired process and methodologies. This situation is especially true today with the popularity of the Agile process where requirements may be articulated directly by the users to the designers and programmers. (Please see the Suggested Reading section.)

The following guidelines might apply to a planning situation in which the requirements process and methodologies need to be either acquired or generated:

1. Determine whether there is a need for a requirements process. If there is a need, continue to Step 2. Otherwise, consider the next type of process planning, which is design process planning.
2. Plan for the tasks or activities to be included and defined as part of the requirements process, outlining the order and the sequencing of the activities:

- Requirements solicitation
- Requirements analysis
- Requirements prototyping
- Requirements documentation
- Requirements review
- Requirements sign-off
- Requirements change and impact management

3. For each of the chosen activities, ensure that either a methodology already exists or the plan includes the definition of methodologies.
4. Include education on the process and the methodology, if necessary, as part of the plan.

In deciding which activities to include as part of the requirements process, the software project management must take into account several parameters, such as the type of software project, the goal of the project, and the measurements needed.

Design Process Planning

Like the requirements process, the design phase may consist of several activities. Thus it may be viewed as a phase that also requires a process. The following activities may be considered as candidates for the design process:

- Architectural design
- Application-specific high-level design
- Application-specific low-level design
- Design analysis
- Design review
- Design change and impact management

Once again, the project management team needs to decide which of these activities should be included in the design process. The architectural design differs from the application-specific high-level design in that the former design focuses on the overall system, including all external subsystems with which the software project must interact, whereas the latter design focuses on the components within the project application itself. For example, an architectural design for enterprise resources planning software will include the decomposition of enterprise resource management into its major components, such as planning, production, inventory, and financial activities; the architectural design also includes the interfaces that depict how these components interact with one another as well as how these components utilize a common technology such as the Internet, which is external to the components. However, the application-specific high-level design will focus on the functions and characteristics related to a specific area, such as how accounts payable information is stored, queried, and reported within the financial application component.

For each of the chosen activities, the plan should include the definition of the specific methodology to be used and the education plan for that methodology, if one is necessary. As noted earlier, these design methodologies fall within the domain of software engineering rather than software project management. For more details, readers should consult the widely available material on software engineering (see the "Suggested Reading" sections at the end of this chapter and previous chapters).

Implementation and Programming Process Planning

The implementation and programming phase is most likely the best-understood phase. In addition to code development, it should include document and publication development activities. To streamline this phase, many software project managers are acquiring existing software code and using it "as is" or with some modifications rather than implementing the complete project from scratch.

Focusing on Reuse Goals

There are multiple technical issues related to reuse of code or designing for reuse with which software engineers should be concerned. For software project managers, however, the key is to understand and decide what the organization's real goal is. If one of its goals is to reduce expenses, then reuse should be viewed from that perspective, and well-defined measurements must be taken to determine whether that goal can be achieved. If reducing risk is one of the organization's goals, then reuse should be measured from that perspective. Software project managers should not allow themselves to be dragged into lengthy discussions on the technical merits of reuse, but rather should focus on the goals of reuse and on monitoring the status to see whether those goals will, in fact, be reached. Similarly, as the project managers consider outsourcing their documentation and publications efforts, their major focus should be on defining the goals for the outsourcing effort, on defining the process or methodology to use for outsourcing the documents and publication efforts that will achieve those goals, and on monitoring the status of the outsourcing process.

The following list of activities may be considered for the implementation and programming phase:

- Programming standards definition
- User documentation, help text, and other information standards definition
- Software code acquisition, procurement, and reuse management
- Program documentation
- Program and information review
- Program unit testing

The programming standards definitions to be included depend on the nature of the project and must be included in planning. Otherwise, implementation and programming might become a task in which each member of the project team codes using his or her own style, which could potentially turn future code changes and support by others into an extremely difficult task.

As an example of how things can go wrong, consider the situation in which a support technician—let's say maintenance programmer A—needs to correct a program that was written by another programmer B, who used her own unique convention for naming variables. Now suppose that support programmer A discovers that another program written by a third programmer C needs to be modified as part of the correction. If programmer C also utilized his own unique set of naming conventions for the same variables, then one can imagine the potential confusion inherent in learning yet another set of variables and making changes to the code that affect the same variables referenced with different names. A problem fix that spans four or five programs written by different programmers who did not follow a common standard can quickly turn into a massive bookkeeping nightmare, thereby increasing costs and the potential for introducing a new error as part of the putative fix.

In the case of acquiring and reusing code, the documentation and programming standards of the acquired material should match that of the project's own code implementation. If the acquired code will be integrated with the code written by the implementation team and will be supported by only one support team, then the problem scenario discussed above might reappear if two different standards are used. Integration of acquired software is both a management and a technical problem. It is a management issue in that software project managers must recognize that software artifacts do not naturally merge together effortlessly; the integration must be thoroughly planned. To ensure that this integration is achieved with minimal problems, knowledgeable resources must be specified during the planning phase. Furthermore, software code acquisition and reuse methodology (a technical methodology for defining, constructing, and policing the interfaces between the old and the new code) must be put in place to address the issues that pertain to software reuse and integration.

Test Process Planning

The testing phase of a software project may be quite complex and may include an assortment of activities:

- Test planning
- Test scenario development
- Test case and test script development
- Test scenario and test case review
- Test result tracking and analysis
- Test execution, problem reporting, resolution, and fix-integration management

Test scenario A description of a set of interactions between the system and an external agent, which may be a user or another system, to accomplish a desired user task or goal. These scenarios are often directly derived from the requirements specification document.

Test case A description of a specific interaction between the system and an external agent; the interaction has defined inputs and defined expected outputs or results. Test cases are usually developed from a test scenario.

Test script A test case written in a language that may be used directly by some test tool to conduct the actual test.

The test planning activities include the definition of the types of testing that will be conducted for the project, such as unit testing, functional testing, component testing, system testing, performance testing, and regression testing. Test process planning might not define the exact methodology to be used, but must include the overall test process, tools utilized, skills required, and schedule. The description of the overall test plan includes a listing of which type of testing (e.g., unit test, functional test) will be conducted, by whom, and in what order. The application of tools to the different types of testing is specified during test process planning. The skills needed to run the tools and to conduct the different types of testing are also included in the test process planning. The definitions of the specific methodologies to be used may be included in the definitions of the various test activities, which constitute the test process. Test case development activity, for example, will be defined separately.

Product Release Process Planning

The release phase of a software project is the final phase during which the software project is coming to a conclusion and the various components of the software product are integrated, packaged, install-tested, and sent out to the customer. Several activities are involved, some of which (e.g., the shipping and distribution of software or other relatively easy-to-describe tasks) may be outsourced. In particular, the following activities are part of the software release phase:

- Integration, packaging, and installation
- Product order, release, and shipment management

If the product installation mechanism was not described as part of the requirements, then the project management team must clearly state it before an integration and packaging methodology can be described. Testing the installation mechanism must be part of the integration, packaging, and installation activity as well as part of the product release phase planning.

Other Process Planning Considerations

Cross-Functional Process Planning In addition to the activities related to the major phases of a software project, some activities cross boundaries or are independent of any specific project phase. These activities also must be defined and understood by the software project team before they can be carried out properly. Thus the processes and the methodologies associated with these cross-functional activities are process resources that should be included as part of the project plan. Some of the major cross-functional activities are listed here:

- Configuration management
- Outsourcing and procurement management
- Quality assurance
- Project change management
- Project reporting and escalation process

The cross-functional nature of some of these activities may not be obvious to new software project managers. We will describe two of them in more detail here.

Configuration management is often associated with a tool that controls the changes to code made by multiple programmers. This description is an extremely limited view of configuration management; in fact, it describes code control only. The broader issue of configuration management is the management of the various versions of all the software artifacts developed as part of the project. Such a broad view of configuration management includes the naming and describing of all the pieces of the software artifacts. Configuration management also encompasses how these artifacts are controlled as the project moves from the requirements phase to the software release phase.

Consider the situation in which a test scenario is associated with a requirement scenario. If we want to ensure that all requirements scenarios have been covered by test scenarios and, therefore, that the system has been adequately tested, then a configuration management scheme that defines all parts of the requirements and the test scenarios must first exist. Furthermore, an automated tool will most likely be needed to keep track of and control all of these parts, as well as to match up the parts. This example of configuration management illustrates how a cross-functional activity permeates software development activities ranging from requirements specification to testing and how it affects multiple artifacts. One can also readily see how configuration management might be helpful in the product support environment: A software engineer, for example, might want to trace through the original requirement, design, code, and test case for a reported software problem before actually changing the software.

Another example of a cross-functional activity is *project change management.* When taken by itself, a legitimate change request may or may not be implemented. Conversely, an illegitimate change that was conjectured by some programmer might slip into the software without anyone else's knowledge.

Later on, because no one ever tested for the unplanned modification, such an uncontrolled change could turn into a serious problem. Software project managers need to recognize and plan for all potential change activities. Thus a project change management process–definition, education, promotion, and policing–must be considered during planning.

Process as Intellectual Capital Other cross-functional processes and methodologies may need to be defined as well. The important thing to remember is that the processes and methodologies are not obvious and free resources. Rather, they must be planned for and included as resources that will be made available to the project team–just as people, hardware, or software tools are resources to be made available to the project team.

The timing at which these processes and methodologies enter the picture is also important. Early on, the overall project process must be defined and agreed to by the team. As new team members are brought on board, it is vital that they receive education on the same process. As the software project moves through its various phases, the specific methodologies to be used within each phase must be introduced to the team members. Where knowledge of those methodologies is lacking, team members should complete their education while they are working on the methodology.

All of the process and methodology definitions, education material, and documentation should be viewed as the "intellectual capital" of the software project. These process materials are valued resources that should be safeguarded. Many software and consulting companies today conduct their businesses based on these processes; some provide processes at prices that exceed tens of thousands of dollars. Examples of commercially available processes and methods include Express Delivery from Computer Associates, Navigator from Ernest and Young, and Team Fusion Object Oriented from Hewlett-Packard. (Method/1 from Anderson Consulting was also gaining a great deal of momentum prior to the demise of Anderson.)

Intellectual capital Knowledge that is considered an asset and ultimately has financial value.

As mentioned in Chapter 3, the Software Engineering Institute (SEI), a U.S. government-supported organization on the campus of Carnegie Mellon University, has been studying and promoting various process models. The SEI also educates organizations on process models for a fee. The institute's Capability Maturity Model for Software (CMM for SW), with its five levels of process maturity and Capability Maturity Model Integrated (CMMI), have been utilized by many software project managers in planning and assessing their organizations. One perhaps unexpected place where CMM and CMMI have taken hold is India. Many Indian IT outsourcing companies—including TaTa, Satyam, and Info Sys—have achieved the highest level (level 5, Optimizing) of the CMM assessment. These companies are able to enhance their stature with potential customers by providing evidence of their software development maturity.

TOOLS AND EQUIPMENT

Many of the processes and methodologies discussed in the previous section may be totally or partially automated and have some tools associated with them. Indeed, unless the complete software project is outsourced and the project manager is just acting as the facilitator between the customer and the provider, there usually is a need for some type of equipment and tools. These tools and equipment must also be planned for as resources for the project.

The most obvious type of hardware needed is the desktop computer. If the project is large enough to require the services of several people to thousands of people, then these desktops will need the help of servers, which act as coordinating and communication machines. Some details concerned with hardware are as follows:

- Desktop computers: Specify capabilities in terms of CPU speed, main memory size, disk storage size, number of ports (for printers, communications, and connection to other peripherals); specify number of desktop computers
- Server computers: Specify capabilities in terms of CPU speed, main memory and auxiliary cache memory sizes, disk storage size, number of ports; specify number of server computers
- Printers: desktop versus shared; specify number of each kind of printer
- Network equipment: controllers, lines, modems; specify number of each

Along with hardware requirements, the software systems requirements must be identified. In particular, the operating systems, database systems, and communications software need to be specified:

- Operating system: specify the number of copies required for the desktop and server computers
- Database system: specify the number of user seats required
- Middleware system: specify the type of communications middleware or transactions-processing middleware, set to the needed number of users or to some number of transactions
- Browser: specify the number of copies needed for the client desktop computers

Once the basic hardware and software operating environment resources are identified, the software project managers must consider which tools are needed. These tools may be classified into the following categories:

- Development and implementation tools: libraries of executable code, editors, compilers, and debugging aids; specify the number of copies or number of user seats for each
- Requirements management tools: specify the number of user seats
- Design tools: specify the number of user seats
- Documentation tools: specify the number of user seats or number of copies
- Test tools: keystroke capture tools, test execution monitoring tools, performance measurement tools, code coverage analysis tools; specify the number of copies or number of user seats
- Support tools: customer call management, release management; specify the number of copies
- Management and general-use tools: library systems, configuration management, diagramming and flowcharting tools, word processors, spreadsheets, project schedulers, statistical function packages; specify the number of copies or number of user seats for each type

Development and implementation tools are some of the most fundamental tools and are used in practically all software projects. Most of today's software project managers also realize the importance of keeping the various software artifacts properly versioned and locked. As such, library and configuration management tools, as described in the previous section, are becoming as vital a resource as compilers and debugging aids. The choice of tools and aids for the particular software project depends on the processes and methodologies chosen, the type of personnel recruited, the management style, and the funds available.

COMBINING THE RESOURCES

Resources planning is a lengthy but a very important project management activity. Ultimately, the more time and attention that are spent on this type of planning, the more likely that the rest of the project will flow smoothly. The resources required to satisfy the software project depend on the deliverables, tasks, schedule, and project goals. These resources themselves are interrelated and may be identified in a comprehensive resources plan.

Table 4.5 presents one such simplified summary. In this example, all of the main software development phases will be utilized, and the process will be close to a waterfall (nearly sequential) process. Clearly, a separate document describing the overall process in more detail is needed for the software project organization. The project managers should ensure, during the planning phase, that such a document exists and that the team members will be educated to perform according to the overall project process. Not all the details are specified in Table 4.5—for instance, the operating system and hardware are merely listed, not described in detail. Each software project team will have to create its own summary table, reflecting its unique needs. Of course, the more detailed and accurate the summary, the more complete the plan.

Table 4.5 Combined Resource Matrix

Project phases	Requirements processing	Design	Implementation	Testing	Product release	Support
Methodologies	Requirements solicitation Requirements prototyping	Class design Sequence and interaction design User interface design	Java and JavaScript coding	Black-box testing White-box testing System and performance testing	Installation method Packaging	Customer call management
Specific tools and equipment	Requirements management tool	UML tool Visual Java	Visual Java development workbench	Test management tool Performance testing tool	CD read/write tool	Service tool
Specific human resources	2	3	8	4	1	3
General methodology	Project management Quality assurance Change management					
General tools	Project schedule Document library and configuration management					
General support human resources	1 Project manager 1 Quality assurance statistician 1 Configuration management administrator 1 Database administrator					
Hardware and operating environment	20 Desktop PCs (256 MB memory and 3 GB hard drives) with Microsoft Windows NT and Internet Explorer 1 Development tool server (1 Hz, 512 MB memory, 50 GB hard drive) 1 Network controller 1 Relational database					

Table 4.5 addresses only the planning for the types and amounts of resources needed for the example software project. The timing of the resources' availability is also important, however, and should be specified in the plan. In addition to the questions of *what, how many,* and *when,* the software project managers may face the problem of *how* to provide these resources. This consideration leads to the next topic in this chapter: deciding whether to outsource activities or to develop the necessary resources in-house.

OUTSOURCING VERSUS INSOURCING

Some or all of the resources needed for the project may come from external and remote sites. This possibility must be addressed as part of the project planning. If any resources will be acquired from outside (outsourcing) as opposed to relocated and transferred within an organization (insourcing), that fact must be noted in the plan. The primary consideration in making this decision is often the cost involved.

Outsourcing Physically moving work to external sources.

Insourcing Physically bringing in external human resources to perform work. These external resources may be from different organizations within the same company.

One possibility in human resources planning is not hiring any additional employees for the particular project. Instead, the team may be cobbled together by "borrowing" personnel from other organizations within the company. If this approach is preferred due to cost or workload imbalance issues, then some of the personnel might operate out of remote locations and need to be "tied" together as a team. The project plan needs to identify how this linkage will be accomplished by answering the following questions:

- Who are the remotely located human resources?
- What additional resources are required to manage remote sites?
- What modifications are needed to the process and methodologies to account for the remote resources?

If the project management decides to outsource all of the human resources needed so as to realize an immediate cost savings, to pursue a long-term strategy, or for some other reason, then the project plan would have to focus on a "remote management" plan, identifying the resources needed for managing an outsourced group.

Many successful outsourcing examples can be cited. For example, a large company, Eastman Kodak, chose to outsource its entire data center to IBM, and a relatively small firm, Mapics, chose to outsource its software programming to an Indian company. Each remote management plan will inevitably differ in content, based on a variety of factors such as the size and type of the project, the risks, and the distance. Although each remote outsourcing experience is different, some common resources should be identified in every remote management plan. Such resources might include the following items:

- Extra network and communications equipment
- Additional methodologies and processes to ensure that reports on project status and problem escalation are not delayed
- A project leader with special skills or experience in remote management
- Travel and meeting policies

Of special significance is the project leader's experience and skill in remote coordination and management. The remote workers may be located in different countries. To counteract potential problems, the project manager must make an extra effort to bring the differing cultural experiences and expectations of these team members out into the open. Including extra time in the project schedule for harmonizing the group is critical. In some cases, the initial task schedule might need to be subsequently revisited and modified. Additional time and effort to understand any concerns that arise due to cultural differences might have to be included in the plan, for example by undertaking informal meetings. Extra traveling budgets also need to be included in the plan. Furthermore, if the remote sites are in different countries, international laws and tax regulations must be considered during the planning phase.

IBM's Rejuvenation Through IT Services

In the past decade, IBM has gone through an amazing turnaround—from almost going bankrupt in the early 1990s to reassuming its role of an industry-leading company in the early 2000s. At the heart of that turnaround is IBM's global service business, which provides IT services to its customers—that is, IT outsourcing.

> The company's rebirth has its roots in 1989, when IBM and Eastman Kodak entered into an agreement under which IBM designed, built, and managed a new data center for Kodak in Rochester, New York. By 1993, IBM had won a 10-year, $650 million contract to provide data center management and other services to Equifax. In that same year, IBM entered into another 10-year, $415 million contract with Southern Pacific to handle the company's information technology functions. These contracts and many other follow-on outsourcing contracts had a dramatic impact on IBM's fortunes and contributed directly to the company's renaissance.
>
> For all of these services, the planning effort was meticulous. The number of items considered and planned for each of these outsourcing engagements could easily take several volumes to list and to describe.

If there is a need to move and relocate equipment or office space for this project, as opposed to acquiring new equipment and allocating permanent new space, then use of these temporary resources must be properly planned. Many times, leasing equipment is preferred due to cost issues or rapid technology changes. This choice must be stated explicitly in the plan, and some type of leasing policy must be established. The plan should also address the length of the leasing period and the desired terms and conditions.

The final plan will identify the *what, who,* and *when* of the resources that need to be outsourced or leased. The challenges in organizing and preparing software projects that have outsourced and leased components are discussed in Part Two of this book.

KEY CONCEPTS

The team members are the most important resource in any software project. Planning for human resources focuses on the types and number of skilled people who will be directly applied to the development and support of the deliverables. At the same time, indirect human resources (such as administrative support personnel) must be included in the overall project resources planning. Because significant effort is expended in the recruiting and hiring of these human resources, skilled people should be viewed as the project's "human capital."

Processes and methodologies are a second resource; they play a key part in the success or failure of all software projects. As such, their specification, education, and documentation must be viewed as significant "intellectual capital" and should be protected accordingly. Each software development phase may be viewed as a separate process, and the methodologies applied and utilized within that phase must be defined, agreed to, documented, and disseminated.

Hardware and software tools and equipment constitute the third type of resources that are required for a project. The project plan must not only specify the tools, but also relate those tools to other resources, such as through a description of who is to use each tool and what preparation is needed for its use. The availability of the tools must also be specified and folded into the project schedule.

All three types of resources should be merged into a single combined resources plan that may be viewed as a template for resources acquisition. Resources may be either obtained through outsourcing or developed (or borrowed) in-house. If human resources will be outsourced, especially from other countries, then the plan must take into account the unique demands related to remote management of people and other resources.

EXERCISES

1. Investigate the SEI's Capability Maturity Model (CMM) and CMMI and discuss how you might use it for project planning.
2. Discuss the difference between direct and indirect resources.
3. List the activities that a software project manager may be involved in during the personnel recruiting period and discuss how that may affect the availability of the manager for other activities.
4. Compare and contrast the concepts of human capital and intellectual capital.
5. If human resources are partially outsourced, what are some concerns that arise? How might you prioritize these concerns?
6. Compare and contrast insourcing and outsourcing.
7. This chapter discussed how to plan for what type and how many resources are needed. How could you extend the planning to cover when the resources need to be available for the software project, especially if the resources will be obtained through different avenues?
8. Discuss the difference between process and methodology.

9. List some of the functions that a configuration management tool should have.
10. Discuss the notion of cross-functional process and use the quality assurance process as an example in that discussion.

SUGGESTED READING

S. W. Ambler, *Agile Modeling–Effective Practices for eXtreme Programming and the Unified Process,* John Wiley & Sons, 2002.

—— Agile Requrements Best Practices, www.agilemodeling.com, 2010.

C. A. Bartlett and S. Ghoshal, "Building Competitive Advantage Through People," *MIT Sloan Management Review,* Winter 2002, 34–41.

Carnegie Mellon University/SEI, *The Capability Maturity Model: Guidelines for Improving the Software Process,* Addison Wesley Longman, 1995.

M. Fowler and K. Scott, *UML Distilled: A Brief Guide to the Standard Object Modeling Language,* Addison-Wesley, 2000.

W. Humphrey, *Managing the Software Process,* Addison Wesley, 1989.

I. Jacobson, *et al., Object-Oriented Software Engineering, A Use Case Driven Approach,* Addison-Wesley, 1992.

P. E. McMahon, *Virtual Project Management,* CRC Press, 2001.

R. Murch, *Project Management Best Practices for IT Professionals,* Prentice Hall, 2000.

J. R. Persse, *Implementing the Capability Maturity Model,* John Wiley & Sons, 2001.

D. Phillips, *Software Project Manager's Handbook: Principles That Work at Work*, IEEE Computer Society, 2000.

Chapter 5

Risk Analysis and Planning

Chapter Objectives

This chapter discusses the following concepts:

- What the concept of risk is—namely, an anticipatable uncertainty that may be identified and analyzed
- How risk items can be identified from previously planned areas, such as project deliverables, tasks, schedules, goals, and resources
- What is involved in planning for risk: identification of risk items, prioritization of risk items, and analysis of risk mitigation alternatives

RISK DEFINITION

It is a rare situation in which a software project carries no risk. There always seems to be something that is not well described, not well communicated, not well understood, not well documented, or not well thought out that somehow causes a problem at the most inopportune time. The planning activities described so far in this book have focused on identifying and understanding deliverables, task analysis and scheduling, goal setting, skills and people identification, process and methodology identification, and tools selection. It is very difficult to identify and fully plan for all of these items at the outset of the project. As a consequence, this long and complex list of planning activities, by itself, carries risks. Typically, some parts of the plan must be modified as the project moves on.

A risk is often viewed as a problem that *may* occur. The probability of it materializing is greater than zero but not 100%. If the probability of its occurrence is 100%, then it *is* a problem. If the chance of it occurring is zero, then it will never occur and thus is not a risk. A problem is something that has a negative value associated with it. For example, a miscommunication about a staff meeting time may not cause any harm in that a missed meeting or a part of a meeting may lead to only a small loss of information that can be easily recovered. In contrast, a miscommunication about a sales presentation time may lead to the loss of a sale, which is associated with a large loss of revenue and may not be easily recoverable. We will usually attach a negative value in some normalized form such as cost in dollars. Thus a risk is defined as an uncertainty that has a negative value associated with it.

Risk A problem that has a greater than 0% but less than 100% probability of occurrence.

Problem An event that has a negative value associated with it.

Unforeseen uncertainties, such as losing a critical resource or using an unreliable new technology in a software project, are examples of risks that bring the possibility of potentially worse risks, such as schedule slippage or cost overruns. All of these outcomes may lead to customer dissatisfaction and possibly legal action. It might sound contradictory to discuss and plan for these "unknowns." But at the planning phase of project management, the risks represent the foreseen uncertainties. They can be listed, categorized, and potentially managed. The earlier these risks are handled, the better the chance of project success. It is critical that any anticipatable risks be addressed as early as possible during the project planning phase. Later, the unforeseen unknowns will actually be captured during the project monitoring phase, and management adjustments to them at that point must be made quickly in real time.

All risks need to be managed. During the project planning stage we need to initiate the planning aspects of risk management. The phases and tasks related to risk management fold naturally into the general stages of POMA. Figure 5.1 shows that risk management is a part of general project management.

RISK IDENTIFICATION

In software projects, just as in projects in other disciplines, some risks are indigenous to the specific discipline. Those that occur more often in software

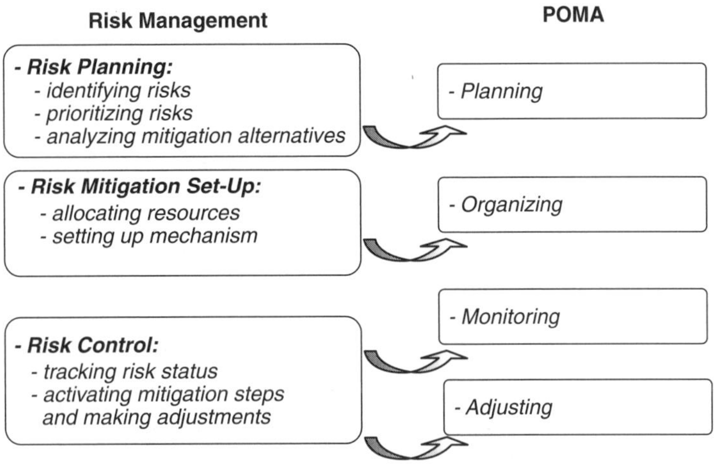

Figure 5.1 Risk Management and POMA

sometimes result from the misconception that software is difficult to define but easy to create and modify. Schedule overrun is one of the most often mentioned risks. Another well-known risk in software development is quality. The following list identifies some of the major sources of risks in software projects:

- Overly optimistic assumptions about the availability of some technology
- Misunderstanding of the real impact of some new methodology
- Miscalculation of the robustness (e.g., extensibility) or constraints of software design
- Misunderstanding of customer requirements
- Uncontrolled continuous changes of customer requirements
- Unrealistic promises to customers made by overzealous salespeople or company executives
- Inadequate due diligence while choosing external sourcing
- Incompetence of key project personnel
- Miscalculation of teamwork and group effectiveness
- Unrealistic expectations about the availability or productivity of special skilled human resources

These causes may themselves be viewed as risks, though they usually lead to other, potentially more dangerous risks. For example, uncontrolled continuous change is a major cause of a risk item known as "scope creep" (i.e., work expansion), which in turn causes schedule elongation. In this case, uncontrolled continuous change itself is a risk because it is a problem that has a greater than zero but less than 100% probability of occurrence. It may also trigger a chain of more risks.

Identifying and Listing the Anticipatable Risks

Each project manager should perform a risk identification activity, in which he or she lists the anticipatable risks associated with the project. This list may be updated as the project progresses. A frequently asked question is, how does one start such a list? Recall that project management is managing the product, the process, and the resources to achieve a set of goals. Consequently, the software project managers may begin by covering each of these areas. Essentially, they revisit the items that went into the previously completed planning activities.

First, list those characteristics of the product that may not be well defined. Examining these characteristics requires reviewing the specified requirements and thinking about what is still unclear. Create a list of those "unclear" items for each deliverable. These items form the initial list of potential product-related risks.

Second, list all unresolved issues for the tasks that will be performed in conjunction with the software project. Start by asking whether any process is defined, documented, and practiced in the organization. If not, then any process that has yet to be specified for the project would represent an untested entity for the team. As such, the process may be a risk. In addition, the methodologies associated with the tasks and the processes may be risks if they are not clearly defined, thoroughly documented, and well understood by the team. Processes and methodologies are especially fraught with risk when the project deals with new enabling technologies that are as yet unproven but labeled as the next panacea for software projects. Identify all of these items to create the list of risks associated with the software project's tasks, processes, and methodologies.

Third, identify risks associated with the management of resources. Do the project managers understand which resources are required and how much of each kind is needed? The risks related to resources will differ depending on the type of resource.

For known hardware and software systems required for the project, the associated risk may simply be the capacity or amount of these resources. For example, we may underestimate the number of simultaneous users of a software package and purchase fewer licenses than are really needed.

In terms of tools, the risk may be related to the underlying technology or the quality of the acquired tool. For example, one may acquire a requirements management tool, but that tool might be built upon a specific requirements management model that conflicts with the requirements management process of the project at hand.

Sometimes this risk may be the timeliness of the availability of the tool for the project. If several different tools are involved, there may also be the risk of the tools working when utilized individually, but not as a set. Consider the situation in which requirements have been solicited and a requirements management tool has been purchased, but the education of the users is not scheduled until the requirements are already gathered. Instead of waiting for the delayed education, the original requirements might be captured via a generic tool such as Microsoft Word and then later transferred to the requirements management tool. Even though most requirements management tools support data importation from Word, the integration of information may not be accomplished automatically. That is, the imported information might need to be further manipulated within the requirements management tool to truly take advantage of the tool's functions such as requirements categorization, prioritization, and tracing. The risk here is that many of the activities that follow the data importing operation may not take place, and the requirements may not be properly prioritized or categorized, even though an expensive requirements management tool was purchased and is available.

As noted in Chapter 4, human resources represent an especially important type of resource for software projects. Here risks may arise at all phases of the project, from the initial recruitment effort to the final separation of the people. Obtaining the needed skilled people in a timely manner is always a problem, and it is further intensified when the field experiences a technology boom or a shortage of some special skill. After the team is assembled, the team may not fully cooperate or the members may even sabotage one another's work. Keeping the people focused and productive is also a very difficult challenge that may affect general productivity, which may in turn affect the project as a whole. (Refer to Chapter 14 for more information about the formation and development of project teams.)

All of these potential risk areas can result in failure to meet the schedule, poor product quality, functionally incomplete deliverables, dissatisfied users and customers, or a demoralized project team. Such a negative result is not a risk as we have defined it, in that something else caused the poor outcome; that something else is the uncertainty that we want to identify as early as possible.

To do so, the software project managers' first task is to identify risks in areas in which one can foresee uncertainties. For software project planning, that initial identification of risks may cover the major planning categories:

- Deliverables and product specifications
- Tasks and initial schedule
- Goals, metrics, and measurements
- Human resources
- Processes and methodologies
- Tools and equipment

While creating the initial risk list, the software project managers should encourage the participation of as many people as possible, including peer groups and executives. The more problems that can be anticipated during the planning phase, the better the chance of project success. Items on this list will also be used as monitoring targets as the project progresses.

After the risks are identified and an initial list created, additional analysis of these risks is needed. The next step is to prioritize the risks so as to better avoid them.

RISK PRIORITIZATION

All risks are uncertainties that may lead to negative outcomes, but not all risks are likely to carry the same level of importance. Also, there may be too many risk items to consider each one in depth. For these reasons, risks need to be prioritized. As stated in the previous section, a risk is a problem that has a greater than zero probability of occurring. One should consider the consequence of the problem should it occur or the severity of the associated negative outcome.

Risk prioritization The activity of ordering risks based on some criterion or set of criteria.

A negative consequence resulting from erroneously designing a function due to a lack of understanding or a misinterpretation of the requirement may range from being extremely drastic to being quite tolerable. For example, the geographical misplacement of an input field on the screen may be due to a misunderstanding, but it will merely create an easily correctable inconvenience. On the other hand, the requirements for an input data check function that differentiates valid inputs from invalid inputs must be clearly defined and recorded. If they are not, the input of invalid data into the system can create system problems that are extremely difficult to detect, especially if the requirements related to distinguishing valid inputs from invalid ones are misinterpreted. Imagine the extreme situation in which an analyst misinterpreted a corporation's valid retirement age of 62 as 60. Although the age field may be properly checked for numerical data, the invalid value (60) will cause many people's retirement compensation to be dramatically miscalculated.

Similarly, the unavailability of a key resource may create a problem of dramatic significance or little significance. For example, most software development managers are quite familiar with the outcome of failing to have a key designer be available at the right time. A slippage of one day in an interface design, which happens to interact with 10 or more components, will force the slippage of all the affected components' designs. The slippage of all the components during the design phase will affect the programming schedule of all the delayed designs. This will, in turn, affect the schedule of downstream testing of the delayed code. Often, a one-day delay in the early phases of the software development cycle can produce a dramatic cascading effect across the entire schedule.

Prioritization by Recovery Cost

To prioritize these different types of risks, the problems—or the negative values—must be measured with a normalized metric that can be ordered. One approach is to devise some scheme whereby the risks can be assigned to ordered categories. For example, one might divide the categories based on the perceived cost of fixing the problem should it occur—that is, the recovery cost.

> **Recovery cost** The cost in terms of effort or financial expense to solve a problem should a risk materialize.

The costs assigned may not be exact but rather identified as merely high, medium, and low. Thus risk items may be categorized as high, medium, or low based on the perceived level of recovery cost, as shown in Table 5.1. What is viewed as a high, medium, or low risk depends on each organization. For example, $100,000 or 20 person-days may be viewed as a high cost or as

Table 5.1 Risk Prioritization by Recovery Cost

Risk item	Problem recovery cost	Risk priority
Item 1	High	High
Item 2	Medium	Medium
Item 3	High	High
Item 4	Low	Low

a medium cost depending on the organization. Thus risk prioritization is subject to a different interpretation by each organization. Because of such potential differences in interpretation, this method is most applicable *within* an organization (rather than *across* organizations) and should be used with care when applied to interorganizational risk prioritization.

Risk prioritization by recovery cost is a very simple, easy-to-apply scheme. A major drawback, however, is the perceived cost. The perceived cost itself may be a risk if it is not gauged accurately. Unfortunately, substantial inconsistencies may arise when different people are asked to provide the recovery cost assessment. In particular, an inexperienced management team should employ this scheme with care. At a minimum, the recovery cost assessment should be reviewed by others. One can not overstate the value of an experienced manager in risk management activities. For an organization that has kept historical data on projects, one may review the past problem recovery costs and create categories for the project at hand using the desired interval of cost for each category. Note that a prioritization scheme using just high, medium, and low categories is not very descriptive; one cannot say precisely how much worse a high-risk item is than a low-risk item, for example.

Types of Recovery Cost Prioritization

Many types of risk prioritization schemes based on recovery cost are possible. One alternative is to increase the number of recovery cost categories, thereby increasing the number of priority categories. This strategy may be viewed as a refinement of the fundamental risk prioritization scheme.

Another variation is to use numerical categories, still based on the recovery cost, such as 1, 2, ..., 10; here, either 1 or 10 is the highest priority. These numerical categories may be designed in such a manner that the recovery cost is divided into 10 equal increments. Such a scheme is actually an improvement, in that it provides more than just simple ordering. It allows us to quantify risk to some extent, by saying that a risk in the priority 7 category is two units higher in priority than a risk in the priority 5 category (assuming that 10 is the highest priority level). We may also think of a risk item with priority 6 as being twice as important as a risk item with priority 3, because the recovery cost of the risk priority 6 problem is twice as much as that of a risk priority 3 problem.

There are several ways to divide the recovery cost into equal increments. One easy method is to examine the risk list and to pick the item with the largest recovery cost and the item with the smallest recovery cost. Divide the difference between the two into equal increments. If L is the largest recovery cost and S is the smallest recovery cost, then

$$\textit{Each increment} = (L - S)/Z$$

where Z is the desired number of priority levels.

For the most part, this scheme would work fairly well. In some situations, however, updating the risk list may cause the L and S values to change. If the priority increment values change, that may, in turn, require a reevaluation of all risk items.

Prioritization by Risk Value

Further sophistication may be introduced in the prioritization of the risk items. Since each risk is an uncertainty that has a nonzero probability of occurrence, the probability of occurrence may be included in the prioritization scheme.

It makes sense to view risks with a low chance of occurring as requiring less attention. In other words, a risk with a high recovery cost but a very low probability of occurring should not command the same amount of attention as a risk item with a high recovery cost and a high probability of occurring.

Let's define the risk value of risk item j, $RV(j)$, as follows:

$$RV(j) = P(j) \times RC(j)$$

Here $P(j)$ is the probability of risk item j becoming a real problem, and $RC(j)$ is the recovery cost for risk item j when it turns into a problem. The risk value, RV, may be used as the scheme for prioritization because it is also ordered.

Risk value A recovery cost that is influenced and modified by another criterion or set of criteria. The probability of the risk turning into a problem is such an influencing factor, and when such a factor is taken into account in modifying the recovery cost, the result is the risk value.

Table 5.2 shows five risk items with different probabilities of occurrence and different recovery costs. These five risk items may be prioritized based

Table 5.2 Risk Prioritization by Risk Value

Risk Item	Probability of occurrence	Recovery cost	Risk value (*RV*)
Item 1	0.4	$600	240
Item 2	0.7	$400	280
Item 3	0.3	$3000	900
Item 4	0.6	$1200	720
Item 5	0.3	$700	210

on the computed risk values, *RVs*. In this case, the risk items will be prioritized in the following order:

1. Item 3
2. Item 4
3. Item 2
4. Item 1
5. Item 5

That is, item 3 has the highest risk value and item 5 has the lowest risk value.

This scheme is more sophisticated than the one that considers only the recovery cost, but it has the disadvantage that it adds more variables and hence more complexity. The probability of problem occurrence must be estimated, and in addition the estimate of the recovery cost must be made. As always, these estimations may be wrong and thus may pose their own risks. Risk prioritization is a task that definitely requires experience. The technique can be used more effectively if historical project data can be used as guidance.

Once the risk items are prioritized, the software project managers may decide to consider all of them or just to focus attention on some of the risk items, such as the top 30%. Alternatively, such decisions may be postponed until the managers have had a chance to examine the possibilities of mitigating the risks.

RISK MITIGATION

Once the foreseeable risk items are identified and prioritized, the next step is to plan how to mitigate those risks. For many of the risk items, several ways to mitigate the risk might be available; for other risks, no mitigation options may exist.

Risk mitigation An activity that may reduce, minimize, or totally avoid a risk.

First, list all the potential ways to mitigate a risk item. For example, if there is a risk of not being able to complete a system integration task with a specific tool because only one person possesses that special skill, there are several possible ways to mitigate that risk:

1. Hire an extra person with the needed skill as a backup helper.
2. Provide extra incentives to persuade the current employee to stay.
3. Use an alternative system integration method that does not require this specific tool.

Software project managers may employ any one of these options, or even a combination of them, to improve the odds of mitigating the risk.

Cost-Based Mitigation

Which mitigation alternative should be chosen when several choices are available? And which criteria should be used in the decision-making process? One may use any of several parameters as the basis for decision making, including the ease of mitigation, probability of success of mitigation, and the cost of mitigation.

Cost of Mitigation

First, let's examine the last of these–the cost-of-mitigation approach. Each mitigation alternative for a risk item has some cost associated with it. Suppose there are several mitigation alternatives; a mitigation cost value must then be estimated for each alternative. Next, choose the one with the lowest cost. For a particular risk item *j*, Table 5.3 shows the estimated costs of the mitigation alternatives.

The cost of each mitigation alternative is just an estimate, and it carries a certain amount of risk, too. For the alternatives shown in Table 5.3, alternative 2 would be the preferred option because it has the lowest estimated cost.

Probability of Success

Each of the mitigation alternatives likely has a different potential for success. For example, while alternative 2 in Table 5.3 may be the lowest-cost option, it may also have a low chance of success. It might be better to choose alternative 1 if it has a better chance of success. The chance of success reflects the probability that the mitigation alternative can actually bring the risk close to zero. Although it is possible that one might not be able to carry out

Table 5.3 Estimated Mitigation Costs for Risk Item *J*

Mitigation alternative	Cost of mitigation
Alternative 1	$65,000
Alternative 2	$50,000
Alternative 3	$120,000

the mitigation alternative, we will assume here that the option can be performed successfully. For the example in Table 5.3, alternative 1—hiring an extra person who has the special skill at a cost of $65,000—will bring (with close to 100% assurance) the risk to zero. In reality, the chance of success is probably less than 100%. Also, there is no guarantee that such a person can be hired in time, though our example makes that assumption.

Mitigation Value Cost

If the probability of success is taken into account, a new cost value is defined. The mitigation value cost for each alternative is defined as follows:

$$MVC(k) = P(k) \times MC(k)$$

where $MVC(k)$ is the mitigation value cost of alternative k. The probability of mitigation alternative k's success in bringing the risk to zero will be viewed in a reverse manner here; that is, this factor will be represented by the probability of failure, $P(k)$. The original raw cost of mitigation for alternative k is $MC(k)$. Table 5.4 shows the same three alternatives, with their probability of failure, and their respective mitigation value costs.

Mitigation value cost The cost of risk mitigation after taking into account another criterion or a set of criteria, such as the probability of mitigation success.

Alternative 2, which has the lowest raw mitigation cost, does not look very good after we discover that the chance of failure is 0.6. That is, even if we give the $50,000 bonus to the employee with the special skill, there is a 60% chance that the system integration task will not be accomplished. After all, a bonus may excite the person only temporarily, so the mitigation value cost is relatively high. Conversely, the more expensive mitigation alternative of using a different technical solution has a much higher chance of success,

Table 5.4 Mitigation Value Cost

Mitigation alternative	Raw risk mitigation cost	Probability of failure	Mitigation value cost
Alternative 1	$65,000	0.1	$6500
Alternative 2	$50,000	0.6	$30,000
Alternative 3	$120,000	0.05	$6000

so it carries a lower mitigation value cost. In this case, we would be wise to choose the alternative with the lowest mitigation value cost, alternative 3.

Note that if we changed *P*(*k*), the probability of failure, to become the probability of success, then the alternative with the highest mitigation value cost would be the proper choice. We used the failure probability in this example because it is counterintuitive to choose the most expensive alternative.

Fixed Budget for Risk Mitigation

Sometimes software project managers face the prospect of planning with a fixed budget for risk mitigation. First, they rank the risk items. Then they explore the risk mitigation alternatives. Next, they choose a mitigation alternative for each risk, using one of the previously discussed methods. Starting with the top risk item, the managers subtract the cost of the chosen corresponding risk mitigation alternative from the budget and then they examine the budget to see whether it is still adequate. If more funds remain available, they then continue sequentially on to the next risk item until the budget runs out. Table 5.5 shows an example of this kind of sequential application of a fixed budget for risk mitigation.

This technique offers a simple and straightforward way to plan for risk mitigation. In the example in Table 5.5, we start with a budget of $500,000, and the risk mitigation budget is allocated to the top four risk items. That leaves only $50,000, which is not enough to cover risk item 5. Even though not all risk items are covered, this approach has indeed lowered the risks of the overall project.

Other budget-based approaches are also possible. One that may deserve some attention is the tactic of looking at a number of top-priority risk items

Table 5.5 Sequential Application of a Fixed Budget for Risk Mitigation

Risk Item	Raw risk mitigation cost	Available budget ($500,000)
Item 1	$185,000	$315,000
Item 2	$105,000	$210,000
Item 3	$95,000	$115,000
Item 4	$65,000	$50,000
Item 5	$60,000	Not enough funds left

and attempting to allocate the budget in such a manner that the total risk value, *RV,* is maximized. Consider the same set of risk items as in Table 5.5, except that now the risk values are also shown (see Table 5.6). Each risk item has an associated risk value, which is chosen based on the minimal mitigation value cost. The *raw* mitigation cost in Table 5.6 is the same as that shown in Table 5.5. Note that this approach may potentially give a different answer than planning purely by sequential priority order.

Table 5.6 shows that risk item 4 may be skipped, but two more risk items may be picked up while still staying within the budget. In this example, the total risk value is 3290. In the previous scheme, in which the budget was allocated sequentially, only four risk items were covered and the total risk value was only 2950. Maximizing risk value would allow the application of risk mitigation to risk items 1, 2, 3, 5, and 6—that is, it enables coverage of one more risk item.

A scheme that considers the total risk value may sometimes be preferable. For example, by not choosing the highest-priority item, a higher total risk value and more risk items might be covered with a fixed budget. However, since these risk values and mitigation costs are generally estimates, we would still need management's subjective experience to double-check and agree with the plan.

At the end of risk planning, the plan should include the following items:

- A list of identified risk items
- Prioritization of the list according to some defined scheme
- A mitigation alternative for each of the prioritized risk items

Table 5.6 Allocating a Fixed Risk Mitigation Budget by Maximizing Risk Value

Risk item	Risk value	Raw risk mitigation cost	Available budget ($500,000)
Item 1	950	$185,000	$315,000
Item 2	700	$105,000	$210,000
Item 3	680	$95,000	$115,000
Item 4	620	$65,000	Omit this item
Item 5	560	$60,000	$55,000
Item 6	400	$50,000	$5000

Table 5.7 Risk Removal Plan

Prioritized risk items	Expected removal date	Removal dependency
Item 1	06/30/2010	Risk mitigation completed
Item 2	07/15/2010	Task 3 completed on schedule
Item 3	01/30/2011	Task 8 target met and risk mitigation completed
.	.	.
.	.	.
.	.	.

RISK REMOVAL AND THE RISK PLAN

A risk plan would be of only limited utility if it did not include target dates by which the risks were supposed to be eliminated. A risk item may be removed from the list after the successful application of the risk mitigation alternative or a change in some other dependency factor. As an example, Table 5.7 shows a prioritized risk item table in a risk plan.

The risk removal plan table consists of the prioritized risk items, the expected date or time frame by which the risk items will be removed from the list, and the events that will trigger the removal of the risk items from the list. This table is one of the many entities that are tracked in the monitoring and adjusting phases of a POMA-compliant project.

As risk items are mostly born out of uncertainties that can be anticipated to some extent, there is a high chance that the risk item list itself will be incomplete or even erroneous. Risk analysis and planning may be revisited frequently over the course of the software project, and the risk plan may be revised several times. The project managers should continuously be on the lookout for the previously unforeseen uncertainties and check for any sign of new risks.

KEY CONCEPTS

A risk is defined as a problem that has greater than 0% but less than 100% probability of occurrence. A problem has a negative value associated with it. Only the foreseeable risks may be planned for. Three main risk analysis and planning activities are pursued as part of POMA: risk identification, risk prioritization, and risk mitigation.

The first activity, identifying risks, seeks to establish a list of risk items. Many anticipatable risks may be identified from the descriptions of project and product deliverables, from the task definitions and initial schedule, from the goals and metrics definitions, and from the project resources plan.

The second activity, determining the priority of the risk items, can follow any of several approaches. One possible approach is to use the estimated recovery cost of each risk item as the prioritization criteria. A more sophisticated approach is to compute the risk value, which takes into account the estimated probability of risk occurrence, and then ranks the risks by these risk values.

The third activity, mitigating risks, focuses on the analysis of risk mitigation alternatives. The various mitigation options are listed, and their respective cost values are estimated. The optimal alternative may be chosen because it has the smallest mitigation cost. A mitigation value cost (*MVC*) is defined so as to include both the estimated probability of the mitigation alternative succeeding and the actual dollar cost of the option. Using the *MVC* value in the decision-making process is a more intricate approach to determining the optimal risk mitigation.

The final risk plan should also include a set of dates indicating when the prioritized risks may be removed from the risk list. The status of these risks and their projected removal dates should be monitored throughout the project.

EXERCISES

1. Define risk, and discuss how unforeseeable risks may be handled.
2. Discuss some of the sources of risks in software projects.
3. Describe one way to prioritize the risks.
4. What are the three major categories of risk management?
5. Why might software reuse be attractive to many software project managers, from a risk management perspective?
6. Why is it important to include risk removal in the risk plan?
7. What are the criteria for risk removal?
8. How can software project managers identify the mitigation alternatives for each potential risk?
9. Explain how risk management folds into POMA.

SUGGESTED READING

B. W. Boehm, "Software Risk Management: Principles and Practices," *IEEE Software*, January 1991, 32–41.

R. Fairley, "Risk Management for Software Projects," *IEEE Software*, May 1994, 57–67.

E. M. Hall, *Risk Management Methods for Software Systems Development*, Addison-Wesley, 1998.

ISO 31000: 2009, "Risk Management–Principles and Guidelines," www.iso.org, January 2010.

A. D. Meyer, C. H. Loch, and M. T. Pich, "Managing Project Uncertainty: From Variation to Chaos," *MIT Sloan Management Review*, Winter 2002, 60–67.

M. Myerson, *Risk Management Processes for Software Engineering Models*, Artech House, 1996.

J. Ropponen and K. Lyytinen, "Components of Software Development Risk: How to Address Them? A Project Manager Survey," *IEEE Transactions on Software Engineering*, February 2000, 98–111.

Part Two

Organizing and Preparing

(POMA)

ORGANIZING

After the initial planning phase is complete, the software project team now has documented descriptions of the following:

- Project deliverables and product attributes
- A task list and initial schedule
- Project goals, metrics, and measurements
- Resources
- Risks

Now it is time to organize and to put the project in action. It is important to note that planning and organizing phases may overlap. That is, some organizing activities, such as human resources recruiting and organizational structure design, may be initiated and performed simultaneously with resource planning activities. This phase of the software project management is especially dynamic, because the project managers are starting to act on their share of the project plan. At the same time, the nonmanagement-related activities of the software project, such as early requirements solicitation and feasibility analysis of technical risks, should be in full motion.

As with planning, the organization and preparation of a project is not just one task but rather a group of diverse tasks. From the project management perspective, this "O" (organizing and preparing) phase marks the start of the execution of the project plan. Ideally, the software project plan has been approved before the project team engages in activities related to the organizing and preparation phase, because a fairly large sum of money will be expended once acquisition of resources begins. Each type of resource mentioned in the plan requires a different approach to attain, organize, and prepare it. For example, goals and measurements must be set up so that they may be communicated, reviewed, understood, and accepted by the team members. The purchasing department is now contacted. Risk items and their respective mitigation alternatives need to be set up for tracking and for continuous evaluation.

HUMAN RESOURCES

As noted in Part One, human resources are the most important resources for any software project. The acquisition of human resources often requires much more effort than acquiring a software tool, methodology, or hardware. Recruitment of people may be necessary, but it is merely a first step. People need to be placed in an organization and given clearly designated responsibilities so that the planned tasks can be accomplished within the target schedule and cost. Unlike tools and process resources, human resources have emotions. Thus a different set of preparations—and one that is exceedingly more complex than equipment maintenance—must be established for the retention and growth of the personnel. In addition, because all projects must eventually end, there needs to be proper preparation of the team members for the close of the project. Even if the plan calls for outsourcing, there is still a significant amount of preparation needed.

PROCESSES, METHODOLOGIES, AND TOOLS

Other resources that must be prepared and made available along with human resources are those related to the immediate needs of the project team members:

- Work space for the individual offices and team meetings
- Communication facilities, such as phones, wall boards, and video conferencing mechanisms
- Computational facilities, such as desktop computers, laptop computers, computer networks, group-share software tools, and access to servers and services

Broader project resources are needed as well, such as software development or support processes, specific methodologies for some activities, and hardware and software tools to support the project as a whole. It is essential to verify that these resource components, as addressed in the plan, will be available at the required time and can be acquired at the expected prices. As part of the preparation, the project managers need to ensure that the purchase orders are completed and that the budget allows for the release of the needed funds. If training and education for the tools or methodologies are required, then reservations for educational facilities and instructional engagements must also be made during the organizing and preparation phase.

If an outsourcing plan calls for forging an external partnership, then appropriate partners must be found, evaluated, and selected. The project management must ensure that the legal and contract group is included in, prepared for, and ready with the drafting of contracts. Sometimes, the software project managers will directly participate in negotiating these contracts. Direct participation of project managers in contract negotiation is often a preferred approach in that such participation allows both sides to work much more closely later in the monitoring and adjustment phases. The topic of purchase and supply chain management is covered in a later chapter in Part Five of this book.

GOALS AND MEASUREMENTS

The preparation for the downstream phase of monitoring occurs at this stage of the project as well. The software project managers must define the types of data needed to measure and track the project. These data are used to assess the attainment of the expressed goals and the status of the risk items identified during the planning phase. The management reporting structure needs to identify the following items:

- Who should receive the project status reports
- When, where, and how long should the project status meetings be
- What format the reports and presentations should take
- How the organization as a whole can prepare for the effort required to collect and analyze the data

During the organizing phase, the software project managers may discover shortcomings flowing from the planning phase. For example, the planned resources may be inadequate. The software project managers should not hesitate to adjust the plan and seek both agreement to and approval of any necessary adjustments.

Chapter 6

Human Resources

Chapter Objectives

This chapter discusses the following concepts:

- What software organizational structures are possible, including those for both software development and software support organizations
- What preparations are needed to acquire human resources—recruiting, hiring, and bringing new people on board

SOFTWARE PROJECT ORGANIZATION: AN OVERVIEW

For software project management, human resources are often viewed as the most vital resource. How many times have we heard industry leaders claim that they can give up their buildings, their equipment, their processes, and their money, but not their people? This declaration is especially applicable to the software industry.

In the early days of the computing industry, software development focused mostly on programming. Programmers' activities and teams have been discussed extensively by authors such as Weinberg and Kraft (see the "Suggested Reading" section at the end of this chapter). In particular, various ways to organize these programming teams have been examined thoroughly. Centralized team control exercised through a chief programmer, as suggested by Fred Brooks in his book *The Mythical Man-Month,* has yielded mixed results. Other centralized and decentralized team structures have been suggested and tried. In addition to organizational and team structures, different leadership styles have been tested. Today, many software projects require a large number of people who possess a wide variety of skills. Multiple teams featuring specialized skills beyond just programming skills, such as system testing and database administration, are used extensively in many software projects. In addition, we continue to outsource large portions of our organizations. To deal with these unique situations, software organizational structures have necessarily become much more complex.

While the software organizational structure is being prepared, personnel recruitment activities may be initiated in parallel. Using the software project plan as a guide, the project management team must now hire the needed people, bring them on board smoothly, and assign them to the appropriate organization. As the project progresses, the project team members may need some special training and growth. Finally, these individuals must be reassigned as the project winds down.

Organizing the software groups effectively and defining specific positions requires some understanding of the functions that the groups will perform. This understanding is achieved by breaking down the tasks, the planned processes and methodologies, the goals and measurements, and other items outlined in the software project plan. The organizational structure may be improved if the software project managers take into account some items that may not be clearly identified in the plan, such as the communications channels available, the team members' personalities, and so on.

Let's look first at several potential software project organizational structures, beginning with software development structures and then continuing with software support structures.

SOFTWARE DEVELOPMENT STRUCTURES

During the creation of the Work Breakdown Structure (WBS) and the planning activities, tasks were broken down and assigned to people with different skills. Although one can start the hiring activity by using this list of needed team members, it is better to spend a little time and put together an organizational chart first.

General Organizational Structure

Figure 6.1 shows an organizational chart for a general software development and service project organization. The general organizational structure reflects

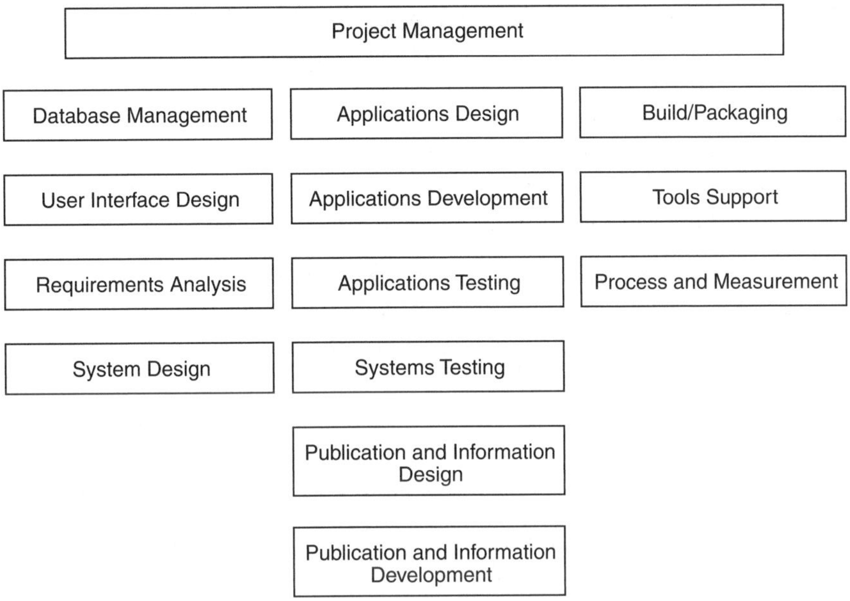

Figure 6.1 General software project organization

the major tasks that a software development and service organization must perform. The particular organization required for the project at hand may be developed based on this structure.

> **General software development organization** An implementation-independent general organization that includes all the major activities required to develop software artifacts, from inception to release. The specific implementation details such as relationships among the activities, expected sourcing of the people, or the deployed organizational structure are added onto the general organization.

In the process of putting together an organization, project managers may discover the need for some additional, but indirect positions. A person who is assigned to an indirect position usually performs some support task that is not directly related to the completion of the project's deliverables. For example, a project administrator might coordinate the various activities and ensure that communication flows properly. The position of project manager—another indirect position—might not be needed until the number of people on the project reaches a certain size. Conversely, if the project is small enough that multiple tasks are assigned to the same people, the number of indirect positions required may be minimal. Such trade-offs may not have been fully analyzed during the planning phase.

Refining the General Organizational Structure I: Matrix Versus Hierarchical Orientation

The final organization selected may to some extent depend on the company's project management philosophy or the corporate culture within which the software project will be conducted. Although most organizations are hierarchical in nature, some adopt a flatter, matrix type of orientation.

> **Hierarchical organization** An organizational structure in which all the people associated with a project are grouped into functional departments that report directly within the vertical line of command of the organization.

> **Matrix organization** An organizational structure in which people are grouped based on the functions they perform. These people may not report directly within the vertical line of command of the organization.

In a matrix organization, not all the functions have to be performed by the people who are part of the official project organization. For example, a "central" test department might specialize in all sorts of testing. This group might provide services to, and be shared by, all of the software project organizations within the company. Similarly, a common software tools support organization might be shared by the various project organizations.

One advantage offered by a matrix-type organization is that there is less likelihood of duplication and better focus on specialized skills compared to a hierarchical organization. The potential downside is that there may not be as much "team loyalty" toward any one project. In addition, there is the potential for confusion in the matrix organization due to the dual-boss situation. By comparison, within a hierarchical organization, team loyalty and team security can be cultivated much more readily.

Many hybrid organizations utilize a combination of hierarchical and matrix structures. One such hybrid is the "functional team" concept, in which members from different departments are temporarily brought together to perform a project while still formally reporting to their own departments. The members of this temporary team take directions from the project manager during the lifetime of the project. At the conclusion of the project, all of them return to their original departments.

With the current trend toward cost cutting and organizational flattening, many structures may be forced into a temporary, functional-team construct in which all the people report permanently to a professional human resources manager. With this approach, every software project is performed by a temporary functional team. In such a flattened structure, the project manager directs all project-related tasks and is responsible for the outcome of the deliverables. The project managers themselves may be chosen from a pool of software project managers, all of whom report to a human resources manager. The human resources manager handles the personnel-related subjects, such as career development issues.

Furthermore, with the trend toward globalization and away from extensive travel, along with much improved communications capability, many organizations no longer require co-location of their employees. Instead, they prefer to form virtual organizations.

> **Virtual organization** An organizational structure in which many of the project personnel are located physically apart and are bought together as a temporary functional team.

Figure 6.2 shows how the organization depicted in Figure 6.1 may be modified so as to set up a hybrid matrix organization that features separate programming and information development centers. Any of the functional groups in such a matrix organization may be virtual, in that they may be located physically apart from the rest of the project team.

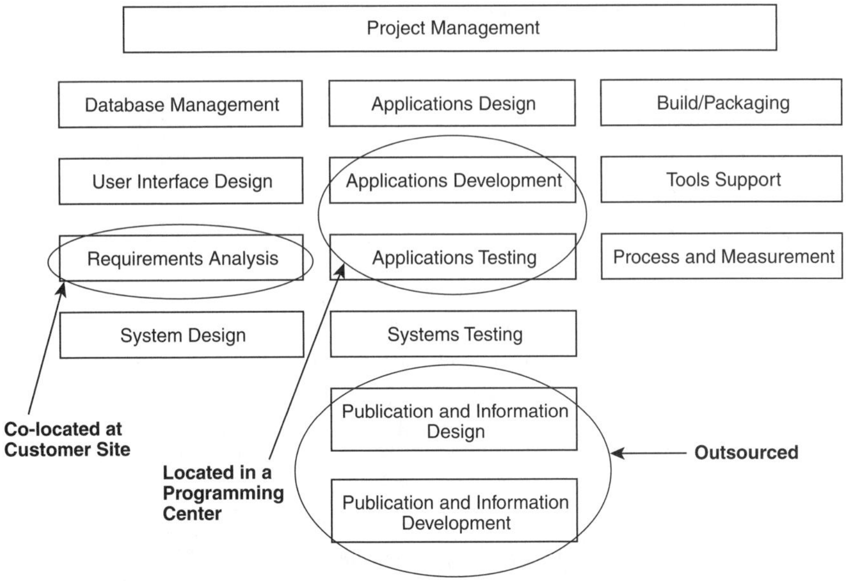

Figure 6.2 Modified general software project organization

Refining the General Organizational Structure II: Functional Orientation

This general organizational structure may be further refined to show a more precise structure. It is important that the organization be defined down to a level where each individual can see his or her name. Figure 6.3 shows a diagram of a software organization with a functional orientation.

The software project organization illustrated in Figure 6.3 is quite small: a total of six people report directly to a project manager. Several assumptions underlie such an organization:

- Managers have a duty to "take care of their people" and will spend a considerable amount of time guiding the professionals' careers, but not directly doing their work. (Today, this is becoming a luxury of the past.)
- A smaller organizational size is conducive to faster team bonding.
- Many members of the group have worked well with one another in the past.
- The "yet to be hired" positions represent 33% of the overall team, but the actual raw number of new employees is only two; the project manager will be able to find the right people without having to compromise much.
- Each position has a specific title, including titles for the open slots, allowing for easier requisitions for hire.
- The requirements and design activities are viewed as front-end activities that set the tone for the project, so it is more important to have direct control over them.
- The implementation activities are sourced from a different group, such as a centralized programming and development implementation center.
- The information and publication activities are also sourced from a different group, possibly from the same programming and development implementation center or perhaps from an external source.

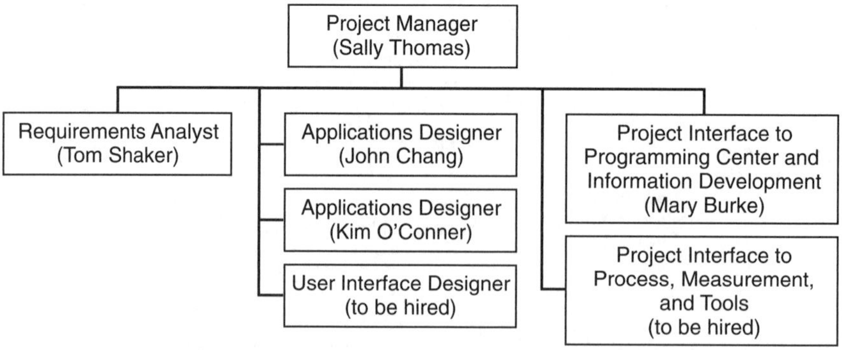

Figure 6.3 Refined software organization: Functional orientation

- The infrastructure activities, such as those focusing on processes, measurements, and tools, are also sourced from other specialized groups.
- One person serves as the designated liaison to the outsourced activities.
- The group does not have to be co-located; instead, members of this small group may reside in different locations and yet communicate effectively with the available technical tools, such as e-mail, cell phones, and servers that provide Web access to a common set of central files.

Many software projects rely on this type of organization, in which the activities are dispersed but all of the responsibilities are still put into the hands of a small group of people. This is quite different from a strictly hierarchical organizational structure in which everyone involved must report directly to one responsible project manager. Such an all-encompassing organization, as mentioned before, tends to have more overhead, including several people engaged in activities indirect to the immediate project. This organization requires a manager to spend more time conscientiously promoting rapid and effective communications. Members cannot conveniently stick their heads into others' offices and strike up a quick discussion pertaining to the project.

Refining the General Organizational Structure III: A Highly Specialized Organization

Let's look at a small section–just the software development group–of a large organization; see Figure 6.4.

This organization is a bit more specialized in that it reflects a group that is responsible for only the development of software, but not the information development and publication tasks. This group does not perform any of the requirements gathering and specification activities, nor does it handle any independent testing. Likewise, no project service activities, such as those dealing with processes, methodologies, measurements, configuration management, and tools, are the responsibility of this group. The group members may depend on and use many of the services provided by other groups. Let's assume that this software development group is part of a larger software project organization, where many of the required services are available. The development manager in this group still needs to ensure that the interfaces to the other departments within the same organization are well defined and operational. This group also faces a big recruiting challenge because it has many unfilled positions.

One advantage that this type of group offers by reporting within a large project organization is the flexibility it brings to the large organization. If this group was part of a separate central design and programming department,

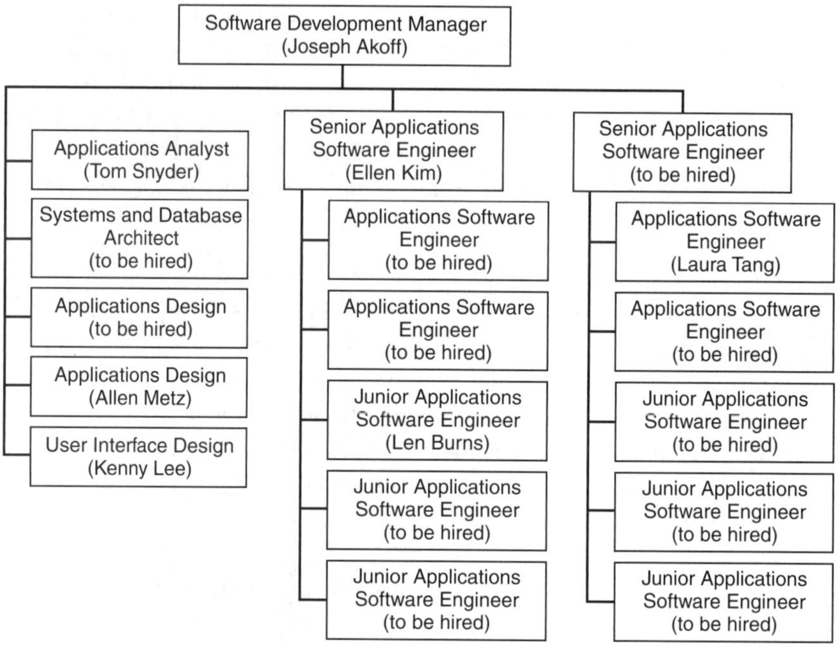

Figure 6.4 Refined software project organization: Software development specialization

every change and modification might have to be "officially" negotiated and approved. The flexibility is especially valuable in large projects, which are more complex and much more prone to changes.

SOFTWARE SUPPORT STRUCTURES

After it is released to the customers, the software still needs to be supported by the software development company. A software support and service organization may share many characteristics of the general software project organization.

> **Software support and service** Post-software-release activities related to clarifying user questions and fixing software problems encountered by users.

Software support and service has one especially important component, however: customer management. Customer management requires the software project managers to organize and set up an extensive customer interface group, such as the customer call service department that handles the following duties:

- Answer calls
- Analyze each problem
- Respond to the customer if a possible solution exists
- Generate a problem report when an immediate solution does not exist
- Track the problem resolution activities
- Report and deliver solutions to the customers
- Close problems

Customer management The set of activities related to ensuring that the customers' needs are properly served.

A different set of skills and tools may be needed for a software support organization as opposed to the software development organization. A software support organization might take the form shown in Figure 6.5.

Note that the support groups in Figure 6.5 are divided into "levels," a term often applied to the types of software support. The support levels are described below.

The *Level 1* support service provides customer call services where problems are reported via the phone or on-line. If the problem is a minor one, for which a simple answer can be delivered immediately on the phone or on-line, then it is resolved quickly and the problem report is opened and closed within that call service cycle. If more extensive research is needed or a software

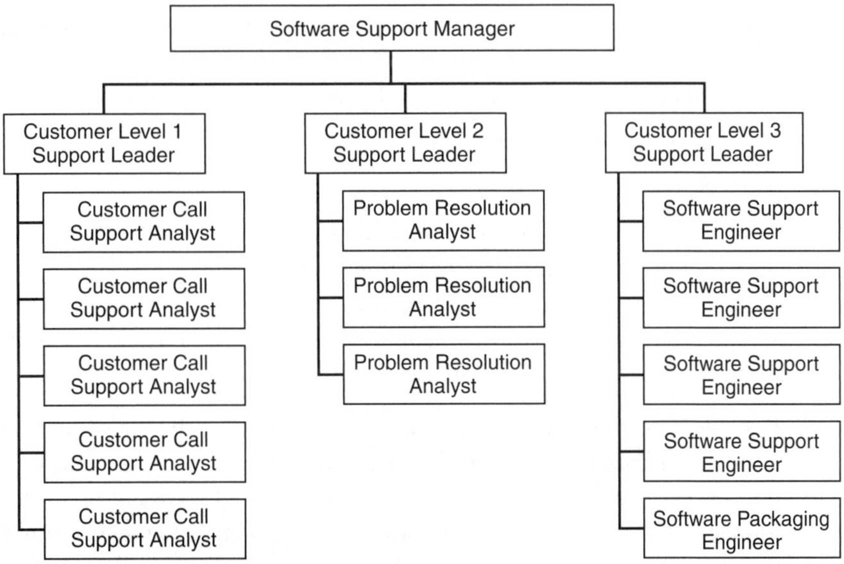

Figure 6.5 Software support organization

change or fix might be necessary, however, then a problem report is opened and sent to the Level 2 service group.

The *Level 2* service group examines the problem description in the opened report, analyzes the problem, and searches—possibly using a solution database—for an existing solution that will avoid modifying the software. If a solution that does not require a code change exists or can be devised, then the customer is provided with that solution and the problem is closed. Otherwise, the problem is passed to the Level 3 service group, whose members will develop the necessary fix.

The *Level 3* service group resembles the development organization. It will make the necessary design, code, information, and publications changes, test those changes, package them, and deliver the changes to customers. If the severity of the problem is high, then the fix may be delivered to the customers immediately. Fixes for lower-severity problems may be aggregated and delivered (or made available via Internet) to the customers at regular intervals, such as monthly or quarterly.

RECRUITING AND HIRING SOFTWARE PERSONNEL

Once the organizational positions are outlined, the software project management needs to fill the open slots. The actual hiring of the employees starts with having a clear definition of the open positions in terms of the skills, training, and character of the candidates required for each position. Not all of this detailed information may appear in the software project plan, however.

Recruiting

In the project plan, the type of software-related skills needed may be classified differently by different search and professional recruiting organizations. For this reason, simply providing a general position title to the human resources recruiters may not suffice. The following are examples of some of the common software positions and related skills descriptions:

1. *Database design and administration:* Technical skills include setting up a relational database, designing queries and reports to access information in the database, and administering backup and recovery processes for the database, which may require direct working experience with a specific database from the database vendor. Formal education includes a bachelor's degree in computer science or information technology.

Professional training includes a certification in the particular database and two or more years of work experience with that database. The candidate must possess good communication skills and enjoy detail-oriented work.

2. *Applications designer:* Technical skills include translating requirements in the industry for which the application is designed into systems solutions and expressing those solutions in the selected design language by utilizing the specified methodology. Formal education includes a bachelor's degree in computer science or information technology. Professional training includes the completion of training in the vendor's design tool, more than three years of experience in software implementation in the industry targeted by the application, and familiarity with the designated software packages used in that industry. The candidate must possess good communication skills and be highly organized.
3. *Application testing:* Technical skills include reading and analyzing designs expressed in the chosen design language, analyzing program listings in the specified programming language, and designing test scenarios and test cases. Formal education includes a bachelor's degree in computer science or software engineering. Professional training includes the completion of training on the selected test tool and two years of experience in generating and executing test scripts with the script language associated with the tool. The candidate must be detail-oriented and have a positive, upbeat attitude.
4. *Applications developer:* Technical skills include reading and analyzing designs expressed in the chosen design language and converting those designs into programs written in the selected programming language. Formal education includes a bachelor's degree in computer science, software engineering, or information technology. Professional training includes a certificate in the programming language and five years of programming experience, preferably in the industry targeted by the application, with progressively sophisticated usage of the programming language and debugging with the chosen tool. The candidate must be detail-oriented and work well under constant schedule pressure.

Each position should have a description, whether it is open or not. Each skill area may also be divided into levels characterized by different expectations and different degrees of reward and compensation. Furthermore, there should be descriptions of the career paths, including the progression through the levels, for the various technical and supporting roles. Employees are interested in their immediate responsibilities, but they naturally want to know about their longer-term prospects as well. As part of the recruiting effort, the project managers should be able to clearly define each position, lay out their expectations, and articulate the potential for growth in that position. The software project managers should therefore prepare their recruiting strategy in concert with the broader corporate human resources strategy, especially when it comes to short-term positions versus long-term retention policies.

The initial screening of the applicants may be performed by professional recruiters or by the personnel department. If recruiters are being used it is beneficial for the project manager to actually sit down and go over each open position with them, explaining the specific needs of that position. Spending this extra time up front will help in filtering out and qualifying the candidates. In this way, preparation of the recruiters can save a lot of otherwise wasted interviews and frustrations.

Hiring

The actual interview of a candidate may be conducted in several stages. The initial conversation may take place via telephone or via video conferencing. This first interview is a two-sided information exchange intended to determine whether a mutual fit and interest exist. A common mistake made by many new managers is to spend too much time describing or "selling" the position and the project. It is important to also listen to the candidate and assess that person's qualifications, specific skills, and personal traits. Sometimes the project manager may include some other members of the project team in the interview to help ascertain the level of some special skill or to assess potential team chemistry. If the open position has any special requirements, then those needs must be brought out. Similarly, the project managers must ask the candidate about any special constraints that the person might have, related to issues such as the amount of travel required or the amount of potential overtime.

Many project managers find it beneficial to use an interview prompter sheet to ensure that each topic is covered. Such a prompter sheet may include questions about the following topics:

- General technical skills
- Specific technical skills
- General educational background
- Years and types of experiences
- The best and worst moments of past projects
- Tasks that the person wants to do the most and the least, and why

- The person's career goals
- Any constraints, including absolute minimum salary
- Why the person is leaving his or her current position
- When the person is available
- Description of the project
- Description of the position
- Description of the team
- Description of the company business and company culture
- Description of the company benefits
- Description of the compensation system

The interview does not necessarily follow the topics in this order. Instead, most interviews will start with the project manager giving a brief description of the project and the open position. Then the conversation will flow naturally from topic to topic. It is important to keep track of the topics, and the interviewing project manager is responsible for ensuring that all relevant subjects are covered within the interview time slot.

The question on minimum salary is important to ask, especially if the project has a very tight budget. Many candidates will not give a straight answer when asked; however, if the issue of budget is explained, then they will understand that the project manager may not be able to recruit him or her without some rough estimate of the salary. Sometimes the candidates will provide a range rather than a specific compensation figure. In today's volatile high-technology and software sector, the mode of compensation has moved from offering a large amount of company stock to a modest amount of stock but more rewards related to job satisfaction, educational opportunity, or health benefits. The project manager must be knowledgeable about the latest trends and must be able to describe how the organization's total benefits package matches up.

After a successful first round of interviews, the candidate may be brought in for a face-to-face follow-up interview. If the project manager chooses to conduct a second interview, then the candidate should be someone whom the project manager is already willing to hire. The second interview may include the candidate talking to other members of the team, other project managers, and the interviewing manager's immediate manager. This meeting will also allow the candidate to assess the environment in which he or she will be working. Sometimes, a skills test in some programming language or tool may be administered at this point. For positions that require high coordination and communications skills, character tests may also be given.

If both sides remain interested after the follow-up interview is completed, the project manager should provide the candidate with a target date for a formal decision and an offer. If the decision is already made, then the offer may be extended at the end of the second interview. This immediate offer is often made verbally for those companies that require drug or other substance clearances before final hiring.

The offer letter should clearly define the position and provide a brief description of the tasks. The total compensation package should be spelled out, including reference to any documents that explain the details; these should also be enclosed with the offer letter. The name of the new employee's immediate manager, the new hire's starting date and time, and any documents that must be brought in on the first day should all be specified. Such a letter may be written and sent out by the human resources group, rather than the software project management.

Bringing People on Board

Once the candidate accepts the offer, the project manager needs to prepare for that person to be brought on board to the project as smoothly as possible. This seamless transition is important for several reasons. First, it gives an initial–ideally positive–impression to the new employee. Also, many hours may be wasted if the new employee just sits at his or her desk with nothing to do or no capability to do anything.

The following list identifies some of the items that must be prepared by the project manager or a project administrator prior to the new employee's arrival:

- Physical space and physical facilities, such as a desk and chair
- Office supplies
- Computing equipment
- Communication facilities, such as telephone numbers, user IDs, and passwords
- Special software tools
- Scheduling of special project education, if necessary
- Printed or electronic documents on project processes, policies, methodologies, and other items relevant to the project

Most project managers will be too busy "running" the project to take the time for these activities. Other project managers may postpone these tasks to a later time–perhaps too late. Although the actual tasks of preparation may be delegated to someone else, the project manager must ensure that the preparation does, in fact, take place and that the appropriate requisitions for the new employee are all signed, approved, and sent out in time.

Finally, the project manager should prepare the other project team members for the arrival of the new employee. Giving the existing members information about the new member can promote positive project chemistry. In particular, the project manager should explain the role and relationship of the new member to the rest of the team.

KEY CONCEPTS

This chapter introduced two general software organizational structures: the software development structure and the software support structure. Working from the general software development structure, organizations may adapt it as necessary to fit their unique set of needs. Similarly, the general software support structure, with its three levels of support reflecting increasingly more complex problems and solutions, may be altered to better fit the needs of different organizations. These structural differences mostly arise from differences in parameters such as size, location, skill groups, finance, efficiency, management, and corporate culture.

After the organizational structure is built, then all the open slots need to be filled with people. Recruiting and hiring of human resources is an important process because people—unlike pieces of equipment—cannot be "returned" easily. After a candidate is hired, the new employee must be brought on board as smoothly as possible to ensure that the software project team will continue to work effectively.

EXERCISES

1. In extreme programming, it is often mentioned that two software programmers should share the ownership of a module and that two people should actually code the same module together. Investigate the topic of extreme programming (see the "Suggested Reading" list) and discuss any concerns you may have about filling a software development position that will be "occupied" by two people.
2. Construct a series of descriptions that outline software designer positions ranging from the entry level to the senior level.
3. Compare and contrast the applicability of hierarchical and matrix organizational structures to a software support and service organization.
4. Discuss which organizational structure will minimize the usage of indirect personnel and under what conditions?

5. What is a virtual organization, and what are some of the reasons to consider such an organization?
6. What are some of the reasons that an employment candidate may be: (a) initially screened out, and (b) later screened out?
7. What is required to successfully bring a new employee on board?

SUGGESTED READING

R. Agarwal and T. W. Feratt, "Crafting an HR Strategy to Meet the Need for IT Workers," *Communications of the ACM,* July 2001, 59–64.

K. Beck, *Extreme Programming Explained: Embrace Change,* Addison-Wesley, 1999.

F. P. Brooks, Jr., *The Mythical Man-Month,* Addison-Wesley, 1975.

L. Constantine, "Working Organization: Paradigms for Project Management and Organization," *Communications of the ACM,* October 1993, 34–43.

M. Goold and A. Campbell, "Do You Have a Well-Designed Organization?," *Harvard Business Review,* March 2002, 117–124.

W. Humphrey, *Managing Technical People,* Addison-Wesley, 1999.

P. Kraft, *Programmers and Managers,* Springer-Verlag, 1977.

H. J. Leavitt, "Why Hierarchies Thrive," *Harvard Business Review,* March 2003, 96–102.

M. Mantei, "The Effect of Programming Team Structures on Programming Tasks," *Communications of the ACM,* March 1981, 106–113.

R. S. Pressman, *Software Engineering: A Practitioner's Approach,* 4th ed., McGraw-Hill Companies, 1997.

L. D. Schaeffer, "The Leadership Journey," *Harvard Business Review,* October 2002, 42–47.

L. A. Slade, T. O. Davenport, D. R. Roberts, and S. Shah, "How Microsoft Optimized Its Investment in People after the Dot-Com Era," *Journal of Organizational Excellence,* Winter 2002, 43–52.

C. Stevenson, *Software Engineering Productivity: A Practical Guide,* Chapman & Hall, 1995.

S. D. Teasley et al., "Rapid Software Development Through Team Collocation," *IEEE Transactions on Software Engineering,* July 2002, 671–683.

G. M. Weinberg, *The Psychology of Computer Programming,* Van Nostrand Reinhold, 1971.

Chapter 7

Processes, Methodologies, and Tools

Chapter Objectives

This chapter discusses the following concepts:

- Why a process may have been chosen for the project during planning, but must be revisited, properly positioned, and controlled for the project team during the organizing and preparing phase
- How the details concerning methodologies, which are typically not included in a project plan, are defined, specified, and introduced to the team
- Why the tools, which accompany the processes and methodologies, are an important productivity aid for the project team

PROCESSES

Besides organizing and preparing for the use and introduction of new human resources, the other resources necessary for a software project must be considered, acquired, established, and installed during the organizing and preparing phase of POMA. One of the first steps in process preparation is to clarify what the plan states about the process that is to be used. No single process is applicable to all software projects. Even if the plan calls for a generic type of software development or support process, each software project must have its process further tailored depending on some of the following factors:

- The size and complexity of the project based on the deliverables
- The maturity of the organization

- The structure of the organization
- The history of the working relationship of the people
- The size of the organization
- The goals of the software project

Many software project managers will refer to the definitions and guidelines from ISO 9000, Software Process Improvement and Capability dEtermination (SPICE), or the Software Engineering Institute's CMM and CMMI bodies of knowledge in preparing for his or her software project's specific tailoring needs. These standards and assessment models provide guidance as to what the "experts" around the world believe are good practices for software development, support, and maintenance. For example, if a software project manager contemplates outsourcing a part of thc activity, hc or she could consult the Subcontract Model described in CMM for Software instead of inventing a methodology within a process from scratch.

Setting Software Standards: ISO, SPICE, and SEI

The International Organization for Standardization (ISO) includes delegates from 146 countries and is headquartered in Geneva, Switzerland. Its mission is to promote the widespread adoption of international standards, most of which are highly specific to particular products. ISO 9000 is probably its most widely recognized and successful family of standards, having become an international reference for quality management. ISO 9001 specifically addresses the development, supply, installation, and maintenance of computer software. ISO 9000-3 specifies quality management and quality assurance issues and describes how these quality aspects apply to ISO 9001 for software.

Software Process Improvement and Capability dEtermination (SPICE) is an initiative to support the development of international standards for software process assessment. SPICE has three specific goals: (1) to develop a working draft for a standard for software process assessment; (2) to conduct industry trials of emerging standards; and (3) to promote technology transfer of software process assessment into the worldwide software industry. The working draft for an international standard for software process assessment was completed in 1995, and the follow-on standards development is now controlled by the ISO/IEC JTC1/SC7/WG10, the Process Assessment Working Group of ISO. SPICE relies on five technical centers around the world, including one in the United States at the Software Engineering Institute.

> The Software Engineering Institute (SEI) initially created the Capability Maturity Model (CMM) to promote the assessment of an organization's software process maturity. While CMM is now widely recognized in the software industry, it did not address the complete software product cycle–specifically, issues related to software support, service, and maintenance. To fill this gap, the SEI developed a new model, Capability Maturity Model Integration (CMMI), which is built on and extends the best practices from three other models: Capability Maturity Model for Software (CMM-SW), Systems Engineering Capability Model (SECM), and Integrated Product Development Capability Maturity Model (IPD-CMM). CMMI for Software Engineering (CMMI-SW) is a version of CMMI without the System Engineering (e.g., SECM) portion. The CMMI-SW document is available through SEI at Carnegie Mellon University in Pittsburgh.

Recently, Agile process has gained wide acceptance. This process methodology is especially popular among small- to medium-sized projects.

Whatever software process is chosen, it must be communicated to the entire project organization, and the project team must be properly disposed to follow the process. In addition, the project management needs to ensure that the various methodologies, which are to be used under the process, are established, communicated, and implemented. Implementation of the methodologies includes educating the people and providing the necessary tools to support the automation of the methodologies (see the "Methodologies" section later in this chapter).

Process Map

Even though the type of process to be employed was deliberated, debated over, and decided on during the planning stage, there is still a need to map the overall process, to clearly list the activities carried out within each step, and to explain any relationships among the steps. To see how this mapping works, let's consider an example.

Suppose an organization is interested in putting together a waterfall-like development process that covers the production of major artifacts, ranging from requirements specification and code, to test scenarios and reference manuals. The planned process also includes defect prevention and defect removal activities.

Figure 7.1 illustrates how this map may be structured based on the summary table of a resource plan from Chapter 4 (see Table 4.5). Table 4.5 shows which activities are desired and a rough sequence of the development activities. The process map in Figure 7.1 portrays not only the sequence but also the interrelationships among the activities. In this first example, many of the details within a process step, such as those relating to design or information development, are left out. Otherwise, a single diagram will be too confusing to read. This level of the process map is meant simply to communicate the general flow and relationships among the parts.

In particular, note that the project management activities are included in the overall process map; they span the complete project cycle. This choice is made deliberately, to ensure that the team will not develop an "us" against "management" mentality. Once such an attitude takes hold, it becomes very difficult to build a cooperative team in which the project management and the professionals work together as trusting partners. When the project management activities are viewed as an integral part of the overall project process, then implementing measurements and collecting data become less threatening, and the introduction of any change or improvement based on the collected status information will be more readily accepted.

Another step shown in Figure 7.1 is an activity that is rarely included as part of software project management but is absolutely crucial to the success of an organization. This activity, which is labeled "Initial Requirements and Business Case," appears in front of all process activities. Too many software

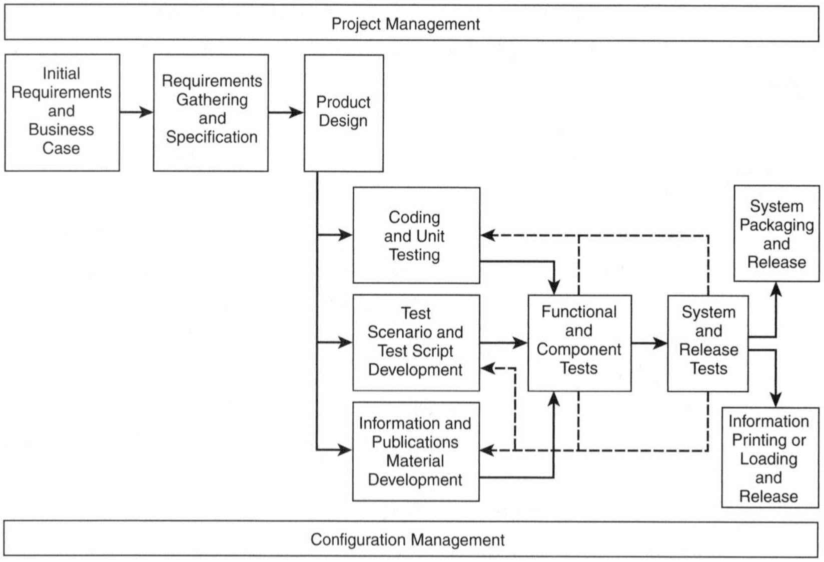

Figure 7.1 Overall project process map

projects have been initiated without taking a moment to assess their business viability. As a result, unrealistic constraints on resources or time may be placed on the project. The project management team is somehow expected to figure out the solution even when there may be no better answer than turning down the opportunity. Thus analyzing the business case for the project should be the first step. The software project managers should be "looking out" for the incoming business and seek to participate in its analysis as early as possible.

Process Flow

The arrows in the overall process diagram in Figure 7.1 show the flow of activities. The first three major sets of activities are fairly sequential. Before the set of design subactivities is completed, the coding, test scenario development, and information development activities may all start and overlap with the design step. The actual testing, however, cannot proceed unless the particular function is coded, functional test scenarios and scripts are written, and the functional help text and usage guide are developed. The testing for a component follows the same logic, in that all the functions within a component must first be tested, and then the system and release testing follows. Upon completion of the system and release tests, the code portion of the product–which may include source code, executable objects, and test scripts–is packaged and set for release. Similarly, the information portion of the product–which may include user manuals and design documents–is set for printing and set for release. If the information product is to be provided through an on-line mechanism, then it must be released to that on-line mechanism.

Figure 7.1 includes some dotted lines with reverse arrows to indicate the potential for backward flow of activities. Although changes and modifications to the artifact developed in a previous step may be needed for every activity, testing as a set of activities will uncover problems and cause more rework to the artifacts in the form of fixes. In Figure 7.1, the dotted line from "Functional and Component Tests" points to "Coding and Unit Testing," "Test Scenario and Test Script Development," and "Information and Publications Material Development." But in fact, depending on the problem discovered, sometimes the team may need to modify the design or even change the requirements specifications. In such a case, the reverse arrows may go back to more previous activities than just the ones shown in Figure 7.1.

A reverse sequence may be initiated when a problem is found during testing. It kicks off a fix cycle that touches upon programming and information development, which in turn may necessitate changes to the project's design. Thus, if we were to modify this general process map, more reverse arrows might be drawn from coding and information development to design and requirements. Also, problems may be discovered during design that may in turn result in some modifications in requirements. Lastly, inspections or reviews within each of the major steps may uncover problems introduced by the previous major step and necessitate changes to the artifacts produced in that earlier step. Some process charts separate out the review and inspection activities. In our example, we will not show all of these reviews and potential reverse flows of activities with dotted lines to avoid cluttering the general process map.

The arrows in the process map may also represent the "successful" completion of events prior to starting the successor activities. The conditions for successful completion or the exit criteria of a step, which allow the work flow to continue to the next step, need to be provided as a companion to the process map. In Figure 7.1, the arrows from the design activities to the three subsequent activities require a bit more discussion. After the high-level and architectural design is completed and as each component and functional area is designed, the corresponding component and functional area may be converted to code. The test scenario and test scripts for those completed component and functional areas may also be developed. Similarly, the information write-ups for help text and manuals for those already-designed areas may be created. Thus the arrows from the design activity to its subsequent activities carry a little more semantics than meeting the usual exit criteria and flow to the next activity.

A typical set of exit criteria from the design process may include the following conditions:

- All the functional and nonfunctional requirements are designed including the following:
    - The user interfaces and workflow
    - The systems and communications interfaces
    - Database and file structure
    - Special constraints: performance, security, back-up/recovery, etc.
- All of the design is documented and represented in the previously specified format and language.
- The design document is stored in a configuration management tool.
- The design document is reviewed and all errors found have been fixed and captured in the updated design document.

The defined exit criteria for the process steps provide a management and a team approach to controlling the flow of the activities. Exit criteria is critical to management and to team process control.

Consider the downstream activities following design (e.g., coding, test case development, and reference manual development) and the listed design exit criteria. If there were no such list, then the question of when the downstream activities should start might be answered only when the design was "complete." Unfortunately, design completion may be interpreted capriciously by different groups. Some groups, facing heavy schedule pressure, might start before the entire design is documented. For example, programmers might code the application functions prior to the "completion" of the nonfunctional parts of the design, such as those related to performance. This rush into coding may lead to later rework, and it may actually elongate the schedule instead of shortening it.

The existence of exit criteria does not necessarily prevent all downstream activities from starting prematurely. For example, one might choose to initiate a downstream activity while one or two exit criteria items remain incomplete. Exit criteria, however, bring out awareness and force conscious decision making in controlling the process. For this reason, all exit criteria should be defined for the various activities shown in the process map. The definitions may be written as a companion document to the process diagram.

Configuration Management

Another activity that is included in the process map in Figure 7.1 is configuration management. Configuration management is made up of a complex set of activities that relate to management of the artifacts generated through the project (see Chapter 4 for more on this topic). It includes the following key activities:

Part I
Configuration management activities: (Definition & Setup)

- Defining and listing the artifacts that need to be managed
- Defining the granularity of managing the artifacts and designing the directory scheme to accommodate that level of granularity
- Defining the rules for accessing the artifacts

Part 2
Configuration management activities: (Control & Track)

- Defining the security and controls needed to manage the artifacts

- Storing, retrieving, locking, and unlocking artifacts based on the predefined set of rules
- Maintaining all of the tools employed to help in configuration management

Configuration management A set of procedures that define, track, and control the artifacts produced during the development, support, and maintenance of software.

Since project artifacts are generated across the entire project life cycle, the set of configuration management activities is also a natural part of the project and these need to be executed through the complete project. It is thus a central concern in managing both the artifacts and the project as a whole. Configuration management will be discussed in more detail in the "Methodologies" section later in this chapter.

Processes and Subprocesses

Within each of the major steps in the general process map, there may be several further expansions that resemble subprocesses within a process. If an expanded subprocess such as the general requirements management activities discussed in Chapter 1 is needed, then that subprocess description must accompany the overall project process. Many of the variations in process models are studied in software engineering, and historical information pertaining to the success and failure of the different process models is discussed in a variety of software engineering books and reports (see the "Suggested Reading" list at the end of this chapter for some sources). For example, Barry Boehm has stated that only 15% of the software development effort is typically devoted to programming and that reviews catch 60% of all errors. Armed with this type of information, quality-conscious software project managers may insist on including software reviews in requirements specification and design activities, but not necessarily in coding, as an integral part of the software development process. The project management would be wise to consult such sources before putting the organization's process into play.

All of the materials related to the general project process must be reviewed and agreed to by the project team management and the technical leaders of the project. It is the project management's responsibility to transform a high-level process plan into a specific project process model. The transformation may involve an emphasis on quality and the inclusion of reviews in requirements and design activities but not in the programming activity. For very small software projects, configuration management may be reduced to only code control. The actual work may be delegated to a process "expert," if the team includes such a person. The transformation from high-level process plan to project-specific model includes the following tasks:

- Identifying and organizing the major components or steps of the process
- Providing the details of subprocesses, if necessary
- Explaining the relationships among the components
- Showing the flow from one component to another
- Identifying the exit criteria from one component to another that facilitates the flow

Process Introduction and Education

Once they have a defined general project process with all the accompanying materials, the software project managers must communicate this information to the rest of the team. Members of a project team may come from a variety of backgrounds, all of which use some form of a process. Some may come from chaotic organizations in which the process is formulated as the project progresses. Others may come from organizations with well-established processes, although different from the one that will be used on the current project. If the team members come in with relatively open minds, then the establishment of a common process for the project may not be very difficult. If they are resistant, it may take some major effort to transform the team so that it will embrace a "new" project process.

In either case, there is a need to provide a period of time for the assimilation of the process. During this time, a combination of education on and communication regarding the process must take place. It would be a horrible mistake for the project managers to assume that much of the education and communication may be accomplished by producing a "comprehensive" process document and then leave it to the team members to read it at their leisure. Likewise, education about and communication of the project process should not be done in one fell swoop. That approach would not be much better than handing the team members a thick process document and then expecting them to absorb and accept all the information. Instead, the education and communication should come in stages.

There are many ways to parcel out the education and communication activities. One possible approach is as follows:

Stage 1: Process Introduction

- Provide the introduction and education, if necessary, to the general project process chosen for the project.
- Provide the rationale behind the specific process.
- Point out both the positives and the negatives as well as any portion of the process that is still untested.
- Point out any past history, if available.

Stage 2: Feedback and Modifications

- Allow team members to debate and study the process on their own.
- Ask for written feedback.
- Collect and analyze the responses.
- Make appropriate modifications and prepare for responses to those changes.
- Bring the team together, providing the team members with feedback on which suggested modifications were accepted and explaining what was done with both the accepted and the rejected suggestions.

Stage 3: Acceptance

- Ask whether any further education is needed and provide it as appropriate.
- Ask for concurrence and acceptance of the process.

Stage 4: Reinforcement

- Quickly review the process and ask for any further input prior to its implementation.
- Make any adjustments and update the process as needed.
- Reemphasize that the process is expected to be used and followed.

The effort required to organize, communicate, educate, and gain acceptance of the process may be longer than many people would like. Indeed, the length of time expended in organizing and setting up the project process might surprise even the best of software project managers. The reinforcement activities (Stage 4) may be performed repeatedly as needed, but not excessively. As new employees come on board, they must also be introduced to the project process. The right balance of process reinforcement versus process bureaucracy must always be maintained. The management of that balance will be discussed later as part of the monitoring and adjustment phases of project management (see Parts Three and Four of this book). At this phase of the project, however, the software project management simply needs to ensure that the team is clear about, and ready to follow, the process map.

METHODOLOGIES

A methodology is a prescribed set of steps to accomplish a task. As such, it may be viewed as a further drill-down on the definition of the activities within a process. The process provides the macro steps, whereas the methodologies provide the micro steps that sometimes may transcend the macro steps. For example, setting up a naming convention for files as part of configuration management is a micro step, but it transcends the macro steps in that it affects requirements documents, design documents, test cases, code versions, and multiple releases. Thus the difference between a methodology and a process is a matter of degree.

Software project managers have traditionally loved to be involved in lengthy discussions of methodologies. One reason for this fascination is that software engineering is a relatively new discipline. As a result, new methodologies are constantly being invented and frequent changes in methodologies come about because of the accelerated pace of technology. Another reason for the high interest in methodologies is that many software project managers were promoted into their positions because they were the "best" performers in some aspect of the software project development using a particular technology and methodology. Clearly, it is to the software project managers' advantage to be familiar with that methodology. However, their ultimate responsibility is to ensure that the most appropriate methodology is selected and that the chosen methodology is properly implemented. They do not have to be methodology experts themselves.

During the planning stage, software project managers became involved in putting the plan together by choosing the main methodologies. Sometimes the rationale behind the specific choice of methodology needs to be reviewed one more time during the organizing and preparing phase to ensure that nothing major has changed since the plan was developed. As the software industry is such a fast-paced environment, the software project managers may have to alter some part of the plan prior to implementing it.

There are different ways to describe and prepare a project team for using a particular methodology. For example, the methodology may be described at two levels: The higher level is a more process-oriented way, in that the major substeps to be employed are listed and their relationships are shown; the deeper level takes each substep and describes the specific method involved in performing it. In other situations, the methodology may include several steps in a process. In the object-oriented methodology, for example, the methodology may cover several major process steps from requirements to programming.

The preparation for introducing such a methodology would be relatively complex. Let's look at how the software project management can organize and prepare the project team to deploy the chosen methodologies by examining first the definition of "methodology" and then by looking at methodology preparation.

Methodology Definition

Let's look at an example in which the methodology may be described in two levels. Let's consider the functional testing activity from the software development process. The general methodology may be described in a high-level fashion as follows:

- Review the requirements specification for the description of the desired functionality.
- Review the design document for the design of the solution to provide that functionality.
- Review the code, if necessary.
- Develop the usage scenario and break down the usage scenario into test cases for that functionality.
- Execute the test cases and record the result.
- Report any problems found.
- Incorporate the fixes and retest to ensure that the fixes are correct.
- Promote all of the correctly tested functional code to a library.

Within this general methodology, very different, specific methods may be employed to accomplish any of the particular substeps. To see how, consider the substep that addresses the generation of test cases. It may be further expanded into a white-box test case generation method, in which the internal workings of the design and code are reviewed to determine how many predicates (i.e., decisions such as in an "if" statement) exist. (The alternative to white-box testing is black-box testing, in which the development of test cases is based on requirements or design documents but not on a review of the actual code.)

Predicate A relation (e.g., $x = y$) that has a value of either true or false. In programming constructs, an "if" statement is often used to evaluate the truth or falsity of a relation.

White-box testing A testing methodology in which the actual code is reviewed during the development of test cases. With this strategy, predicate constructs such as "if" or "case" statements in the code can be counted.

Black-box testing A testing methodology in which the development of test cases is based on requirements or design documents but not on a review of the actual code. With this strategy, the code is viewed as a "black box."

From those predicates, the combinations for a test data set may be prepared to ensure that all paths of the program associated with a particular function are executed. Then specific test scripts need to be developed for each test case. The generation of an actual test script will depend on the particular tool utilized, but generic test scripts may be developed first.

Another specific method may address how to report the discovery of any problems during this white-box testing. In this case, the actual reporting simply involves filling out a problem reporting form on paper or electronically. But after the form is completed, where does it go and who takes responsibility for this reported problem? Thus, in setting up a simple step within the functional testing methodology, one may discover the need for two more items:

- A problem reporting form, which may be electronic, must exist or be designed.
- A subprocess that defines the flow of the problem reporting form, from the opening of a problem report to the closure of that problem, must exist or be designed.

If both the problem reporting form and the problem opening-to-closure process need further work, then the preparation for the "reporting problem found" step may be quite time-consuming. Although it is not difficult to design a simple form to record the opening of a problem, a major piece of preparation work is required to design an information-gathering form that will allow the tracking of the problem from beginning to closure. The problem opening-to-closure subprocess may also need to be defined, reviewed, and communicated as part of the methodology.

Software project managers should not be surprised to find such holes as they prepare to introduce the methodologies to the project team. Could some of these issues have been addressed at planning time? Yes, but it is not likely that they would have been identified at that time. Besides, the details of process and methodology implementation rightly belong to the organization and preparation phase of project management. Furthermore, no plan is perfect, and the discovery of holes in the process and methodology plan is a very common occurrence.

Methodology Preparation

If the plan includes a complete methodology that crosses several steps, such as the object-oriented programming methodology or Ken Beck's extreme programming methodology, then the preparation for it may be quite difficult for project management. This was especially the case when object-oriented methodology was first introduced more than a decade ago. Even though both object-oriented programming and extreme programming utilize the term "programming," each covers more than just programming activities. By now almost everyone is familiar with object-oriented methodologies, but some may not be familiar with extreme programming. As this book is not meant to be a treatise on software engineering, interested parties are directed to Ken Beck's *Extreme Programming Explained: Embrace Change* or A. Cockburn's *Agile Software Development* for more details on this approach to software development and programming (see the "Suggested Reading" list at the end of this chapter).

It is extremely difficult for project managers to stay out of the detailed technical discussions of a methodology, especially if it is an up-and-coming one such as aspect-oriented programming (AOP), which is viewed as a potential post–object-oriented programming era methodology. The lengthy debates and discussions over a new methodology form a trap into which many technical managers fall. As a result, a large amount of good technical exploration is done, but no plan or preparation for that methodology is made.

Aspect-oriented programming (AOP) A new software development methodology that emphasizes cross-functional features or concerns that may arise in the requirements, design, or implementation steps. Examples of aspects include design constraints, system properties, and system behaviors.

The software project managers do need to facilitate the debate over a new or complex methodology, so that all fears and apprehensions about it may be exposed and resolved before the next stage of preparation. During this debate, the project managers must stay objective and ensure that accurate information is provided during the discussion stage and that the discussion is geared toward making a decision. Thus the parameters for decision making and embracing of a methodology need to be spelled out. From a software-project point of view, a methodology should be judged by the following criteria:

- Whether it will accomplish the task
- Whether it will accomplish the task in some advantageous way that improves productivity, reduces complexity, and enhances quality
- Whether the actual project cost will be reduced and the schedule improved

This is a tall order. Nevertheless, the software project managers must be prepared to answer these questions as part of the organization and preparation of the methodologies.

If the methodology is new to the team, there is also a front-end cost in terms of the potentially steep learning curve and extra time required to master the methodology. Once the debates are over and the team is mentally prepared to embrace the methodology, then team education is needed to ensure that everyone will practice this complex or new methodology in the same way. The project managers should insist that all members participate in the education process so that the entire team will be on the same page.

Sometimes the team may already include a few experts who do not need the technical education. If so, then the project managers should take advantage of the situation and have those people mentor and help the rest of the team get up to speed on the methodology. It is very tempting to try to utilize these experts and get an early start on the project. However, it is much more valuable to have the software project team work harmoniously on a complex methodology. Thus preparing the team as a group is important. Just as in process preparation, the team receives the same experience as they go through the first three stages of preparation:

1. Introduction
2. Feedback and modification
3. Acceptance

In addition, a reinforcement stage (Step 4) may be needed from time to time.

TOOLS

One of the main reasons for using tools is to reduce work effort and, thereby, to increase productivity and efficiency. Tools represent a significant set of resources for software projects. They range from compilers and databases to requirements modelers and configuration managers. Tools, like other technologies and methodologies, are often presented as a panacea for all ills afflicting a software project. At times, high improvement numbers, such as 50% to 200% gains in productivity, have been thrown around as evidence of a particular tools' effectiveness. Such grandiose claims should raise a red flag for software project managers. Unfortunately, many software technical leaders and project managers have embraced those highly optimistic numbers and organized their projects around a tool, rather than the other way around. In the early days of computer-aided software engineering (CASE) tools and again in the early days of object-oriented methodology, for example, several tools were thought to provide very aggressive savings of effort and schedule, but many of the expected gains did not materialize.

As part of the preparation and facilitation of tools for the software project, the project managers need to first take a realistic account of what should be expected and what effort will be required to achieve those expectations. In the general process map shown in Figure 7.1, the configuration management activities are portrayed as a subprocess that must be carried out throughout the complete software project. Several tools are available to help in many of the substeps within that subprocess. The question is which one to bring in and what preparation is needed for its use.

Tool Identification and Preparation

During the planning phase, it may have been recognized and determined that a configuration management tool is needed. Thus the plan may have listed it as a necessary tool and resources may have been set aside to acquire it. Now the software project management is responsible for "making it happen." The following are some of the major activities that the software project managers should carry out to prepare for acquisition and use of the tool:

- Identify the specific steps and activities that the tool is expected to automate or improve.
- Explore realistic expectations for the tool, stated in terms of productivity gain or efficiency gain that the automation of these steps will bring.
- Review the various tools available that will meet these expectations.
- Review the training needed to attain the level of competency for the expected gains.
- Choose the specific tool to be acquired, working out the needed terms and conditions.

- Announce the decision.
- Set and communicate the realistic expectations in terms of productivity gains that the team should be experiencing.
- Schedule and facilitate the necessary training.
- Acquire and set up the chosen tool.
- Ensure that proper and continuous support of the tool is in place.
- Communicate the project policy for usage of this tool.
- Set up the mechanism to enforce the usage policy.

This extensive list of activities is not only applicable for introducing a sophisticated tool for configuration management, but should also be consulted as a prompter for introducing less complex tools.

The first step in the list is an especially important one. Even though the project team may have already recognized the need for a tool to carry out some of the activities during the planning phase of the project's management, the software team members and the project managers should understand and agree on exactly which steps the tool will try to automate and improve. This clear identification will allow the project managers to address and calculate the potential productivity and efficiency gains in a realistic manner. Using this information, they can set achievable goals related to productivity and efficiency gains. Identifying the specific activities to be supported by the tool will also help in setting the tool usage policy.

Tool Selection

Another key step is the actual selection of the particular vendor and the vendor's tool. This step may be extremely time-consuming and perhaps charged with strong emotions. To avoid problems, the software project managers must establish an objective set of criteria for tool selection. These criteria will draw upon the information gained from reviewing and studying the various vendors and their offerings. In particular, the criteria should take into account an analysis of the following information:

- The functions that the tool performs and automates
- The expected gains in productivity and efficiency from the tool's functions
- The number of users who may simultaneously access the tool
- The tool's performance capacity and reliability
- The vendor's expertise in the tool
- The vendor's past history in supporting the tool
- The amount of training needed to use the tool

- The effort required to maintain and support the tool
- Contractual terms and conditions for the tool—especially the financial terms

Some "scoring" mechanism must be established for each criterion. For example, a range of weights (e.g., 1, 3, 5) may be assigned to each criterion, and the sum of the weights calculated for each tool. With this scheme, in the actual assignments of weights, one must be careful about the semantics of each criterion. Assigning a value of 5 to the "vendor expertise in the tool" criterion highlights vendors' richness in expertise, whereas assigning a value of 5 to the "amount of training needed to use the tool" represents the need for little training on the tool. The choice of the tool is then made based on the scores, which are the different sums for the contending tools. The scoring mechanism may be modified to accommodate the particular class of tools, but something similar to this approach is needed so that the project team will accept the decision and embrace the chosen tool.

Tool Usage Preparation

Bringing in a tool is one thing; using it properly is another. To ensure that the expectations will come to fruition, the project team must be trained how to use the tool correctly. The software project managers should realize that even with the team's formal training in the use of the tool there is an early period of time, when the usage of the tool is still new, during which the team may lose some productivity. The team will inevitably go through a start-up period marked by exploration, some frustration, and further learning. The software project managers must account for this early experimentation phase while setting expectations for the tool and sending a message about it to the team.

Even with all the software project manager's good intentions, preparation, and facilitation, some team members may still find reasons not to use the tool. In the author's own experiences, there have been several occasions in which people did not want to use a certain tool simply because they did not want to attend the necessary education. Their egos prevented them from going to a class! In the situation where the tool is targeted at helping improve only the individual's productivity, a few team members' refusal to work with the tool may not lead to too much of a loss in team productivity. Nevertheless, this "revolt" may still create a negative team morale. In the situation where the tool is targeted at helping the team as a whole and its effectiveness depends on everyone's participation, then even a few "renegades" must not be tolerated. It takes only one recalcitrant worker to thwart the effort to use such team-oriented tools and achieve the desired benefits. And the problem may be bigger than just the missed realization of expected productivity gains—total project chaos can ensue. Such would be the case with failure to use library control or configuration management tools, for example. For all these reasons, the tool usage policy must be clearly communicated and enforced. In devising a policy, software project managers must put thought into devising the enforcement mechanism of the policy as well.

This last point on policy development and enforcement also applies to processes and methodologies. For the process and methodology to really work, they must be adhered to and properly utilized by all team members. Thus the software project managers must set the tone for the project by establishing a usage policy, which in turn must be supported by an effective enforcement mechanism.

KEY CONCEPTS

Plans to adopt and deploy certain processes, methodologies, and tools need a substantial amount of software project managers' preparation efforts before the plans can be transformed into real practice. The organization and facilitation of this transformation is a vital project management task. One may view these activities as "getting the resources ready" for the software project monitoring phase.

To demonstrate how a software project team may tailor a process for its particular situation, this chapter considered a generic waterfall process. Its process map included some extra activities, such as the initial requirements and business case establishment, project management, and configuration management. The exit criteria for each activity in the process map controlled the process flow, whether forward or reverse.

Defining and specifying the details of a process must be accompanied by proper preparation of the team members. The communication and education of the team should proceed through four stages: (1) introduction of the process; (2) feedback and modification; (3) acceptance; and (4) reinforcement.

Methodologies may be viewed as a drill-down on the process definitions. For each activity in the process, a methodology provides a set of steps to accomplish that task. Software project managers should avoid spending too much time themselves in debating the various methodologies. Rather, they must work to facilitate the discussion in such a manner that the methodologies are chosen, defined, and introduced to the team by following the same four stages as found in process communication.

The tools that are needed and desired for the software project must be determined up-front. The selection of a particular tool from a specific vendor is a time-consuming activity that must be performed during the organizing and preparing phase. The software project managers should understand and establish the expected degree of productivity and efficiency gains from these tools. In addition, they should identify how these tools will be utilized and supported.

Clear usage and enforcement policies must be established for all processes, methodologies, and tools selected for the software project.

EXERCISES

1. Choose an iterative process and tailor it to an organization that has fewer than 20 people who take on projects that are normally not complex and typically last less than one year. Show and explain the process map and the process flow.
2. Discuss the advantages and disadvantages of including management activities into the general process flow.
3. Discuss the merits of having exit criteria. Are there any drawbacks?
4. Discuss how you, as the software project manager, might commission the selection of test tools for your project. What selection criteria would you recommend?
5. Discuss some of the reasons why a software process might fail.
6. Review the steps involved in introducing a process, and discuss how you may or may not modify the approach in introducing a new, but untested methodology.
7. Devise a tool usage policy, taking into account the tool types (e.g., team or individual). Should you include reward and punishment in managing tool usage?

SUGGESTED READING

P. G. Armour, "The Laws of Software Process," *Communications of the ACM,* January 2001, 15–17.

K. Auer, R. Miller, and W. Cunningham, *Extreme Programming Applied: Playing to Win,* Addison-Wesley, 2001.

K. Beck, *Extreme Programming Explained: Embrace Change,* Addison-Wesley, 1999.

B. Boehm, "Industrial Software Metrics Top 10 List," *IEEE Software,* Vol. 4, No. 5, September 1987, 84–85.

A. Cockburn, *Agile Software Development,* Addison Wesley, 2001.

T. Elrad, R. Filman, and A. Bader, "Aspect-Oriented Programming," *Communications of the ACM,* October 2001, 29–32.

K. E. Emam and A. Birk, "Validating ISO/IEC 15504 Measure of Software Requirements Analysis Process Capability," *IEEE Transactions on Software Engineering,* June 2000, 541–566.

K. E. Emam, J. N. Drouin, and W. Melo, *SPICE: The Theory and Practice of Software Process Improvement and Capability Determination,* IEEE Computer Society Press, 1998.

L. Mathiassen, O. K. Ngwanyama, and I. Aean, "Managing Change in Software Process Improvement," *IEEE Software,* November/Decenber 2005, 84–91.

G. C. Murphy, R. J. Walker, and E. L. A. Baniassad, "Evaluating Emerging Software Development Technologies: Lessons Learned from Assessing Aspect Oriented Programming," *IEEE Transactions on Software Engineering,* July/August 1999, 438–455.

J. Raynus, *Software Process Improvement with CMM,* Artech House, 1999.

C. H. Schmauch, *ISO 9000 for Software Developers,* ASQC Quality Press, 1994.

I. Sommerville, P. Sawyer, and S. Viller, "Managing Process Inconsistency Using Viewpoints," *IEEE Transactions on Software Engineering,* November/December 1999, 784–799.

F. Tsui and O. Karem, *Essentials of Software Engineering,* 2nd Edition, Jones and Bartlett Publishers, 2009.

I. Vessey and A. P. Sravanapudi, "CASE Tools as Collaborative Support Technologies," *Communications of the ACM,* January 1995, 83–95.

B. E. Wampler, *The Essence of Object Oriented Programming with Java and UML,* Addison-Wesley, 2002.

Chapter 8

Goals and Measurements: Preparations and Costs

Chapter Objectives

This chapter discusses the following concepts:

- How the goals specified during the planning phase can be reexamined to ensure that proper metrics and measurement schemes are defined and implemented
- How the software project team should be prepared so that it will accept the measurement scheme

TRANSFORMING GOALS AND MEASUREMENTS

As part of the planning activities, a number of goals and measurements to gauge and validate the attainment of goals were considered and identified. The project team, as a whole, still needs to be organized and motivated to both understand and accept these goals and measurements. Just as with other parts of the software project plan, the software project managers are responsible for transforming the plan items into executable items during the organizing phase of POMA.

During the planning stage, various product and process attributes were considered. For those attributes considered especially important, goals were set. In setting the goals, the metrics and the measurement scheme for those goals had to be conceived. During the organizing phase, several other important notions need to be weighed by the software project managers:

- Are the goals and their associated measurement schemes clearly defined?
- Has the organization embraced the measuring scheme?
- Has the cost of measuring been taken into account?

Software project managers should be prepared to face relatively more challenges from the project team and the rest of the organization than their peer project managers in other disciplines would encounter. This greater resistance reflects the young state of the software field, where no traditional measurement schemes have emerged as standards.

CLARIFYING DEFINITIONS OF GOALS AND MEASUREMENTS

Even though the importance of different product and process attributes was considered in the planning phase, often the goals for those attributes deemed important may not have been set clearly. As a result, the actual measurement scheme may be confusing to team members. To alleviate this possibility, the software project managers should do the following:

- Review the goals set for the product and project attributes
- Review the measurement scheme and modify it if necessary
- Build an "operational" plan for the measurement schemes

The goals set for each attribute should be clear. By "clear," we mean that there is a way to determine whether a goal has been met. In software projects, many desirable goals are stated in a qualitative way. A prime example is a requirement statement such as "The product should be easy to use." All software project managers realize that "ease of use" is a characteristic that the ideal product will have. Thus, during the project planning phase, this requirement is transformed into some type of a product goal. Is the goal set for this important product attribute still desired at the organizing phase? If so, then the question of whether it is well understood, specified, accepted, and verifiable during the project monitoring phase needs to be answered before going forward.

Decomposing the Ease-of-Use Example

Let's analyze the ease-of-use example further to demonstrate how goals and measurements are clarified. One popular way to clarify a statement is to decompose it into several substatements. Suppose the initial requirement statement "The product should be easy to use" is decomposed and transformed into the following subgoal statement: "Every function in the product can be completed by a user without any other human intervention." This transformation into something more specific may be reasonable, but it may need further clarification. Is this subgoal more specific than the original ease-of-use statement? How would we gauge this transformed attribute? Is there a need for a specific activity that will allow us to gauge its attainment?

The clarification needed, in this case, relates to the measurement scheme. A possible answer may involve setting up a usability test within the testing activities as part of the process. The precise metric and measurement methodology should be defined in terms of this usability test. The following steps might be used:

1. A test case is designed for each function in the product.
2. A numerical count is kept of the number of test cases that are successfully executed by a test subject without any external intervention.
3. This test is repeated with a predetermined number of test subjects to ensure the results' statistical relevancy.
4. All of the unsuccessful test cases are summed.

The goal for the product is to have zero unsuccessful tests—which is probably impossible. A more reasonable goal may be 5% unsuccessful or 95% successful test cases.

Upon further consideration, both the goal statement and the measurement scheme need a little more clarification. More specifically, how many test subjects should be included in the usability test for it to be considered statistically relevant? Would we classify a function as one that was not "completed" if 99 out of 100 test subjects could complete it? How many people must not complete the function before it is labeled as "noncompleted"? One can see the potential areas of contention arising from this example, if the measuring and classification scheme for this goal is not further clarified.

Potentially Misleading Measurements

It is worthwhile to spend a little time discussing the notion of measurement and classification. As in the preceding example, you may want to classify "completed" in a graduated way with a categorization scheme such as the following:

- *Totally completable* means all participants complete all functions.

- *Mostly completable* means 75% or more of the participants complete all functions, but not 100% of the participants complete all functions.
- *Partially completable* means 75% or more of the participants complete at least 75% of the functions, but not 100% of the functions.
- *Not completable* means 25% or more of the participants complete less than 75% of the functions.

The key point to remember when creating categories is that the categories as a whole should exhaustively cover the range of metrics and that each category should be mutually exclusive of any other category. Creating a categorization with the preceding definition of "completable" is just the beginning. The measurement scheme may be further defined by taking each component of the application and applying the categorization scheme to it. You can then tabulate how many components fall into each category.

Once the number of components by categories is known, it is very tempting to perform additional arithmetic operations on those data, such as computing the average. Consider the following scenario, where the categories are assigned a numeric value as follows:

- Totally completable is assigned a value of 8.
- Mostly completable is assigned a value of 4.
- Partially completable is assigned a value of 2.
- Not completable is assigned a value of 0.

Let's further assume that there are 24 components in a software product and that the numbers of components classified into the four categories are as follows:

Totally completable: 6
Mostly completable: 7
Partially completable: 3
Not completable: 8

Utilizing the 8, 4, 2, 0 value system of the categories and considering the number of components in each category, one might be led to compute the average and assert that the average value is $(82 \div 24) = 3.42$. The number 3.42 could then be matched to the closest category, which is 4 (mostly completable). The software project management team would be happy to declare that the product is mostly completable, especially if the goal were to attain a "mostly completable" state.

This sequence of assigning values to the categories and computing values based on the assigned values and the numbers falling in each category

Table 8.1 Effect of Varying Assigned Values

Value assignments	Totally completable	Mostly completable	Partially completable	Not completable	Sum	Average
8, 4, 2, 0	48	28	6	0	82	3.42
10, 7, 3, 1	60	49	9	8	126	5.25
3, 2, 1, 0	18	14	3	0	35	1.46
5, 4, 3, 2	30	28	9	16	83	3.46

may be very misleading, however. Table 8.1 demonstrates that different results may be derived by altering the values assigned to the various categories. In each case, the distribution of components in each category remains the same: 6, 7, 3, 8.

As Table 8.1 shows, if the category value system is changed to 3, 2, 1, 0, then the average is 1.46. This is closest to 1, which is considered "partially completable." Thus picking a different value system yields a different result for the categorization! Clearly, one should be very cautious in assigning values and performing calculations with those assigned values. The scale of measurement can make a huge difference and thus distort the measurement, possibly allowing one to arrive at a different conclusion during the monitoring phase of the software project life cycle.

Sometimes there is a need to decompose and translate the goal statement into a more specific measurement through a more comprehensive activity such as the usability testing mentioned earlier. The parameters that are measured and the classification of the results may then have to be analyzed in more depth. As the preceding example demonstrates, very different conclusions may be reached if one does not take the time to analyze and properly prepare the measurement scheme.

Building a Measurement Operational Plan

Finally, the project team may need to build an "operational" plan for the measurement. Each item in a general plan may require a slightly different operational plan, but there are some common items that need to be considered in any operational plan. Each of the following categories, however, needs to be further expanded by including the following refinement steps:

- Steps to ensure that the process and methodology are modified to include the details needed to implement each plan item

- Steps to ensure that proper resources are made available in a timely manner
- Steps to ensure that necessary metric and measurement schemes are defined for each plan item
- Steps to ensure that goals are defined for the implementation and that the achievement of the goals is validated

Operational plan A plan that contains all the details of how to implement what is contained in a general project plan.

An operational plan for usability testing might include the following sequence of refinement steps:

- The "general" software process must include the additional usability testing step.
- Expertise in terms of conducting usability tests must be brought on board.
- Any physical equipment needed for monitoring the test must be made available.
- The measurement methodology and classification scheme must be defined.
- The criteria for gauging the attainment of the goal must be predefined.

This particular measurement operational plan contains many items and extends the initial plan consisting of goal statements. This level of preparation is needed for successful measurements to take place later during the monitoring phase. Note that the operational plan for each goal and measurement scheme will be different. Also note that it is not possible to fully preplan each goal and its measurement scheme during the planning phase of POMA because, just as the ease-of-use example showed, the definition of the original goal may need to be decomposed and restated in a different form. This deeper level of understanding of a project sometimes does not occur until more analysis is performed during the organizing phase of POMA. More complex measurement schemes will require deeper-level organizing and preparation.

The following items are among those that need to be considered for goals and measurements during this organizing and preparing phase of the POMA life cycle:

- Any additional goal clarification and decomposition
- Well-defined goal validation
- Specific measurement techniques and schemes
- Any process extensions and modifications needed to accommodate measurements
- Additional software/hardware tools needed for measurement activities

EMBRACING THE MEASUREMENT SCHEME

It is one thing to put a plan forward to the software project team. It is another thing to gain the team's acceptance of that plan. Before using the goals and the measurements associated with those goals to track the project status, both have to be explained to the team. As noted earlier, sometimes the measurement scheme may take on quite a bit of complexity. For this reason, further analysis of the planned goals and measurements is required.

Participating in Goal and Measurement Preparations

It is highly recommended that software project managers do not perform all of the analysis and justification studies by themselves. Having various project members and technical leaders participate in the analysis would be much more advantageous, for the following reasons:

- More team members would understand the goals and measurements.
- More nonmanagement team members would feel committed to the goals and measurements.
- Some team members may be counted on to "spread the message" and educate other team members.
- Sharing the burden would lessen the workload of the software project managers.
- Distributing the knowledge would lessen the general fear of being measured.
- Team ownership of the goals would be more likely to be achieved.

Of course, there are also some drawbacks to having the team members participate in the analysis and in the setting of the measurement details. One obvious disadvantage is that the new duties may affect each person's currently assigned workload. That means that the software project managers must monitor the amount of effort the nonmanagement members are being asked to put into these activities, which do not directly affect the product. Many people cannot balance such extra demands effectively or explain to their managers how the extra work placed on their plates will affect the schedule. In addition, some technical people are averse to doing management-related activities, believing that such tasks are not their responsibility. Thus software project managers should be careful in picking the nonmanagement participants in goal and measurement preparations.

Ideally, goal-setting and measurement procedures will be decentralized and lead the team to "own" them. This should neutralize some of the potential resistance to measurement. Minimizing the resistence is especially valuable if the goals set during the planning phase were forged mainly by management personnel. Eliciting positive and cooperative participation at the organizing and preparing stage is crucial.

Basili and Weiss introduced the Goal–Question–Metric (GQM) approach to software metrics. This approach defines a measurement model as follows:

- establish a goal
- develop a list of questions related to the goal
- develop the metrics

GQM has been used quite successfully by many organizations.

Goal Attainability

It is extremely important to take the time and effort to ensure that the project team understands and responds favorably to the measurements process. Sometimes, measurements are put into the project to collect information that will benefit future projects and their immediate value to the current project is not evident to the team. Such measurements may be difficult for some team members to accept, and it requires extra care to explain their benefits. Most people tend to accept that which they understand and to reject that which they do not comprehend. Team members cannot perform their assignments with conviction if they do not understand or believe that the goals are achievable. If the project team starts believing that the goals and the measurements are nonrealistic, team morale will suffer tremendously. As team morale drops, so will team productivity, which may eventually lead to the demise of the entire project.

An example of this situation is one in which an experienced group of software engineers is asked to complete a project in half the time spent on any previous projects of a similar type. An inexperienced project manager may offer justifications for the accelerated schedule such as better tools and methodology when, in fact, introduction of new tools and methodology often takes more time. The experienced software engineers will initially attempt to convince the project manager to alter the schedule goal. If their request is met with unreasonable, stiff resistance, then these experienced software engineers may become demoralized and "let" the project fail just to prove a point.

A less extreme situation occurs when the software development group is asked to keep track of the volume of work and the time expended on it. The software engineers' immediate reaction to such a request is often negative.

The goal here may simply be data collection to use as a baseline for future projects. Achieving acceptance for the data collection requires software project managers to take the time to explain the rationale behind it, especially if the data collected will be used as part of the basis for future productivity estimates and not for modifying the current productivity goal.

Clearly, it is important that team members view the goals and measurements, as planned and established by the project management, as a natural and integral part of the project. These cannot be perceived as management goals for the team or merely bureaucratic goals. Instead, the team members must embrace them as their own goals and measurements. For these reasons, the software project managers, during the organization and preparation phase, should actively and positively communicate the goals, measurements, and measurement scheme. E-mail may be used for this purpose, but one should not approach the communication effort as an electronic broadcast. The message must be sent out with an invitation for all recipients to comment on these items. All team members should be copied on the responses to these comments (both positive and negative), and all concerns must be resolved. The communication must be inclusive, in that no one team member can be left out. In fact, the preferred approach would be face-to-face meetings with the whole team.

To win general acceptance and positive reception of the goals and measurements, the software project management must ensure that the following elements are in place:

- A well-defined goal and measurement scheme
- Attainable goals
- The team's participation in the setting of the goals
- The team's understanding and belief in the goals and measurements
- The commitment of qualified resources for measurement

Measurement Resources: How Do You Find an Expert?

A metrics and measurement "expert" is often a person with special skills in statistics and a thorough understanding of software engineering. This person will be schooled in data collection, analysis, and projection. He or she will also be familiar with tools such as the data management and statistical analysis package from SAS. Such a person may be a member of the process group or quality assurance group if the software organization has strong process and quality assurance departments. The metrics and measurement expert may serve on multiple projects. In smaller enterprises, such a person may come from the testing department because many of the popular product goals deal with product quality or usability. In rare situations, the software project manager may assume this role on a temporary basis.

MEASUREMENT COSTS

One often-asked question is why, if setting goals and measurements is so important, so few software projects do it. Some reasons put forth to explain this contradiction are as follows:

- Software project "success" is often gauged by only a single goal, such as a deliverable's due date.
- The organization may not see the value of setting goals and measurements or may fear the process.
- Management has the misguided view that only "direct" project activities are important and, consequently, fail to fund indirect activities involving measuring the project.
- The team members may not have accepted the goals and, therefore, do not want to be tracked or measured by them.
- Some goals are difficult to define and measure.
- The organization may not have allocated any resources or funding for measurement activities.

All activities within a project must be accounted for–and funded. Setting goals and taking clear measurements are no different in this respect. It is crucial that software project managers take the time during the organizing and preparing phase to explain to the executive and financial managers the project goals, the measurement schemes for gauging the attainment of those goals, and the costs to implement the chosen measurement scheme. One commonly utilized justification for the cost of measurement is comparing the cost of having to rescue a disastrous quality, morale, schedule, or customer satisfaction incident against the cost of measurement and fixing the potential problem prior to it turning into a disaster. This type of argument is especially effective if there is a history of such misfortunes. Having the backing of executive stakeholders will make the goals and the measurements visible. When goals and measurement have a high profile they will, in turn, facilitate requesting the proper funding and resources.

If tools are needed, then the total cost must include the resources needed to maintain each tool. There is a cost related to measurements, which includes the tools, the people, and the procedures. Although project measurement costs are often rolled into a general project management "cost bucket" during project resource planning, they actually need to be delineated separately. Only then will the real cost of measurements be tracked and the value of having the measurements be appreciated.

Consider a relatively simple situation of measuring design review results. The following is a sample breakdown of the effort required. Each has potential costs.

- The effort made to determine and define the data (related to design review) that should be collected
- The effort related to educating the designers and reviewers on the definition of data that will need to be recorded from the design review
- The effort made to acquire a tool for recording and analyzing the design review data (including the tool's purchase price), if a tool is deemed necessary
- The effort made to record or input data into the tool and to analyze the captured data
- The effort required to reorganize and present the analyzed data

As yet, software project managers do not have much hard information on the actual costs of performing software measurements. Not surprisingly, it is difficult to assess the incremental benefits of having goals and measurements without information on the cost side of the equation. Nevertheless, it is clear that without goals and measurements, the project cannot be tracked and monitored.

KEY CONCEPTS

During the planning and organizing phase of POMA, the goals from the planning phase are revisited and refined as necessary to transform them into measurable entities. Sometimes, what appeared to be a well-defined goal in the heat of planning may turn out to require extensive decomposition and transformation if there is to be any reasonable way to gauge and validate it.

The defined metric and measurement scheme must be clear and embraced by both the project team and the project stakeholders. Taking a decentralized approach to setting the goals and the measurement scheme will improve the chance of achieving team ownership. Involving the team members in the refinement of goals and asking them to help in communicating the goals will certainly ease the resistance factor. Likewise, drawing the nonmanagement team members into many of the measurement-related tasks will lessen many of the team members' initial fear of measurement.

There is a cost to measurement. The resources needed to support measurement activities must be allocated and tracked, so as to ensure that the current project's goals are actually met and to guide future projects.

EXERCISES

1. Pick a goal for a software project such as "high productivity." Define it and discuss the metrics and measurement process that need to be put in place so as to achieve this goal.
2. What does it mean to say that a goal has to be "clear"?
3. What is an operational plan, and what are the categories of items needed to be considered to transform a general plan into an operational plan?
4. Why might a team resist having goals and measurements?
5. What must a software project manager ensure and put in place in order to gain general acceptance of the goals and measurements?
6. Discuss the potential perils that may result from assigning values to a categorization scheme of an attribute.
7. List some of the costs related to establishing goals and measurement.
8. In terms of team organization and project structure, where would you place those people involved with measurements, and why?
9. Search for various software measurement tools for quality and productivity attributes and categorize them by characteristics such as data collection, data analysis, or data representation ability.
10. Conduct a mini-research project as follows. Study the three articles related to the CK design metrics (by Chidamber and Kemerer; Chidamber, Darcy and Kemerer; and Subramanyam and Krishnan) in the "Suggested Reading" list and report on the metrics and its applicability to software project management. Also provide your own views on this set of metrics.

SUGGESTED READING

V. R. Basili and D. Weiss, "A Methodology for Collecting Valid Software Engineering Data," *IEEE Transactions on Software Engineering,* 10, No. 6, November, 1984, 728–738.

S. R. Chidamber and C. F. Kemerer, "A Metric Suite for Object Oriented Design," *IEEE Transactions on Software Engineering,* June 1994, 476–493.

S. R. Chidamber, D. P. Darcy, and C. F. Kemerer, "Managerial Use of Metrics for Object-Oriented Software: An Exploratory Analysis," *IEEE Transactions on Software Engineering,* August 1998, 629–639.

M. K. Daskalantonakis, "A Practical View of Software Measurement and Implementation Experiences Within Motorola," *IEEE Transactions on Software Engineering,* November 1992, 998–1010.

A. Glushkovsky, "An Analytical Approach to Software Metrics Management," *Software Quality Professional,* Vol. 4, No. 3, 2002, 34–45.

R. B. Grady, *Practical Software Metrics for Project Management and Process Improvement,* Prentice Hall, 1992.

R. B. Grady, "Successfully Applying Software Metrics," *IEEE Computer,* September 1994, 18–25.

S. H. Kan, *Metrics and Models in Software Quality Engineering,"* 2nd ed., Addison-Wesley, 2003.

R. Subramanyam and M. S. Krishnan, "Empirical Analysis of CK Metrics for Object-Oriented Design Complexity: Implications for Software Defects," *IEEE Transactions on Software Engineering,* April 2003, 297–310.

C. Weber and B. Layman, "Measurement Maturity and the CMM: How Measurement Practices Evolve as Processes Mature," *Software Quality Professional,* Vol. 4, No. 3, 2002, 6–20.

Part Three

Software Project Monitoring

(POMA)

THE ROLE OF MONITORING IN SOFTWARE PROJECT MANAGEMENT

In the eyes of many nonmanagers, regular monitoring of the project and daily fire fighting constitute the majority of the software project management work. For many team members, the previous two phases (of project planning and of project organization) were not visible to them. After planning for the project and having the plan approved, the project managers had to organize and prepare for the beginning of the project. Once the project is started, however, the software project team cannot just be left alone to follow the plan and the course for which it was prepared. As a matter of fact, the plan, the organization, and the preparation work are never perfect. Inevitably, what was planned and prepared for in terms of goals, measurements, and information gathering will go through modifications and conversions during the next phase, the project monitoring phase (the "M" in POMA).

Some mechanism must be put in place to constantly gauge whether the project is progressing on course. That mechanism must collect information about the project, ensure that what is observed is valid and reliable, and analyze the information and report it as necessary. Clearly, the software project team must then make decisions if the data indicate that some aspects of the project need to be altered.

The monitoring activity for software projects is no different from the monitoring tasks performed in other system projects. What is different is that the list of items to be observed for software projects contains only domain-specific items, which are software-related and were planned earlier. In general, the goal is to determine whether the project—no matter what its type—is tracking to plan.

Many times, software projects fail due to the sloppy jobs that the software project managers do during the monitoring phase. Having a wonderful plan is merely the first step. In the previous POMA phase, that plan was transformed into an executable, operational plan with all resources assigned, organized, and prepared. Now that the project resources are assigned and prepared to execute, the project team is ready to start performing. Project managers must continually evaluate this performance by the project team to see whether the way it is carried out would indeed achieve the various stated goals of the project. Here, the project team includes both the technical members and the management personnel. The information representing the status and the results of the project team's activities are used as the basis for this ongoing evaluation.

In software projects, one of the more menacing situations encountered is the scenario in which frequent and large numbers of changes are made to the requirements and design. Thus, besides monitoring the predetermined set of measurable characteristics of the project, the software project managers need to be constantly on the lookout for potential changes to the planned project or unexpected changes to resources, such as the sudden loss of an employee. The ongoing review of the risk items list is also included as part of the monitoring activities.

MONITORING: A THREE-PART OPERATION

Part Three of this book discusses the following three topics related to software project monitoring:

- The regular collection of project information that is considered relevant to the measurement of goal attainment
- The analysis and evaluation of the collected information
- The presentation and communication of the information related to project status to the project team members, upper management, and, potentially, customers

To collect any information, the first issue is what data should be collected. Next, we must determine how that information will be collected. These two questions should have been addressed during the planning and organizing phases. In addition, we must decide how often the information should be collected. Data collection and status monitoring are conducted in two different ways: through formal status reviews and during informal "conscientious socializing." The important thing is to make sure that software project managers handle these duties as a natural part of the regular project monitoring set of tasks.

Even though the data collection process is assumed to be valid, relevant, reliable, and accurate, sometimes the information gathered is not and, therefore, needs to be "cleaned." Data cleaning, for example, might involve recognizing extreme data points or inconsistent situations and excluding those data. Only after cleaning can the information be analyzed. Following that step, the cleaned information can be evaluated and compared against the planned goal.

The analyzed information and the result of the evaluations must be communicated to all affected parties. This communication is critical: The manner in which the information is represented and shared sets the tone for the entire phase of project monitoring. The communication of project status and changes must be disciplined, and the information transmitted must have value to the recipients. Undisciplined project status meetings are a waste of time and will eventually render these meetings useless. The key stakeholders will stop attending, status information will not flow, dependencies will not be understood and fulfilled, and the project will slowly but surely slip into chaos. The remedy is status meetings that are disciplined and to the point. These are the responsibility of the software project managers.

Chapter 9

Collecting Project Information

Chapter Objectives

This chapter discusses the following concepts:

- How to perform formal and regular data gathering and monitoring
- How to hold formal and regular status meetings
- How to perform informal and nonregular data gathering and monitoring

In many ways, software project management, like other types of project management, is highly dependent on the information it collects. What information should be collected and how should one go about collecting it constitute the first set of questions that the software project managers should be prepared to answer. The data that need to be collected are first dictated by what was planned and prepared until now. Of course, no plan or preparation is perfect. Consequently, the metrics and measurements established during the planning phase or the organization and preparation phase of software project management may go through further changes as the project proceeds. It is not uncommon to alter the focus on some details of a specific area when some evidence indicates that the area has changed. For example, even if employee retention had never been a problem, the heated-up economy of the late 1990s forced many software project managers to focus on a new personnel metric, employee retention. Conversely, with today's cooled economy, a hitherto important metric on employee retention might be dropped. In turn, a change in the measurement scheme is required.

Most of the information collected during the monitoring phase of the POMA process is gathered in some formal manner through regular status meetings. At the same time, unplanned information may be collected informally through project managers' conscientious socialization. Conscientious socializing is the purposeful but informal socializing that managers conduct, such as conversations at the water cooler, to get a better understanding of the project status. Electronic conscientious socializing would involve "chatting" or "instant messaging" with the team members. The amount of unplanned and informal information that the software project managers can gather is directly related to how well the managers listen to the team members as they socialize with them at a business level.

Both formally collected data and informally collected information gathered during the monitoring phase need to be analyzed before appropriate decisions can be made to take action or to stand pat. In any event, software project managers should restrain themselves from reacting impulsively following receipt of the information.

FORMAL DATA GATHERING AND MONITORING

The formal gathering of project information is usually performed at regular intervals such as daily, weekly, or monthly, depending on the type of activity and the stage of the software project. For example, the formal gathering of information on project status may be conducted on a weekly basis during the requirements gathering and analysis phase. During the functional testing phase, however, test results data may be gathered upon completion of each test and aggregated on a daily basis. Clearly, the needs of information collection must be balanced against the resource requirements and the impacts to the on-going project. These impact issues and considerations were addressed in the transformation of the project plan to an operational plan.

The frequency of data gathering may also depend on the urgency of the activity. In some situations, time is of the essence, as when responding to a high-severity customer problem. Under normal circumstances, the support manager might collect customer problem reporting and resolution data at the end of each day; however, a high-priority customer problem may temporarily warrant changing the collection status to an hourly basis until resolution of that problem is achieved.

The data collection may be based on project activities or on some project attribute. Some of these criteria may not have been planned and set up in their entirety in the previous planning and organizing phases.

Let's consider an example in which the goal is to see how the project is tracking in terms of schedule integrity. In this case, the manner in which the data are collected depends on the type of activity. Both activity-based and attribute-based methods may be employed for measuring the schedule goal.

Activity-Based Monitoring

In the requirements gathering and analysis phase, assume that information is gathered on a weekly basis. During this phase, the data collected may differ depending on the specific task. During the early stages, for example, the data collected may focus on the team's attempts to meet a set of minor milestones, such as completion of requirements interviews, completion of requirements documentation, or completion of requirements classification. The data desired in this case are non-numeric—that is, the data collected are binary logical values of yes or no, depending on whether the minor milestone is or is not met.

The actual representation of the data collected, in a date format, contains more information than simply whether a milestone has been achieved. Thus data collection may consist of filling in a table on a weekly basis. Consider Table 9.1, where the expected completion date and the observed actual completion date fields are both used to indirectly indicate whether a milestone has been met. This measurement is needed to gauge whether the goal of schedule integrity will be satisfied.

This type of data collection is activity-based in that the team is collecting attribute information—namely, completion dates—about the activities. Note also that with this type of information collection, which goes beyond purely logical values, one can perform arithmetic manipulation and obtain "derived" information. In this case, the derived information is the difference between the expected and actual completion dates (delta, Δ). The Delta column in the table provides a quick overview of the completion status of the various activities.

In Chapter 18 on Earned Value Management, we will see that earned value is a form of activity-based monitoring.

Table 9.1 Activity Completion Status

Milestone activities	Expected completion	Actual completion	Delta
Requirements interviews	07/05/2010	07/10/2010	+5 days
Requirements documentation	07/25/2010	07/25/2010	0 days
Requirements classification	08/20/2010		

Table 9.2 Date Attribute-Based Status

Date	Expected number of panels reviewed and approved	Actual number of panels reviewed and approved	Delta
04/05/2010	12	12	0
04/12/2010	15	13	−2
04/19/2010	20	20	0
04/26/2010	15		
05/02/2010	10		

Attribute-Based Monitoring

Now consider the screen requirements prototyping tasks within the requirements processing activity. In measurements taken so as to assess schedule integrity, it is not enough just to be interested in the simple answer of whether prototyping is complete, because the activity may stretch over several weeks. In this case, the data collected are based on an attribute. As shown in Table 9.2, the actual data are numerical figures representing the number of user panels that have been developed, shown to the users, and approved by the users.

This type of data collection is attribute-based in that the team picked an attribute—the weekly time interval—to assess the result of an activity. The result, or the metric, is the number of completed items given in terms of panels reviewed and approved. The attribute in this case is a date, so this is a date-based collection mechanism. The data collected are numerical, so the normal arithmetic operations may be applied to them. The delta values are, once again, derived information.

Note that Table 9.2 does not explain what happened to the two panels that were not reviewed and approved on April 12. The Delta column shows the −2, but no +2 has appeared in the table yet. Thus the derived information column can provide an additional view to help in tracking the status. In this case, based on the date attribute, the project seems to be two screens behind the number expected to have been completed at this point. If the project is to maintain schedule integrity, the sum of the numbers in the Delta column needs to be zero on the last day of the screen requirements prototyping activity.

MACRO AND MICRO LEVELS OF MONITORING

Generally, activity-based data collection would apply better at a "macro" level, in that we list only those activities that are considered to be at least minor milestones. Attribute-based data collection would be a better fit for a "micro" level of data collection, in that we will collect the smallest unit of the attribute. As the preceding example shows, we would record a number as small as 1 panel reviewed in Table 9.2. Of course, both types of data collection may be applied at either level.

The data that are collected for measurement purposes may be traced back to the planned goal and the preparation work that went into designing the metric and measurement. Every project–software or otherwise–is concerned about schedule integrity. The other major goals and measurements for software projects include the following and will be illustrated later in this chapter:

- Completeness of function
- Quality
- Budget

These considerations are not necessarily listed in any priority order. Because satisfying all of these attributes is important, software project managers need to monitor all of these characteristics.

In the following sections, examples from attribute-based monitoring and activity-based monitoring are used to demonstrate both the micro and macro levels of project status collection. The completeness-of-function goal, the quality goal, and the budget goal measurement and monitoring are explored.

Monitoring Completeness of Function

Attribute-Based Monitoring

Completeness of function is an attribute of the end product, so it seems logical to consider attribute-based data collection methods first. A table may be built listing all the required functions and the number of features within each function that have been completed (see Table 9.3). This presumes that the requirements document is complete and sufficiently detailed. Here the metric is the number of completed features, which is a countable figure.

> **Completeness of function** An attribute of a software product that describes the number of features implemented versus the number required for that software product.

Table 9.3 Function Attribute Completeness Monitoring

Functions	Expected number of features	Completed number of features	Delta
Function X	13	9	−4
Function Y	7	7	0
Function Z	9	8	−1
.	.	.	.
.	.	.	.

In Table 9.3, the attributes, as expressed in terms of number of features in a function, are shown in the form of columns. The attribute of completeness may be viewed in a more detailed form by further subdividing each feature into three subcategories, such as basic, intermediate, and advanced. Using such a table allows the software project team to collect and record information indicating how much of each feature is completed for each of the functional requirements. Along the way, this functional attribute-based data collection mechanism facilitates the detailed counting of the features, so it serves the software project managers well at the micro level.

Again, the derived information in the Delta column needs to eventually be zero for each row of the table. A positive delta value would indicate that the function contains more features than required. This inclusion of "extras" may not necessarily be a good sign: Having more than the expected number of features may indicate uncontrolled scope creep.

Activity-Based Monitoring

At a macro level, the software project managers may want to collect information on project activities completed using an activity-based method. The activities, in this case, would be the software process tasks that contribute to the production of the desired software functions. Table 9.4 shows an example of data collection based on functional completeness within each activity. In such a table, the activities displayed will depend on the specific process. The level of detail that is chosen to be portrayed will dictate the amount of data collection required. Table 9.4 uses a macro level, presenting the activities in a simple sequential order.

The activity-based data collection method indicates where each function is in terms of the activities that must be performed. In Table 9.4, F1, F2, and

Table 9.4 Software Process Activity-Based Monitoring

Activities	F1	F2	F3	...	Total
Requirements defined	Y	Y	Y		20
Function designed	Y	Y	N		15
Code implemented	Y	Y	N		12
Function tested	Y	N	N		10
Function integrated	Y	N	N		8

so on are the functions. Y (yes) indicates the completion of the activity for that function, and N (no) indicates a status of incomplete. The direct data collected give the team a global picture of the status at the different activity levels. Clearly, the desired end is to have all activities completed for every function.

The Total column provides a numerical representation of the status of each activity in terms of the number of functions completed. Each activity's Total column entry should match the number of total functions before the software project manager can consider the activity to be completed. What would be viewed as completed functions are all those functions that have been integrated (i.e., those in the Function integrated row). Thus, if there are n number of functions, then the Total column entry for the Function integrated row should also be n.

Table 9.4 illustrates a much higher-level status than the attribute-based data collection example discussed earlier, in which the team simply tracked the number of features within each function. Once again, it is apparent that activity-based data collection is well suited for handling the macro level of data.

Monitoring Quality

An important goal for software projects, as discussed extensively in previous chapters, is quality. Software projects have suffered from the image of poor quality for so long that some software project managers have unfortunately become very cynical about controlling quality. The goals and measurements of product quality must nevertheless be defined and prepared prior to the monitoring phase.

> **Software quality** An attribute of a software product that describes how well the product satisfies and serves the needs of the users. It offers a broader view of quality than the attribute that addresses only the defects in the product.

Attribute-Based Monitoring

As an example, let's consider one possible goal of quality: to achieve the level where there is no known severity level 1 problem in the product prior to its release. Assume that the different severity levels have already been defined. Then attribute-based data collection for product quality purposes may be expressed as shown in Table 9.5, with data being gathered just prior to the product's release. Note that the metric for the quality goal is the number of severity level 1 problems.

In this case, the teams collect data based on the quality attribute of each functional area at release time. All entries in the Delta column must reach zero before the product may be viewed as reaching its quality goal. As long as the Delta column includes one nonzero figure, we cannot proclaim that this goal has been attained.

Again, the attribute of quality may be viewed in more detail by including problems found and resolved not only for severity level 1, but for all the severity levels. In this way, the project team can take this micro level of monitoring to an even lower micro level.

Activity-Based Monitoring

The data collection mechanism for the quality goal may also be activity-based. The results will look much like the activity-based data collection for completed functions.

Suppose the activities list is based on the sequence of defect detection and removal activities that will be performed as part of the software project. In this case, the activities list clearly depends heavily on the software process. The defect identification and removal activities listed in Table 9.6 are a simple example. In reality, the defect detection and removal activities may be

Table 9.5 Functional Attribute-Based Quality Monitoring

Functional area	Severity level 1 problems found	Severity level 1 problems resolved	Delta
Function X	20	20	0
Function Y	12	10	−2
.	.	.	.
.	.	.	.

much more expansive. Also, remember that to simplify the discussion, this example focuses on only severity level 1 problems, because the goal was expressed in terms of severity level 1 problems. In most large software projects, all levels of problems found and fixed are collected and tracked.

The pairs of numbers in Table 9.6 are the entries for each function (F1, F2, and so on). The first number in each pair is the number of defects detected during that activity. The second number represents the number of defects resolved and removed as a result of that activity. The metric is a pair of countable numbers.

Table 9.6 provides a global view of each functional area as different quality-related activities are applied to it. The Total column indicates the number of severity level 1 problems that are as yet unresolved from applying the specific quality activity. The goal is that all entries in the Total column be zero; in other words, there should be no unresolved severity level 1 problems remaining from any of the defect prevention and detection activities carried out prior to the product release.

In the case of quality, the attribute-based and activity-based data collection mechanisms are very similar. Both provide a global view of the quality status of all the functions. However, the attribute-based data collection mechanism may be easily expanded to include lower severity levels, and it can achieve a more detailed view of quality by functional area.

Monitoring the Budget

Meeting and not exceeding the budget of a software project, while sometimes less emphasized by the technical community, is actually one of the most important goals. It must be met if the organization is to continue in existence.

Table 9.6 Defect Removal Activity-Based Quality Monitoring

Activities	F1	F2	F3	...	Total
Requirements review	(5,5)	(6,5)	(4,4)		1
Design review	(6,6)	(7,6)	(9,9)		1
Functional testing	(3,3)	(2,2)	(5,5)		0
Component testing	(2,1)	(2,2)	(4,4)		1
Systems testing	(0,0)	(1,1)	(0,0)		0

Software budget An attribute of a software project that describes the financial resources allocated and expected to be followed, by some time period such as monthly or quarterly and by areas such as tools, people, travel, or education, for that project.

In software projects, this particular attribute is often managed at a somewhat higher level than the traditional, first-line project managers' level. Indeed, sometimes it is managed by the financial community, and the software project managers are not directly involved in managing monetary considerations except to treat the budget as a process where funds are requested and granted. Until the software project managers understand and begin managing the financial aspects of the project (at least the budget), however, they will remain naïve and nonappreciative of the key role that finance plays in most projects.

If the software project has gone through business case analysis, then the organization has likely determined that the project is worth pursuing with the planned budget. For most software project managers, the revenue portion of the financial goal is not a concern, because they most likely will not manage that aspect of the goal. Nevertheless, they need to recognize that what they produce will greatly affect the income side of the financial picture. Today's more aggressive organizations are including the software project managers in the discussion of the budget, recognizing that the sales and marketing organization's commitment to revenue projections usually depends on how the project team reacts to their requests for features and functions. These requests for features and functions must be weighed against the estimated expenses for those features and functions as well as the feasibility assessments provided by the software project managers.

For all these reasons, the software project managers should participate in the organization's discussions of its financial goals. They should also include revenue status as a focus of their project monitoring.

Attribute-Based Monitoring

Budget-related data may be collected with the attribute-based methodology as well as with the activity-based method. Table 9.7 illustrates one possible attribute-based data collection method. Although not all software projects can break down product revenues based on functional areas, Table 9.7 assumes that such data collection is possible. A Revenue column is included in this example, even though most software project managers are not responsible for that parameter. Nevertheless, its inclusion will give the software project managers something to contemplate as they monitor the expense side

Table 9.7 Functional Attribute-Based Expense and Revenue Monitoring

Functional Area	Month 1		Month 2		...	Accumulative Data			
	Expected	Actual	Expected	Actual		Expected	Actual	Revenue	
Function X	4	3.5	5	5		9	8.5	54	0
Function Y	2	2.5	4	5		6	7.5	60	0
Function Z	7	6	9	10		16	16	350	2
.									
.									
.									

of the product equation. Expense data are collected on every function at some regular interval, most likely monthly. The example in Table 9.7 uses thousands of dollars as the metric for the entries.

The data collected in Table 9.7 show both the expected budget (Expected column) and the actual expense (Actual column) by month as the software project progresses. The table also includes some derived data, in the form of cumulative expected and actual expenses. The revenue portion of the table (Revenue column) shows the up-to-date expected and cumulative actual revenue information.

Clearly, this effort involves monitoring the expense side of the budget at a monthly level. If the project budget attribute needs to be managed tightly, the software project managers may change the monitoring interval to semimonthly or weekly.

The items that go into each table entry must have been planned and prepared during the planning and organizing/preparing phases. Most of the time, the expense entry for each (nonacquired) software function includes costs for all of the following resources:

- People (compensation in salary, bonus, and so on)
- Tools
- Travel
- Special education
- General overhead (office space, phone service, desktop computer, and so on)

If a particular function is an acquired function, then the expense for it may be spread out in an even fashion over the time interval. The important thing to remember is that the data may be collected on a weekly or monthly basis, but some of the budget may be expended in a lump-sum form, such as

Table 9.8 Software Process Activity-Based Expense and Revenue Modeling

Activities	F1		F2		...	Accumulative Data	
	Expected	Actual	Expected	Actual		Expected	Actual
Requirements gathering	0.5	1	1	0.5		15	15
Prototyping	1	1.5	2	1		18	25
Joint customer design	1		0.5			25	
Detailed design	1.5		1			22	
Design inspection	0.5		0.5			5	
.							
.							

paying up-front for an enterprise license for a software tool before all the team members have come on board. These lump-sum expenses incurred at the beginning of a project may cause the project to temporarily show an expense overflow.

Activity-Based Monitoring

The budget attribute may also be monitored via an activity-based data collection method. As before, the specific activity list may differ based on the software project and the process chosen for that project. For the purposes of this example, the software project activity list is greatly simplified. The metric for the entries in Table 9.8 is thousands of dollars; the accuracy of the data is 0.5 of $1000 (that is, $500).

This activity-based data collection mechanism provides a global view of the expenses of all functions as each function goes through each of the activities. Again, the actual entry is an accumulation of several resources that went into it. Note that there may be an honorarium paid to each customer who participates in the joint customer design activity; the table may need to include this expenditure. For each activity, the preparation for the measurement must be established by working with the financial organization.

For the budget attribute, data collection should be performed in concert with the financial organization. Thus, to monitor the financial goals, the software project managers must collaborate with the financial organization during the planning phase as well as the organization and preparation phase.

There may even be a need to reserve the services of and financially account for a person in the financial department who will spend at least some of his or her time on data collection duties. As a consequence, the data collection expense for the project may need to be charged back to the specific software project, and the data collection activity itself may appear on the activity list for activity-based data collection for monitoring the budget attribute. The actual recording of data will most likely be carried out by the financial organization and the results given to the software project management team.

DATA COLLECTION SCHEDULE

The formal collection of data for the purpose of project monitoring should be performed on a regular basis with the schedule chosen to match the needs of the software project. For longer projects, the interval of data collection for monitoring may be monthly, to match the monitoring time cycle. For smaller and shorter projects, the data collection and monitoring intervals may also be shorter. The data collected at these regular time intervals should be maintained throughout the project and kept for historical purposes. The historical data will be needed for statistical estimation activities in the future. Each batch of data represents a snapshot of the project status at that point in time.

Of course, the project team must balance its need for data with the effort required to collect and monitor that information for the particular software project. Most of this decision making occurs during the earlier organization and preparation phase, but these decisions should be reviewed and perhaps modified as the software project managers start the monitoring phase of project management.

With the sophistication of today's spreadsheet products, much of the data collected in tabular form for smaller projects may be easily placed in these spreadsheet files. If more sophisticated capabilities are needed, then any of the database products may be used along with some of the currently available data drill-down products, such as Oracle's Business Intelligence tool or SAS Institute's SAS tools.

FORMAL PROJECT STATUS MEETINGS

The formally collected data should be brought forward and presented by the project team members to their colleagues at regular project status meetings. The project status meeting serves two purposes: It is a means to collect the data, and it is a way to communicate those data. If the status meeting is used as a means to collect the project status data, then the project managers must constantly think of ways to minimize the amount of data collection time needed. After all, time spent in meetings and data collection is indeed time taken away from direct project development. Automation and tools may be one answer.

Data Collection Automation/Tools

Information from the various stages of software development may be collected as more automation is introduced. For example, one might use a tool such as Borland's Together to develop a design and code for the project. The same tool can provide information on how many objects, modules, or lines of code have been developed. Thus, instead of manually counting and reporting on this information, the team can use the tool to automatically provide the count on a weekly or daily basis.

Another tool from Borland, called CaliberRM, may be used for requirements management. This tool can trace changes made to requirements, thereby providing information on the volume of changes to requirements.

The formal project status meetings should not be so lengthy that most of the people there are "waiting" for their turn to present. Given that key personnel (i.e., managers and project leaders) are likely to attend these meetings, one should definitely not keep them for too long. If once-weekly meetings are held, a three-hour status meeting would consume roughly 8% (3 hours ÷ 40 hours = 7.5%) of a normal working week for the attendees. If the status meetings begin to consume more than 10% of the normal work week, then the project managers should immediately reassess the meeting schedule and agenda. One possible solution is to cut the discussion to only the high-risk items, with normal status information just being provided in a written form that the participants may choose to read at their convenience.

In addition, if any unexpected information or negative data require further discussion or analysis, a separate meeting should be scheduled to focus on that specific topic. Unexpected negative status information is one item to watch out for, because it is so natural to become drawn into a lengthy discussion of a "surprise" item. The risk items list is the source of many such surprises—for example, when a low-risk item suddenly turns into a high-risk item. The software project managers must be disciplined enough to log the surprise item on the list of high-risk items and immediately schedule a separate session attended by just the affected parties. One question that often arises is, What information should be brought to these special meetings? Unfortunately, there is no standard answer because the "surprise" may be anything.

To ensure full and effective status monitoring, the key attendees must not be allowed to send substitutes to these regular meetings except for special reasons such as planned vacations or family emergencies. The software project managers also must not send any substitutes.

These meetings are usually well attended at the beginning of a new software project. The attendance problem tends to appear later in a project, if it happens at all. There are many reasons for poor attendance. For example, if the status meetings are not managed well and are constantly postponed or running overtime, then the key participants will start to disappear. However, if the meetings are running smoothly but turning into a "rubber stamping" of data, then the key participants will also abandon them. In particular, the dangerous sign of unrealistic smoothness must be recognized by the software project managers.

The key to effective formal status meetings is to create an agenda and stay within its bounds, scheduling any subsequent and additional meetings if necessary to cover off-agenda items. The agenda should be circulated prior to the meeting so that all attendees are aware of the topics to be covered and the time allotted for each topic. Each time slot should include a small buffer to allow for a certain amount of discussion and communication on that topic.

What's on the Agenda?

A formal project status meeting should follow a predefined agenda. The agenda items need to correlate with the project goals, because it is the progress made toward attaining those goals that is mainly under review at the meeting. A sample software project status meeting may have the following parts:

1. Review of the project and product progress metrics: schedule, items completed, cost, defects discovered and corrected, and so on
2. Review of personnel and resources: problems, rewards, and so on
3. Review of risk items: number, status, and so on
4. Review of any other items: customer status, industry status, and so on

Software project managers must keep in mind that while project monitoring may be the most important item for the managers, the other team members are equally driven to complete their tasks, and these tasks do not deal with project management per se. Some nonmanagers will view these meetings as bureaucratic and a waste of their time. From their perspective, this perception may be accurate. Therefore, any additional meetings scheduled to tackle specific topics should also require the minimum amount of time for the attendees. For each meeting, time must be set aside for discussions beyond just the presentation of data and information. Managers must also learn to moderate the meetings, keeping attendees focused on the scheduled topic so that the discussion does not turn into a random wandering of conversation that leads to no conclusion.

Sources of Meeting-Related Information

Project managers who need to enhance their meeting management skills or conflict resolution skills may consult books such as *The Art and Science of Negotiation* by Harvard Business School professor Howard Raiffa or attend seminars on these topics. The Project Management Institute, a nonprofit professional association that is headquartered outside of Philadelphia, also conducts seminars on these topics. Interested parties may consult the institute's Web site for more information: www.pmi.org.

INFORMAL DATA GATHERING AND MONITORING

Software projects, more than most other projects, depend heavily on the performance of people. Although formal data collection and monitoring are essential, assessment of human performance is often based on some very hard-to-collect information that requires informal data gathering. Consider the following situations:

- A false rumor about any part of the project may cause workers to engage in lengthy discussions and extensive information seeking rather than focusing on the work at hand.
- A particular tool that is not working well may cause delays and loss of efficiency.

- A process that is viewed as bureaucratic may cause people to find ways to circumvent it rather than fix it.
- A key employee may be seeking new opportunities and getting ready to resign from the project.

Formal data collection efforts may not be able to recognize any of these situations. Instead, the software project managers must realize that a number of factors that contribute to the success or failure of the project may not be apparent from formal data and will not be discussed and disclosed during formal status meetings.

It has been shown that communications among the team members is one of the important factors in successful projects. Please see Tsui in the Suggested Reading section. Informal data gathering is heavily dependent on the communication skills of the project managers.

Physically Collocated Environment

As part of their informal data gathering, software project managers need to perform conscientious socializing. Different from formal information meetings, these informal meetings or encounters should encourage a certain amount of wandering among topics. Often, it is through serendipity that certain vital information pertaining to the software project comes to light. To help such communication take place, the software project managers should pursue the following activities, among others:

- Keep the management offices "open" and accessible to everyone.
- Make daily walks and visits to the team members' offices.
- Invite team members to the project manager's office to chat about the project (Formally schedule these "informal" meetings if necessary at the beginning of a new project.)
- Have scheduled "lunches" with different, small groups of team members.

Note that almost all of these activities require some kind of physical "contact" with the team members.

Physically Remote Environment

Many managers choose—or are forced—to have virtual meetings instead of person-to-person contact, including meetings held via the Internet. For the formal, regular meetings, virtual meetings held through phone, video conferencing, or bulletin boards may substitute for some part of the physical meeting. However, for the informal, conscientious socialization, the rule is this: The less virtual, the more effective the socialization.

With project team members who work at remote sites, the software project managers need to make an extra effort to meet them in person when they first come on board. The software project managers also need to ensure that ongoing communications occur via telephone or e-mail with team members at remote sites; that is, they need to "just chat." The volume of electronic communications that would be considered normal depends on the size and type of project involved. The software project managers must take the initiative to start both one-on-one and group electronic dialogues. Certainly, if either a sudden increase or decrease in the volume of communications occurs, it should prompt the software project managers to immediately follow up. In addition, they must pick up on any voice and intonation changes during a telephone conversation with a particular individual. In terms of e-mail, the choice of words and the length of the messages can offer informal clues as to the team member's state of mind.

Establishing Trust

Informal data gathering requires the software project managers to understand both the team members and those individuals' views concerning the project and its status at different phases of the project. This invaluable information cannot be attained through formal project monitoring.

The underlying assumption here is that the team members have some trust in the software management. Without this trust, people will not disclose their true feelings. To build such a bond, the software project managers must listen and not become defensive, no matter how negative or biased the information communicated may appear. Trust must be earned, and it takes time to establish. But it may be lost forever because of a single instance of broken trust.

Software project managers should also realize that trust is a mutual activity and must be honored by both sides. Thus, before sharing any information, each manager must know the degree of trust that has been established between and among the team members and him or her. Clearly, some information is not appropriate for any sharing or conscientious socializing:

- Employees' personal information
- Confidential corporate information
- Information with a "need to know" designation

Need-to-know information is a special class of information that is intended to be transmitted only to a small group of people who have an absolute need to know it. An example would be the impending closing of a large contract or the potential loss of a large contract.

KEY CONCEPTS

The monitoring of project status involves three major activities: formal and regular data gathering and monitoring; formal and regular status meetings; and informal and nonregular data gathering and monitoring.

Formal gathering and storing of the needed data for gauging the status of the project may follow either of two approaches: (1) activity-based or (2) attribute-based. The activity-based approach gathers information about an attribute based on the activities performed to achieve the goal of that attribute, whereas the attribute-based approach gathers information about an attribute based on a metric defined to measure the attainment of the goal for that attribute. Some goals and measurements may be monitored utilizing both of the methods, although one is usually more effective; the method of choice depends on the specific target.

Project status meetings constitute a mechanism both to collect project information from the team and to disseminate information to the team members. To be effective, such meetings must occur regularly, be kept on schedule, and follow a predetermined agenda. Software project managers should use these formal meetings as one tool for project monitoring.

Informal status gathering and project monitoring is a powerful tool that must be utilized in conjunction with other, more formal methods of data collection. When working with physically remote personnel, software project managers must take extra care in monitoring their electronic communications because conscientious socializing cannot be accomplished in the same manner as with physically co-located team members. In any informal communications, trust is a key ingredient.

EXERCISES

1. Discuss the difference between activity-based and attribute-based information collection methods.
2. For monitoring completion of function, which of the above information collection methods would you use and why?
3. Discuss the difference between formal and informal data gathering and monitoring. If you can implement only one, which one would you implement and why?

4. What is conscientious socializing?
5. Devise a software project status meeting agenda for monitoring and gathering status information about the project schedule, key personnel, and product quality of four different software projects; include the formats for presenting the status information during the meeting.
6. How does trust play a role in project monitoring?

SUGGESTED READING

K. Bassin, S. Biyani, and P. Santhanan, "Metrics to Evaluate Vendor-Developed Software Based on Test Case Execution Results," *IBM Systems Journal,* Vol. 41, No. 1, 2002, 13–30.

T. Hall and N. Fenton, "Implementing Effective Software Metrics Programs," *IEEE Software,* March/April 1997, 55–65.

J. D. Herbsleb and S. Moitra, "Global Software Development," *IEEE Software,* March/April 2001, 16–20.

P. Jalote, "Use of Metrics in High Maturity Organizations," *Software Quality Professional,* Vol. 4, No. 2, 2002, 7–13.

R. Murch, *Project Management Best Practices for IT Professionals,* Prentice Hall PTR, 2001.

R. J. Offen and R. Jeffrey, "Establishing Software Measurement Programs," *IEEE Software,* March/April 1997, 45–54.

H. Raiffa, *The Art and Science of Negotiations,* Belknap Publisher, 1985.

H. Raiffa, J. Richardson, and D. Metcalfe, *Negotiation Analysis: The Science and Art of Collaborative Decision Making,* Belknap Publisher, 2003.

S. Snaker, et al, "Knowledge Transfer in Virtual Systems Development Teams: An Exploratory Study of Four Key Enablers," *IEEE Transactions on Professional Communication,* Vol. 48, No. 2, June 2005, 201–218.

P. C. Tinnirello, ed., *Project Management,* Auerbach, 1999.

F. Tsui, "Information Communications in Software Projects," Proceedings of the 2004 ASEE SE Annual Conference, Auburn University, Alabama, 2004.

Chapter 10

Analysis and Evaluation of Information

Chapter Objectives

This chapter discusses the following concepts:

- Why numerical and formally gathered data (as opposed to data collected through conscientious socialization) must be reliable, accurate, and valid to make analysis and evaluation of those data possible
- What various statistical measures–distribution of data, centrality and dispersion of data, moving averages, and data correlation–reveal about data trends within the software project management context
- How data may be normalized to ensure that any comparisons made are valid

RELIABLE, ACCURATE, AND VALID DATA

It is one thing to collect data, but it is another matter to make sense of what has been collected. As part of the project monitoring, these data need to be further analyzed. It is assumed that the collected data are reliable–that is, that no error was committed in the actual recording and subsequent tabulation of the data. The assurance of data reliability is a non-trivial task, as a large amount of the data in software projects is still collected manually.

Reliable data Data that are collected and tabulated according to the defined rules of measurement and metric.

It is also assumed that the data collected are accurate. The level of accuracy is predetermined by the unit of measurement. For example, if the budgeting information is collected at the $500 level, then all data will be assumed to be properly rounded to and accurate at that level. Because most software attributes are measured in a discrete (countable) form, the topic of significant figures is not much of an issue in software project management, unlike in some other disciplines (e.g., chemistry).

Accurate data Data that are collected and tabulated according to the defined level of precision of measurement and metric.

The third consideration for data is the validity of any data collected. Validity addresses the applicability of the data to assess the particular issue or to measure the particular attribute.

Valid data Data that are collected, tabulated, and applied according to the defined intention of applying the measurement.

To see how these criteria are applied, let's consider an example. Suppose that we want to find the average number of problems detected after a software solution is delivered. Recall from earlier chapters that the problems found are grouped into categories. These categories were labeled according to severity levels 1, 2, 3, and 4 in earlier examples to represent different degrees of failing to meet the requirement. Only these four categories exist; there is no intermediate category such as severity level 2.4, for example.

Consider the following computed measurement of average problem level:

Average problem level =
[SUM (number of severity k problems × severity k)/n]

where

n = total number of problems found
SUM = the summation function
k = a discrete value between 1 and 4

The computed average problem level is a numerical value that is sometimes—and sometimes wrongly—used to assess the quality attribute of the product. Consider a situation where the average problem level computed in this way is 2.7. As 2.7 is closer to severity level 3 than to severity level 2, the average problem level may be "rounded up" and communicated as 3. Worse yet, some may assume that this severity level 3 average is a reputable assessment of the product quality. In fact, equating the average severity levels of problems found in a product to the product quality may be a stretch and may be invalid. In analyzing data, the validity issue is very important. Software project managers need to be extra careful in considering the validity of the data when those data are utilized in the analysis of some attribute. In particular, they need to be careful when using the derived information after applying some computation or transformation to the raw data.

Nevertheless, software managers can and should undertake several common analyses that yield beneficial evaluations of data. As this book is not intended to accompany a course in statistics, no deep discussion of statistical principles is included here. Instead, the goal is to apply some of the knowledge from statistics to the analysis of data in software projects.

DISTRIBUTION OF DATA

Assuming that data collection was reliable, then one of the simplest forms of analysis is to look at the distribution of the collected data. By viewing the "spread," one may be able to readily detect some problems or trends. Software project managers may improve their understanding of the project's status during the monitoring phase by evaluating the data distribution through analysis of the skew of the distribution, the range of data values, and trends in data.

> **Data distribution** A description of a collection of data that shows the spread of the values and the frequency of occurrences of the values of the data.

Example I: Skew of the Distribution

Consider the four attributes of schedule, functional completeness, quality, and budget discussed in Chapter 9. Which attribute is more amenable to the notion of distribution of data? Let's consider the quality attribute first, by studying the number of problems detected by functional component. Suppose the recorded data identify the number of problems detected at each of five severity levels:

Severity level 1: 23
Severity level 2: 46
Severity level 3: 79
Severity level 4: 95
Severity level 5: 110

These data may be viewed graphically to better discern the relative differences; see Figure 10.1.

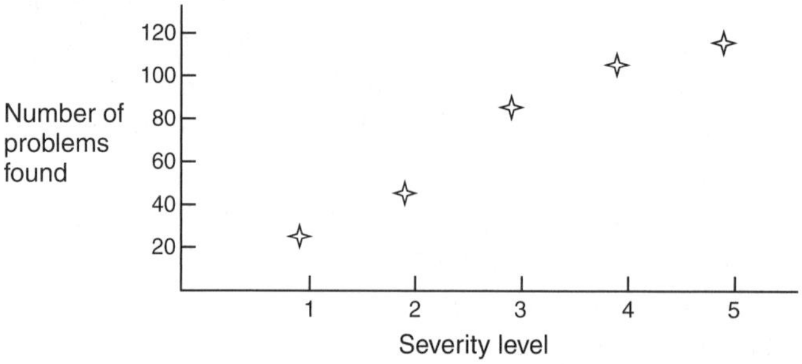

Figure 10.1 Distribution of problems found by severity level

As shown in Figure 10.1, the number of problems found in this project is "skewed" to the higher end of the severity level, that is, the graph rises to the right. Let's assume that the higher severity level implies less serious problems. The distribution does not indicate whether this software artifact is a good product; it says only that the product contains considerably more less-severe problems than more-severe problems. That is, the severity levels of all problems found are skewed toward the less-severe ones. Of course, this outcome is better than the situation in which the distribution is skewed toward the more-severe problems. To determine exactly how good or bad the situation really is, the project managers should then compare this distribution with the distribution of problems from past projects.

Example II: Range of Data Values

Another way to examine collected data is look across functional areas at the distribution of the problem severity levels for a product or the distribution of the number of problems found at a specific severity level (e.g., severity level 1). Consider the following distribution of number of severity level 1 problems by functional area:

Functional area 1: 2
Functional area 2: 7
Functional area 3: 3
Functional area 4: 8
Functional area 5: 0
Functional area 6: 1
Functional area 7: 8

This distribution reveals which functional areas have more problems. It also shows that the number of problems found in the functional areas range from 0 to 8. The lowest number is 0 in functional area 5, and the highest number is 8 in functional areas 4 and 7.

As in the preceding example, the best use of this information is to compare it to similar analyses of other projects. If prior history shows that the high end of the range of severity level 1 problems has never exceeded some value x, then the software project managers can compare the value 8 from this example with x. This comparison would give the software project managers some indication of where this project stands relative to others.

Alternatively, the software project managers might compare the ranges themselves. The range of problems found here goes from 0 to 8. How does that result compare with software projects that have ranges of 3 to 25 or 0 to 3?

The software project managers can see how uniform or nonuniform these functional areas are in terms of quality by evaluating the range of problems found in them. If the range is fairly small, such as 0–3 severity level 1 problems, across all functional areas, one may consider such a software project to have relative uniformity in quality.

Example III: Data Trends

Next, let's consider the distribution of total number of problems found in a functional area across test time periods in weeks. Suppose we identify the following number of problems:

Week 1: 20
Week 2: 23
Week 3: 45
Week 4: 67
Week 5: 35
Week 6: 15
Week 7: 10

Just as in earlier examples, this one distribution of the number of problems found in a functional area does not indicate whether this product is good or bad. It does tell us that fewer and fewer problems have been found as more and more test cases have been run. Such a distribution across test weeks reveals that the product is getting better in that problems are being squeezed out of the product through weeks of testing.

This distribution through time is really a trend—here, the trend is desirable because ever fewer problems are detected in the same functional area as the project progresses. Trends offer a powerful way to analyze data. In trend analysis in software projects, managers are often looking for some form of stabilization, whether in the schedule, the budget, or some other attribute.

CENTRALITY AND DISPERSION

Centrality analysis, another way to study a collection of data, evaluates the central tendency of the data distribution. It provides a convenient way to compare groups of data. Analyzing the centrality and the dispersion of data provides software project managers with a way to characterize a set of related data, whether those data deal with product quality, project productivity, or some other attribute.

Centrality analysis An analysis of a data set to find the typical value to represent that data set.

Average Value

The most common of the centrality analysis methods is the computation of average. The average value is computed by adding up all the observed values of the distribution and dividing that total by the number of observations, assuming that the observed values all have the same probability of occurrence. To see how it works, consider the data taken from Figure 10.1. The average value is computed as follows:

$$\begin{aligned} \textit{Average severity level} &= [(23 \times 1) + (46 \times 2) + (79 \times 3) + (95 \times 4) + (110 \times 5)]/353 \\ &= 3.6 \end{aligned}$$

In this case, the average value of the distribution is the severity level 3.6. Thus we can say that the severity level of the problems found in this product tends toward 3.6.

Average value One type of centrality analysis that estimates the typical (or middle) value of a data set by summing all the observed data values and dividing the sum by the number of data points.

Consider another distribution of problems found by severity levels. Assume that the average value for that distribution is 3.2. Then, even if the two distributions look alike, the project managers can still compare these two averages and get a feeling that 3.6 is much closer to 4 than is 3.2. Therefore, one product's problems (the product with the average of 3.6), as measured by average severity level, tend to be less severe than the problems of the other product (the product with the average of 3.2).

It is well known that the average value may be influenced greatly by the inclusion of one or two extreme data points. Consider the earlier example of the distribution of severity level 1 problems found by functional area. The number of severity level 1 problems found by functional area ranged from 0 to 8.

$$\textit{Average number of severity level 1 problems found} = (2 + 7 + 3 + 8 + 0 + 1 + 8)/7 = 4.1$$

Now consider another product with the same number of functional areas but a much higher average number of severity level 1 problems found. Suppose the set of data is as follows: 1, 3, 4, 37, 3, 2, 1. The average is 7.2, which is much larger than the 4.1 average found in the preceding example. But by looking at the actual distribution, one can easily see that one functional area leads to this large average for the second distribution of data. If the extreme value (the outlier) of 37 were dropped from the average computation of the second data set, the new average would be 2.3—much smaller than the original average value of 7.2. Thus one may still need to look beyond just one computed value, such as the average of the group, to see whether the raw data contain any abnormal values.

Median Value

Another method of measuring centrality, use of a median, may provide a different perspective on the data distribution. To find the median, all observed data are placed in ordered sequence. The value that divides the collected data into upper and lower halves (i.e., the middle value) is the median; in other words, half of the data are larger than the median and half of the data are smaller than the median. In the situation in which there is an odd number of observations, identifying this value is a simple matter. When there is an even number of observations, the values of the middle two observations are averaged to obtain the median.

> **Median** A value used in centrality analysis to estimate the typical (or middle) value of a data set. After the data values are organized, the median is the data value that splits the data set into upper and lower halves.

Let's find the median value for the earlier example, which comprises the 0–8 distribution of severity level 1 problems across seven functional areas. It may be computed by first placing the observations in sequential order:

0, 1, 2, 3, 7, 8, 8

The median value is 3 because it divides the observed data into lower and upper halves. This value also provides information about the group in terms of the centrality. Recall that the average for this group of data is 4.1. Although the average and the median values are different, they are relatively close.

Now consider another example of severity level 1 problems across another seven-functional-area product whose data set includes one extreme value of 37. The observed data are placed in ordered sequence:

1, 1, 2, 2, 3, 4, 37

The median value is 2. Recall that the average value for this second data set was 7.2. The median value method of viewing centrality for this example certainly paints a different picture than the average value for the same group.

If the median values were used to compare the two products, the second product's data would have a lower median value: 2 versus 3. The one extreme value in the second set, 37, had much less effect on the median than it did on the average. Note also that a comparison of the two products couched in terms of the median values gives a different perspective than a comparison of the average values. The second product, except for the one functional area, has fewer severity level 1 problems. The median value portrays that perspective a little better than the comparison of the average values of these two products.

Standard Deviation and Control Charts

Sometimes one would like to know how the distribution of data is dispersed from the central value of either the average or the median. The earlier example of a data set containing one extreme value demonstrated the effect that one extreme data point can have on the group's central value. For example, the more widely dispersed the number of severity level 1 problems in the different functional areas, the more likely that the central value for the entire group of functions will differ from the number of severity level 1 problems in each of the functional areas. Thus, in cases of a large dispersion from the central value, it is more difficult to utilize the central value—whether it is the average or the mean value—to characterize the group as a whole.

Standard Deviation

A very common dispersion measurement is the standard deviation, which is numerically defined as follows:

$$\text{Standard deviation} = \text{SQRT}\ [(\text{SUM}\ (x_i - x_{\text{ave}})^2)/(n - 1)]$$

where

SQRT = square root function
SUM = sum function
x_i = ith observation
x_{ave} = average of x_i's
n = total number observations

Standard deviation A metric used to define and measure the dispersion of data from the average value in a data set.

The standard deviation from the first example, which is the group that included the data points 2, 7, 3, 8, 0, 1, 8, would be computed as follows:

$$\text{SUM}\ (x_i - x_{\text{ave}})^2 = 4.41 + 8.41 + 1.21 + 15.21 + 16.81 + 9.61 + 15.21 = 70.87$$

$$\text{SUM}\ (x_i - x_{\text{ave}})^2/(\text{n} - 1) = 70.87/6 = 11.81$$

$$\text{Standard deviation} = \text{SQRT}\ (11.81) = 3.43$$

One standard deviation is 3.43. This value gives a measure of the variability of the number of severity level 1 problems found in the functional areas relative to the average number of such problems, which is 4.1. Thus one standard deviation covers from (4.1 + 3.43) = 7.53 to (4.1 − 3.43) = .67.

The larger the standard deviation, the greater the variability or dispersion from the average value.

Control Charts

In quality control of nonsoftware areas, such as manufacturing, control charts are used to assess whether the average of any particular group falls within the range of "acceptable" limits. A control chart is used to assess and control the variability of some process or product characteristic. Making a control chart usually involves establishing the upper and lower limits of data variations from the data set's average value (the control limits). If an observed data value falls outside the control limits, then it would trigger evaluation of the characteristic. The usage of control charts and statistical process control may help us improve and diminish the variations in the implementations of a defined software process.

> **Control chart** A chart used to assess and control the variability of some process or product characteristic. It usually involves establishing the upper and lower limits (the control limits) of data variations from the data set's average value. If an observed data value falls outside the control limits, then it would trigger evaluation of the characteristic.

The acceptable upper and lower bounds of a characteristic may be established differently. Sometimes, they may reflect customers' expectations. At other times, the bounds may be based on past management experiences. The standard deviation from the average value may also be used as these limits. For example, if one standard deviation is used as the upper and lower limits, then an observation that falls outside of these limits would be cause for attention and possibly alarm.

In software project management, the notion of a control chart, along with the use of a standard deviation as the upper and lower limits, may be applied to tracking and observing a specific characteristic of a product or a methodology. In the case of a product, the usability characteristic may be observed through usability testing. The question then becomes, When should a software manager be alarmed?

A control chart may help in this decision process. The average number of problems found in previous usability tests may be used as the "typical" number of problems found during a usability test. How many more problems (or fewer problems) than the previous average number should trigger alarms? One can establish the deviation boundaries from the previous average number of usability problems by setting upper and lower limits of deviations. When the number of problems found in usability testing falls outside these limits, then the project manager should be alerted. If the number of usability problems exceeds the upper limit, then the project manager must question whether the product has a true usability problem or whether the test result is just an anomaly. If the number of usability problems falls below the lower limit, then the project manager might reexamine the usability testing methodology to ensure that this round of testing was not less rigorous than previous ones and that the product truly has fewer problems.

To see how this process works, let's look at a specific example. Suppose the product from the preceding example that had seven functional areas is considered by both the managers and the customers as the representative, good-quality product that should be used as the basis of comparison. It had, on average, 4.1 severity level 1 problems with a standard deviation of 3.43. The software project manager could potentially use this information to evaluate other products' functional quality.

The control chart in Figure 10.2 shows the average number of severity level 1 problems found (4.1 problems) as the basis of comparison for each functional area of the product being scrutinized. The upper limit value, 7.5 problems, is one standard deviation from 4.1. That is, adding one standard deviation (3.4) to the average value (4.1) results in the upper limit (7.5). The lower limit value of 0.7 problem is derived by subtracting 3.4 from 4.1.

As another product goes through testing, its severity level 1 problems may be plotted by functional area. As long as the number of problems found falls within the upper and lower limits, that functional area may be considered "under control." If the problems in any area exceed the upper limit, however, the project managers should take a second look at that functional

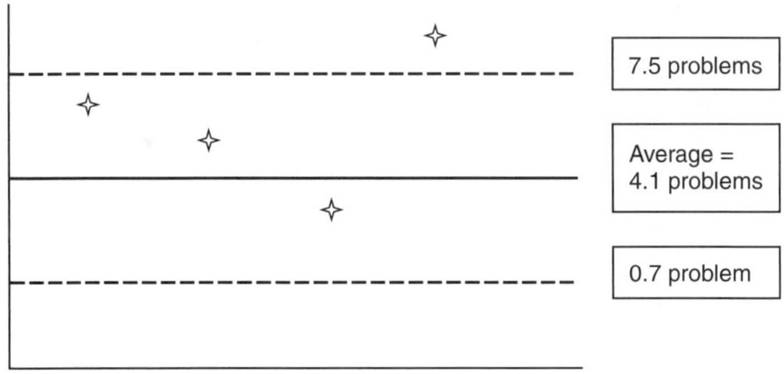

Figure 10.2 A sample control chart

area. Similarly, if the number of problems in a functional area falls below the lower limit, that area may be worthy of some attention. For example, the test cases might be reviewed to make sure that they fully covered the functional area. The process under which the reviews or testing for that area was conducted might also be examined.

This application of the average value and the dispersion from the average value in control charts is quite common in general project quality management, and it is gaining momentum in software project management. The manufacturing industry has for many years used control charts to help manage its production processes and product quality. Extensive statistical studies have been done in the process control area, and readers who are interested in this topic should consult the article by Kotz and Johnson listed in the "Suggested Reading" section at the end of this chapter.

DATA SMOOTHING: MOVING AVERAGES

Data taken at a specific time provide only an instantaneous view. In many cases, the historical trend of collected data is studied and analyzed to yield clues about the product. For example, this approach is popular in software projects during the testing activities. Often testing lasts for weeks or even months, and there may be quite a variation of problems found in some weeks. To "smooth" out these variations and prevent an alarm from being raised by a few spikes, the data from two or three weeks are combined. The resulting combined value is called the moving average.

> **Moving average** A technique for expressing data by computing the average of a fixed grouping (e.g., data for a fixed period) of data values; it is often used to suppress the effects of one extreme data point.

Consider the following example, where the number of problems found during a seven-week test period has been changed slightly from that in the earlier example:

Week 1: 20
Week 2: 33 (was 23)
Week 3: 45
Week 4: 67
Week 5: 35
Week 6: 15
Week 7: 20 (was 10)

The difference in value during week 2—from 23 problems found to 33 problems found—is not a problem, but the increase in value for week 7—from 10 problems found to 20 problems found—shows an actual reversal in trend. This slight change may cause some reservations on the part of the software project managers and prompt them to make a decision on completing the testing activities. That is, the seventh-week reversal may be viewed as a potential instability in testing. On the other hand, it may not mean anything.

To facilitate this type of decision-making process, data smoothing may be helpful. Data smoothing is accomplished by combining data points and viewing the aggregated values. Consider how the moving-average approach can be used to smooth out data variations. In Table 10.1, both two-week and three-week moving averages are computed. The two-week moving average is computed by averaging the previous week's value and the current week's value. The three-week moving average is computed in a similar manner. The two-week moving average does not start until the second week; similarly, the three-week moving average starts at the third week.

Data smoothing A technique used to decrease the effects of individual, extreme variability in data values.

Both the two-week and three-week moving averages show a much less erratic movement of values from the raw distribution of the data. Although it may be meaningless to have "partial problems" found, the moving averages are left with decimal figures just to show the computational results and to provide more precision for comparisons. Trend analysis utilizing moving averages is a little easier, because a few, sudden changes do not affect the

Table 10.1 Moving Averages of Problems Found

Test week	Problems found	Two-week moving average	Three-week moving average
1	20	-	-
2	33	26.5	-
3	45	39	32.6
4	67	56	48.3
5	35	51	49
6	15	25	39
7	20	17.5	23.3

smoothed values as dramatically. In this case, the decreasing trend of the moving averages continues smoothly without a spike.

Note that the range of values in the original data goes from a low of 15 problems discovered during week 6 to a high of 67 problems discovered during week 4; that represents a difference of 55 problems. The two-week moving average displays a smaller variation, from 17.5 problems to 56 problems, for a difference of 38.5 problems. The three-week moving average has an even smaller variation, with a difference of only 25.7 problems from the lowest to the highest. Clearly, the range of values of the moving averages is smoother than the original data. For these reasons, project managers often prefer to use the moving-average technique.

In a long software system test, test managers often use moving averages because the variability in test data values may be substantial. The large variability observed in a lengthy test situation might result from the different numbers and types of test cases run due to employee vacations or it might result from planned slowdowns due to a large amount of retesting of previously fixed problems.

DATA CORRELATION

Correlating attributes is a very useful tool for software project managers, but it must be used carefully. Data correlation speaks only to the potential existence of a relationship between attributes; it does not necessarily imply cause and effect.

> **Data correlation** A technique that analyzes the degree of relationship between sets of data.

One sought-after relationship in software is that between some attribute prior to product release and the same attribute after product release. The software developer might, for example, collect data on the total number of defects found during the three years after the release of one of its products. It could then compare those data with the number of total defects found in the product during testing. This analysis would focus on whether a correlation exists between the number of defects found during pre-release testing and the number of problems found during the three post-release years.

One popular way to examine data correlation is to analyze whether a linear relationship exists. Two sets of data may be plotted and the resulting graph reviewed to see how related they are. A more formal method, called linear regression analysis, may also be applied.

Linear regression A technique that estimates the relationship between two sets of data by fitting a straight line to the two sets of data values.

Linear regression analysis is predicated on expressing one variable, y, as a linear function of another variable, x, in the following form:

$$y = a + bx$$

The slope of the linear equation is the constant b. The y-intercept is represented by the constant a. The slope, b, may be calculated as follows:

$$b = \text{SUM}\ [(x_i - x_{\text{ave}}) \times (y_i - y_{\text{ave}})]\ /\ \text{SUM}\ (x_i - x_{\text{ave}})^2$$

where

SUM = the sum function evaluated over all data points
x_i = the ith observation of the x variable
x_{ave} = the average value of all x_i's
y_i = the ith observation of the y variable
y_{ave} = the average value of all y_i's

The intercept, a, may be calculated as follows:

$$a = y_{\text{ave}} - (b \times x_{\text{ave}})$$

Consider the example of a pre-release and post-release defects relationship over a number of software products developed by one organization. Table 10.2 lists the number of such problems found.

The two sets of data in Table 10.2 look directly related in that an increase (or decrease) in the number of pre-release problems seems to be

Table 10.2 Pre-Release and Post-Release Problems

Software products	Number of pre-release problems	Number of post-release problems (3 years)
1	10	24
2	5	13
3	35	71
4	75	155
5	15	34
6	22	50
7	7	16
8	54	112

accompanied by an increase (or decrease) in the number of post-release problems found. Furthermore, the relationship looks almost linear. One may estimate the constants, *a* and *b*, as follows.

Equating the pre-release problems with the variable x and the post-release problems with variable y, we have

$$x_{ave} = 27.8$$
$$y_{ave} = 59.3$$

Then utilizing the previously given formulae, we compute the values for a and b:

$$b = 2.0 \text{ (approximately)}$$
$$a = 3.7 \text{ (approximately)}$$

The estimated linear equation would be as follows:

$$y = 3.7 + 2x$$

Graphically, this equation gives the straight line shown in Figure 10.3, which provides the best fit through the data points that were recorded.

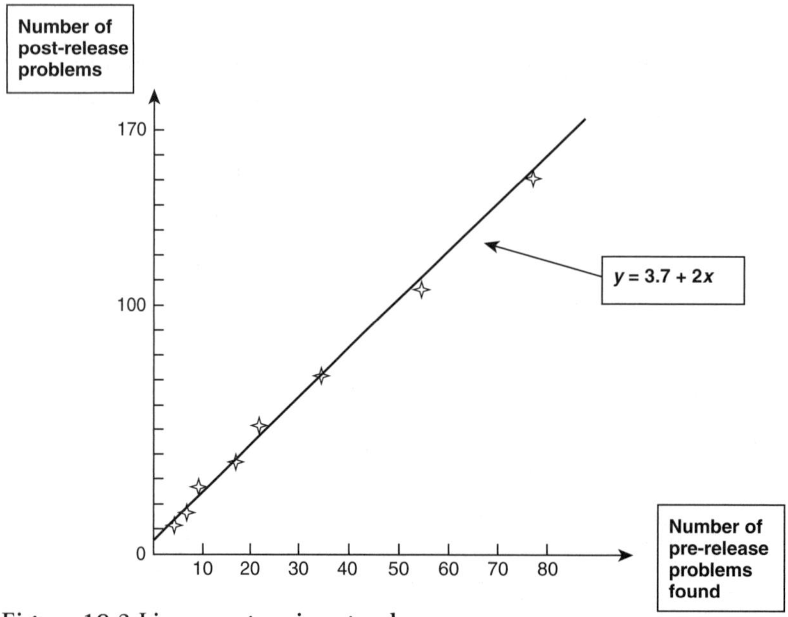

Figure 10.3 Linear regression graph

The equation $y = 3.7 + 2x$ may be used to estimate the number of problems that may be found following the release of a product, given the number of problems found during the pre-release testing of that product.

Assume that a new software product is developed by a similar software project team using the same process as employed for those projects that contributed to the graph in Figure 10.3. If the total number of problems discovered in this new product through the various pre-release tests is 32, then the estimated linear relationship may be used to project the total number of post-release problems: $3.7 + (2 \times 32) = 67.7$, or approximately 68 problems. Software support managers may, in turn, use this projection of 68 problems to estimate the cost of support services for that product.

Linear regression may be used to correlate other project or product attributes as well. For example, a project attribute status value may be used to project the value of a correlated attribute. Based on the projected value of that correlated attribute, certain adjustment actions may be applied to the ongoing project.

A word of caution is in order in using such linear relationships for projections: Interpolation of values is safe, but extrapolation of values may be dangerous. Fitting a linear line through the data points gave a linear equation, for example, but this linear relationship is not guaranteed outside the range of the data points. Put bluntly, extrapolation of the linear relationship outside of the range of the data points may be erroneous.

A linear relationship is one of the most easily identifiable relationships that may exist between two sets of data. Software project managers will find many other relationships and ways to gauge different types of data correlation in the reference books on statistics listed at the end of this chapter.

NORMALIZATION OF DATA

A pure comparison of the raw data sometimes does not provide an accurate comparison. Consider the following situation. The detection of a large number of problems in a functional area A compared with a small number of problems found in another functional area B may be misleading if functional area A is much larger or much more complex than functional area B. The size of the functional area or its complexity should be taken into account rather than just collecting the raw number of problems found in that area. Thus some measurement of size of the functional area or its complexity must be used to normalize the number of problems found.

Normalizing data A technique used to bring data characterizations to some common or standard level so that comparisons become more meaningful.

Even though software engineering reports put forth many arguments against using lines of code as the measurement of software size, it remains one of the most popular options. This measurement will be used as a means of demonstration here.

Consider the case where a total of 76 severity levels 1 and 2 problems are discovered in a functional area A. In a functional area B, a total number of 98 severity levels 1 and 2 problems are detected. Further suppose that functional area A is composed of 3300 lines of newly developed code, and functional area B is composed of 5400 lines of newly developed code and another 2000 lines of integrated code. We may normalize these numbers as follows:

Functional area A: 76/3300 = 0.023 defect per line of code

To make the normalized number easier to remember, lines of code may be recorded in units of 1000 lines of code, or "kloc." Using kloc as the unit, the normalized figures would be

Functional area A: 76/3.3 = 23 defects per kloc

Functional area B: 98/5.4 = 18.1 defects per kloc

Although functional area B may have more detected errors in terms of absolute numbers, its normalized figure–that is, the defect rate given in terms of defects per kloc–is smaller than that of functional area A. Furthermore, if the integrated code consisting of 2000 lines is included in the normalization, then the defect rate for functional area B would be 13.2 defects per kloc. Normalizing the defect numbers and converting the metric to the defect rate enables a more accurate comparison to be made.

Another example involves the evaluation of productivity figures. The average productivity of a software development effort is often cited in the form of lines of code or function points per person-month. Here the normalization factor is a person-month. However, to ensure that truly comparable normalization is possible, a person-month must be clearly defined. One person-month may vary from 15 working days per month to 20 working days per month. Following this definition, there must be further clarification on how many hours are included in one working day.

In many types of analysis, normalized data should be used. In all cases, the normalization factors must be well understood and defined. Examples include efficiency and productivity analysis where the development of 20 test cases should be normalized to 20 test cases per person-month, cost analysis where $3000 of telecommunications line usage should be normalized to $3000 per 1000 hours of telecommunications line usage, and quality analysis where 15 problems discovered during code reviews should be normalized to 15 code review problems per 1000 executable code statements.

KEY CONCEPTS

The earlier planning and organizational phases of the software project management should have properly defined and prepared the measurement schemes for reliable, accurate, and valid data. Nevertheless, this topic should be revisited one more time during the monitoring phase prior to the actual evaluation of collected data.

There are many ways to analyze the data and the status of a software project:

- The distribution of a set of collected data may be analyzed for extreme values, skew, and trends.
- Centrality and dispersion analysis of groups of data may be performed by computing averages, median values, or standard deviations from the central value.
- Data-smoothing techniques, involving the evaluation of trends through moving averages, are often used to lessen the impact of exceptional data points (outliers).
- The correlation of groups of data may be examined through many different methods. One very simple but popular method is linear regression.
- Normalizing the data ensures that groups of data are properly compared.

EXERCISES

1. Discuss the three terms, reliable data, accurate data, and valid data. Can a valid data be inaccurate or unreliable? Give an example.

2. Define the term "data distribution." Why do we care about data distribution?
3. In monitoring the trend of some project attribute, discuss the pros and cons of using data smoothing. Does this strategy conflict with the control chart approach?
4. What are some of the ways to establish an upper and a lower limit of the control chart?
5. Discuss centrality analysis and what a standard deviation represents.
6. Give an example of some software projects for which it may be useful to know the average value of a set of data on some attribute, such as quality or productivity.
7. Give an example of how a software project manager might use linear regression to correlate project attributes.
8. Does the fact that two sets of data correlate imply that there is a cause and affect relationship? Why?
9. Discuss how raw software cost attribute values such as $2 million or $50,000 may be normalized to make them valid for comparison.

SUGGESTED READING

W. Chase and F. Brown, *General Statistics,* 4th ed., John Wiley and Sons, 2000.

N. E. Fenton and S. L. Pfleeger, *Software Metrics: A Rigorous and Practical Approach,* PWS Publishing, 1997.

P. Jalote and A. Saxena, "Optimum Control Limits for Employing Statistical Process Control in Software Processes," *IEEE Transactions on Software Engineering,* December 2002, 1126–1134.

C. Jones, *Applied Software Measurements Assuring Productivity and Quality,* 2nd ed., McGraw Hill, 1996.

S. H. Kan, *Metrics and Models in Software Quality Engineering,* Addison-Wesley, 1995.

S. Kotz and N. L. Johnson, "Process Capability Indices–A Review, 1992–2000," *Journal of Quality Technology,* January 2002, 2–19.

D. C. Montgomery and G. C. Runger, *Applied Statistics and Probability for Engineers,* John Wiley and Sons, 2003.

J. M. Utts, *Seeing Through Statistics,* Duxbury Press, 1996.

E. F. Weller, "Practical Applications of Statistical Process Control," *IEEE Software,* May/June 2000, 48–55.

Chapter 11

Presenting and Communicating Data

Chapter Objectives

This chapter discusses the following concepts:

- Why representing and communicating project status information is important
- What forms may be used to present data, including tabular, bar chart, control chart, pie chart, and histogram formats

SHARING INFORMATION

The project status needs to be monitored by the software project managers, but the gathered information also needs to be shared with the rest of the team as well. Software projects are becoming so large and complex that a team effort is now considered essential for a project's success. To achieve this goal, the software project team needs to be informed of the status and the analysis of various parts of the project because an informed team is usually much more motivated. Conversely, sharing too much information may overload team members and defeat the purpose. Thus communication of information, as part of the monitoring phase, needs to be balanced.

To achieve the proper balance, it is best to pick three or four measurements to share with team members. The following four areas discussed earlier would be a good starter set:

- Schedule status
- Functional completeness status

- Quality status
- Budget status

In addition, the team should be made aware of the status of the items on the risk management list, regardless of the category. Team managers need to pay special attention to and act on all items on this list, but sharing just the high-risk items with nonmanagement personnel might be a wise decision.

A key question is, How should the information be portrayed? This question may be divided into several more specific questions:

- What form should the information take?
- When should the information be communicated?
- Where should the information be displayed?

The answers to these questions very much depend on the project. One should use a graphical form to share data if the goal is to make a single impression because it is very difficult to convey a large amount of data in words. Employing a visual, graphical approach would allow data to be summarized and provide that single impression. Information updates should come at short intervals if the overall project schedule is brief—perhaps only a few months. In addition, the information should reach all intended recipients. Thus it should be posted, electronically or otherwise, where all intended recipients can easily access and view it.

Each type of information that is monitored needs to be viewed and analyzed from a presentation and communication perspective. Some information may be best displayed in a tabular form; other information is amenable to sharing in bar graph or pie chart form. Besides offering a pictorial representation of information, the software project managers may need to summarize in words the key message that the recipient should come away with. As Jean-Luc Doumont notes, sometimes "words are worth a thousand pictures."

COMMUNICATING TIME-RELATED STATUS

When the communication is about the schedule and its status, the information may be shown in various formats, each of which has its own pros and cons.

Tabular Formats

For monitoring and tracking a list of major events, a tabular form may be well suited for the management team members and desktop review. Table 11.1 shows an example of this format.

Table 11.1 Schedule Status Portrayed in Tabular Form

Activities	Target date	Current status	Actual date	Assessment
Test plan	5/20/10	Completed	5/25/10	Late start date
Test scenario design	7/30/10	7 of 9 scenarios completed		Will be close
Test scripts writing	10/15/10	15 of 52 scripts completed		On target
Test case execution	1/25/11	Not started		None

Table 11.1 shows only the activity target completion dates and the actual completion dates. The Current-status column gives a glimpse of where the project is now. The current status of an activity must show the ratio of subtasks completed to the total number of subtasks. In the world of software projects, many joke about a task that stays "90% complete" forever. In reality, this perpetual incompleteness is a serious matter that all software project managers must be cognizant of; it is essential that they should ask for further status explanation on the remaining "10%."

The Assessment column provides this kind of information regarding the status of each activity. For example, in Table 11.1 the lateness of the test plan is attributed to its late start date, not to the actual performance of that activity. Even though the test case execution activity has not started and the Assessment column consequently shows "none," it would be worthwhile to ask about the likelihood of its meeting the start date or any other relevant risk. Software project managers should use the Current-status and Assessment columns aggressively in both analyzing the status of the various activities and communicating that status to others.

A few things are lacking in this representation. For example, ideally Table 11.1 should include a target start date and an actual start date for each activity. This information would provide further insight into the schedule status. If projects are not started on time, the chance of completing them on time is low. The Assessment column then must also include an assessment of the start date integrity of an activity, such as the readiness of all prerequisites for that particular activity.

The project schedule representation, utilizing a tabular form, may be appropriate for this type of detailed monitoring and reporting on a regular daily, weekly, or semi-monthly basis. The information may be presented on paper or as an on-line document. If it is updated daily, then creating an on-line document would save a lot of paper and distribution effort, and it may be the preferred distribution method.

Note that the mere electronic posting of schedule status is not the same as communicating. The intended receivers should be notified of the regular updates as soon as they are posted on-line. If any item needs special attention, then the message to the recipients should highlight that point. Alternatively, if all activities are moving along smoothly according to the target schedule, then the message should give that news. This additional summary message from the software project managers to the other key personnel accomplishes two important goals:

- The software project managers must formulate a quick overall assessment themselves so as to write the summary message.
- The recipients of the message will better understand the managers' interpretation of the data and the significance of the data reported.

In addition, the managers should solicit comments from the recipients of the on-line reports. A minimal response of acknowledging the receipt of the status data should be expected, even if no comment is attached. The software project managers should establish this kind of communication "rule" with their key project team personnel. Otherwise, the posted material may be ignored and will simply be one of the trappings of a costly, wasteful bureaucracy.

The project managers must realize that monitoring the project status may represent a key activity for them, but not necessarily for other team members. Thus special effort has to be made to communicate the status information. This communication is a prerequisite to the next POMA phase, especially if some adjustments need to be made based on team members' feedback. Team members should always be cognizant of the status of the project and the possible adjustments that may be coming.

Bar-Chart Formats

For communicating time-related information to a broader audience, a detailed tabular form may not be suitable because it sometimes requires careful reading of the details. A more graphical representation would be needed for a quicker communication to large audiences.

Bar chart A chart in which data values are represented with graphical bars.

For schedule and completeness of functions, a popular representation is the type of bar chart shown in Figure 11.1.

In Figure 11.1, the dotted-line bar shows the planned units of work over a period of time. The numerical units of work are shown inside the bar. The

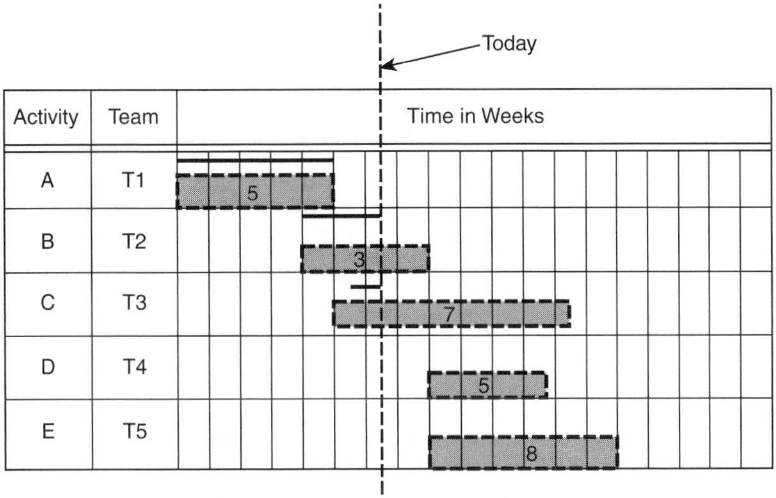

Figure 11.1 Activity status presented in bar chart form

length of the bar covers the planned time, in weeks, to complete the work. The solid line indicates the completed work.

This type of bar chart may be physically expanded to cover a wall, enabling a large number of team members to see it on a daily basis. Such a chart is typically updated weekly.

The bar-chart format helps to give a global view of the status of project activities over time. It provides a natural way to represent the activity schedule and partial or full functional completeness. In addition, it may be used to show a variety of activities, such as the project's spending status plotted against the planned budget for particular functional areas over time.

COMMUNICATING CONTROL-RELATED STATUS

In a way, one may view monitoring the project status as relating current information to planned information. Some status information, however, is more amenable for viewing through a control chart (see Chapter 10). Control charts are especially good for communicating project status to a large group of people because of their graphical form and the ease with which one can spot data values that fall outside the control limits.

The control-chart approach can be seen in the monitoring of quality in terms of problems uncovered through time using a normalized moving average. An example is shown in Figure 11.2.

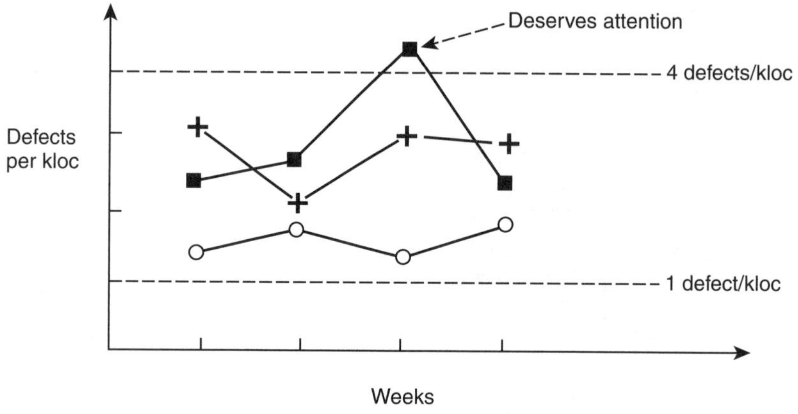

Figure 11.2 Control chart for severity levels 1 and 2

In Figure 11.2, the severity levels 1 and 2 problems of three software components are monitored during the component-testing period over several weeks. The control chart's upper and lower bounds were established based on the organization's past experiences with similar projects. This type of chart provides a quick view of whether the monitored status is within expected or "planned" target numbers.

Control charts may also be used to monitor other normalized information, such as productivity-related data. As long as each data value falls within the limits, then the project is progressing according to plan, and the software project team may view the project as being "under control." Conversely, if a data value falls outside the limits, then some effort needs to be spent on checking out the cause of the outlier. Depending on the reason, adjustments may or may not be needed to bring the project under control.

OTHER COMMON DATA REPRESENTATION FORMATS

There are many other ways to present information, including pie charts and various types of histograms.

Pie Charts

A pie chart is often employed to show the proportion of different categories. As an example, the pie chart in Figure 11.3 shows the breakdown

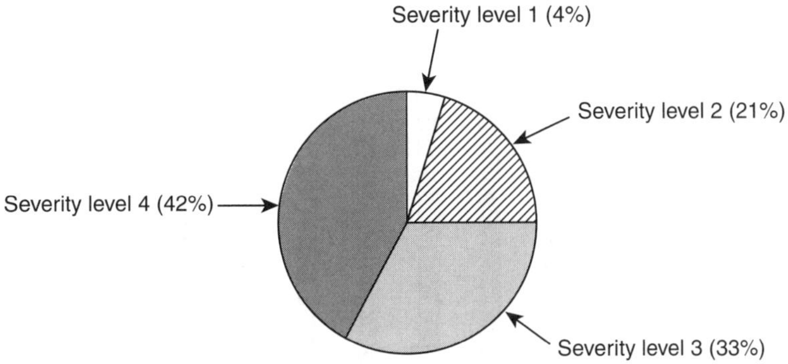

Figure 11.3 Pie chart

(by percentage) of the four severity levels of problems found in a functional area.

> **Pie chart** A technique for graphically representing the proportions of different categories of data values.

Histograms

A histogram is another way to show proportional information by categories. In the histogram in Figure 11.4, the top 10 largest customers' opinions are surveyed on a basis of 0 to 100 index points (e.g., in the form of percent satisfaction).

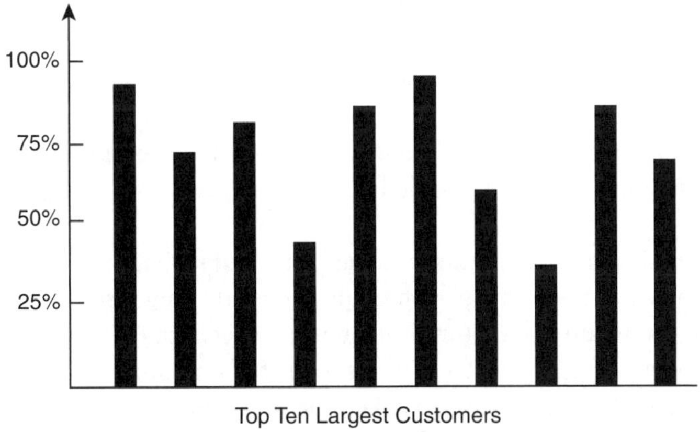

Figure 11.4 Customer satisfaction index: histogram

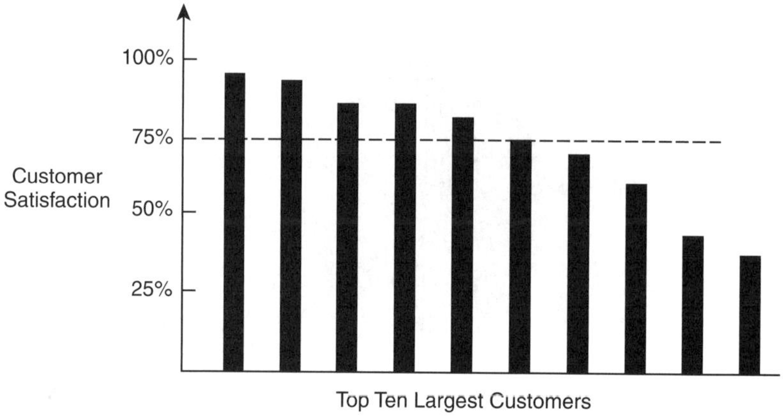

Figure 11.5 Customer satisfaction index: Pareto diagram

Histogram A technique for graphically representing frequency counts of data values via a bar chart.

Sometimes the bars of a histogram are arranged in order from the tallest to the shortest, or vice versa. This kind of sequenced histogram, known as a Pareto diagram, provides a quicker view of the status.

Pareto diagram A histogram modified to show a frequency count of data values in either ascending or descending order. It is named after the Italian economist Vilfredo Pareto.

An additional information line, portraying the "minimal satisfactory" index, may be included in the Pareto diagram. For example, if 75% was the minimally acceptable customer satisfaction index, then a horizontal line might be drawn across the diagram as shown in Figure 11.5. All customers below this line might be considered candidates for immediate management follow-up and additional focus. Thus the monitored status is used as input to the project adjustment phase.

Some newer data representations include the Kiviat diagram and the Tree Map diagram. The Kiviat diagram provides a visual comparison of multiple attributes. In Figure 11.6, three attributes—Defect Rate, Transaction Rate, and Customer Acceptance Rate— are shown for two products, one of which is represented by a solid line and the other by a dotted line. Both are shown with a three-axes Kiviat diagram.

A Tree Map is a method in which to display hierarchial, tree-structured data in nested rectangles. The size of the rectangles provides a comparison of

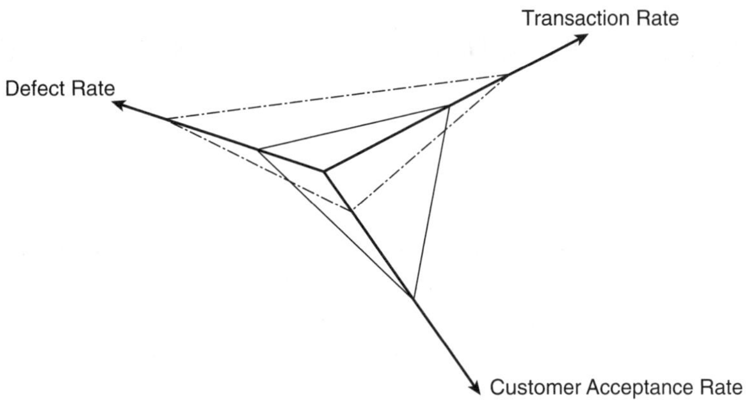

Figure 11.6 Multiple attribute Kiviat diagram

the attribute value of interest. Figure 11.7 demonstrates a breakdown of the subcomponents contained in a software product. The size of the rectangles may represent an attribute, such as memory size required by the subcomponents. For illustration, the hashed area shows a nested breakdown of a subcomponent. The double-hashed area shows further breakdown of the inner subcomponents of the hashed area into even smaller subcomponents. The Tree Map visualization technique may include the use of color.

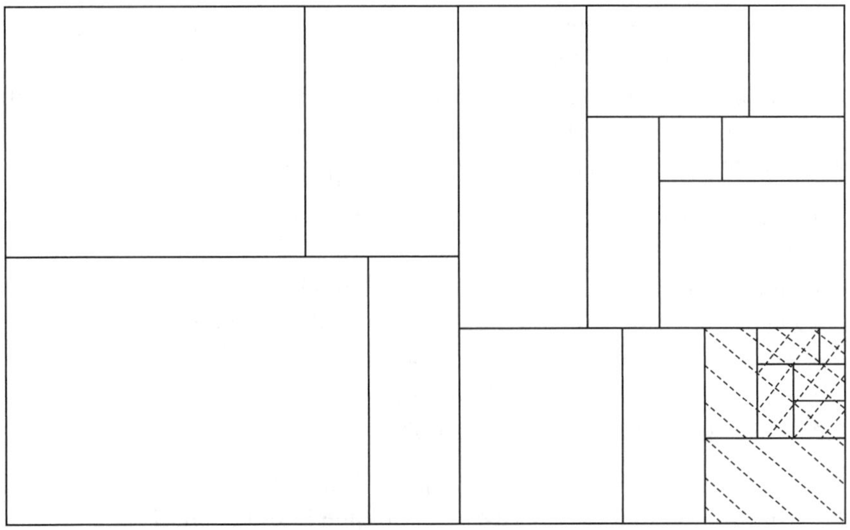

Figure 11.7 Tree map representation of software sub-components

SELECTING A DATA REPRESENTATION FORMAT

Clearly, there are many different ways to present the collected and analyzed data to both project managers and nonmanagers. For some managers, a detailed tabular form is the easiest to use. For others, graphically represented data are preferable. The software managers may try a few different approaches, ask the other team members for their opinions, and decide on a set to conduct project monitoring. The constant, regular representation and communication of software project status will not only serve the project monitoring phase well, but will prepare the team for any needed adjustments.

If the managers decide to use graphical data representations, many of them may be produced via a widely used tool such as Microsoft Excel. In such a case, the raw data are put into the tool and the chart wizard options of Excel are then evoked to produce graphical diagrams in the form of a bar or pie chart. A more sophisticated tool, such as the statistical software from MINITAB or the Chart Fx tool from Software Fx, may be used in a similar way.

KEY CONCEPTS

The importance of presenting and communicating the information gathered from software projects cannot be overemphasized. The specific form of representation and communication chosen will depend on the type of project, the intent of the data representation, and the audience. The following forms are especially popular among today's software project managers:

- Tabular forms–to convey a lot of project detail
- Bar charts–to show a global view
- Control charts–to highlight trends and bounds
- Pie charts–to show relative and proportional information
- Histograms–to show relative comparisons
- Kiviat diagram–to show multiple attributes
- Tree Map–to show hierarchially organized data

The type of recipients and the purpose of the communication will dictate the frequency and medium used for sharing the information. If the information is posted electronically, then the project managers must ensure that it is received and reviewed by asking for some kind of acknowledgment.

EXERCISES

1. Consider the following pairs of numbers, where the first value represents the number of software companies in a certain city and the second value represents the number of employees in those software companies: (3, 5), (5, 10), (10, 14), (22, 20), (5, 45), (2, 70). Which graphical form would you use to represent this information?
2. For conveying the breakdown of problems in different severity levels during a major testing cycle, which graphical form would you use?
3. Use the appropriate diagram and represent the following data of module size, in lines of code, by descending order: modA-300; modB-255; modC-70; modD-185; modE-507. How would you show the average size of these modules in this same diagram?
4. Suppose the information in Exercise 1 includes a third attribute, the number of software products produced, with data points that look as follows: (3, 5, 4), (5, 10, 6), (10, 14, 9), (22, 20, 13), (5, 45, 15), (2, 70, 18). Use a three-axis graph to represent the information. How else might you want to represent these data points?
5. Consider the following activities: initial prototyping–5 days; design–4 days; code implementation–10 days; testing–5 days; user guide–7 days. If you were asked to place this in a graphical form to represent a schedule, what questions might you need to have answered first?
6. Colors and shapes are sometimes used in the graphical representations of data. Discuss possible advantages and disadvantages on the usage of colors and shapes. Convert your discussion into a visual presentation to your class. Use Kiviat or Tree Map as examples.

SUGGESTED READING

J. L. Doumont, "Verbal Versus Visual: A Word Is Worth a Thousand Pictures, Too," *Technical Communications,* May 2002, 219–224.

B. J. Dretzke and K. A. Heilman, *Statistics with Microsoft Excel,* Prentice Hall, 1998.

A. Fiore and M. A. Smith, "Treemap Visualization of Newsgroups," MSR–TR–2001–94, Microsoft Research Technical Report, Microsoft Corporation, Redmond, WA, October, 2001.

G. T. Henry, *Graphing Data Techniques for Display and Analysis,* Sage Publications, 1995.

M. Y. Rabb, *The Presentation Design Book: Projecting a Good Image with Your Desktop Computer,* Ventana Press, 1990.

B. Shneiderman and C. Plaisant, "Treemaps for Space-Constrained Visualization of Hierarchies," http://www.cs.umd.edu/heil/treemap-history, accessed March, 2010.

E. Tufte, *The Visual Display of Quantitative Information,* 2nd ed., Graphics Press, 2001.

H. Wainer, *Visual Revelations, Graphical Tools of Fate and Deception from Napoleon Bonaparte to Ross Perot,* Lawrence Erlbaum Associates Publishers, 1997.

Part Four

Adjustments and Actions

(POMA)

Software projects are performed and managed by human beings. Thus, these projects are subject to changes, imperfect planning, and necessary trade-offs. Even the most carefully planned, best-staffed, and schedule-friendly projects sometimes require midcourse adjustments.

The software project managers should not be afraid to take action and make adjustments when necessary. Some staff beliefs and attitudes actually indicate that a shifting of gears and the taking of an active stance are not only warranted but necessary. Examples are:

- Believing or hoping that a problem will go away by itself
- Believing that the project includes some "sacred cows" that cannot be changed
- Believing that making changes is a sign of weakness and lack of commitment
- Not realizing that changes and actions are needed
- Being afraid of changes
- Not knowing what options are available and what adjustments to make

Many of these reasons for remaining passive may seem foolish. Having a fear of change may sound silly, for example, but it is a very real problem for some people—and not just software project managers. Behind this fear of change may lie a fear of the unknown, in the form of what the changes will bring. Unfortunately, if actions are not taken when needed, several unpleasant outcomes may result:

- Projects may fail
- Projects may fail faster
- Projects may experience a slow-paced failure
- Projects may barely get completed while taking a great toll on the sponsoring organization

Once the software project starts, project status may begin to veer from the plan at any point–there is no single moment at which all projects falter. The software project managers almost have to make a concerted effort to look for those deviations that may require modifications and adjustments to the project.

Similarly, adjustments and actions may need to be made at any time–during the regular project status monitoring meetings, during any off-line meetings, during any emergency or crisis, or during planned changes. There is no simple prescribed period for adjustments and actions. Software project managers will be making adjustments, both major and minor ones, throughout the entire project life cycle.

Software project managers do not and should not need to make all adjustments by themselves. That is, the project team approach should include a certain amount of team management, wherein team members are solicited for their opinions and suggestions about various project management decisions and actions. To help team members group-manage the project, managers may form a permanent "release management" team for each software project. Release management utilizes a group of people from all areas of software development and support, including the software project managers, to set goals, make decisions, take actions, and generally guide the project to its successful completion.

The traditional approach to making unplanned project adjustments in response to problems detected via project monitoring follows a four-step approach:

1. Determine and define the problem. (Sometimes this is the most difficult step because there is very little guideline to the problem identification and determination process, and there are so many different problems. One step that would help is to make sure that the problem is stated in a written form and not just verbally. The mere writing process itself will force some degree of exploration of the problem.)
2. Discover the root cause of the problem (perhaps utilizing a cause-and-effect diagram as an aid).

3. Define the solution and the necessary actions.
4. Assign resources to take the needed actions.

For software projects, the three main solution areas typically involve resources, functionality, or schedule. Thus actions taken will usually touch upon these three main domains of software projects.

Chapter 12

Planned and Unplanned Adjustments and Actions

Chapter Objectives

This chapter discusses the following concepts:

- How to respond to the monitored status of the project
- How to take actions with a sense of urgency
- How to make planned adjustments
- How to react to unexpected situations and make adjustments

If the project proceeds as planned and the status indicates that everything is on track, then there is nothing to adjust. Unfortunately, planning and organizing are rarely perfect in real-world software projects. As a consequence, software project managers must be prepared to take actions to rectify problems, whether they are minor or urgent, planned or unplanned.

TAKING ACTIONS WITH URGENCY

As mentioned earlier, almost all software projects experience at least some changes. Some of the changes are deliberately planned for; others occur in response to an unplanned event. As managers monitor the status of the project, there will be many occasions in which the current status does not match their expectations or the plan. Some minor mismatches are tolerable and may be left alone under continual monitoring for a while. An example of a "tolerable" case would be a situation in which a single test run results in a data point that exceeds the limits on a product quality control chart (see, for example, Figure 11.2) but subsequent test results fall within the acceptable limits; in that case, one may take a wait-and-see approach. Other discrepancies might require quick response and action. If several tests result in data points that fall outside of the planned limits, for example, then immediate actions must be taken to investigate, analyze, resolve, and prevent potential product quality problems.

All software projects follow some preplanned set of activities, like those described in Chapters 6–8 of this book. That is, a process and a set of methodologies are planned and usually implemented. Key metrics and measurements activities are defined as well. As the project proceeds, those measurements are actually taken and analyzed. Whenever any emergency or "crisis" occurs, in the form of a dramatic deviation of the monitored information from the expected result, then the team and the management are alerted immediately. In such situations, software project managers may be forced into taking quick actions.

In addition, deviations from the plans may be discussed at the regular, weekly or semi-monthly project status meetings. Those discussions typically cover a large amount of ground, mostly dealing with immediate problems. If these immediate problems are not solved without delay, the next regular status meeting will simply re-expose the same problem. The solution to the problem, when addressed early, will often be much less painful than it might otherwise be.

For example, if not resolved early, a personnel problem—such as a disagreement about the design approach between two lead people—can create two camps of people working diligently to prove the other side wrong instead of working productively to complete the project. The effort required and time lost in bringing two camps of warring people together may greatly exceed the effort required to adjudicate the differences between only two people.

Steps in Taking Urgent Action

For project management in general, the urgency with which one approaches problems and takes the necessary subsequent actions dictates the tone of the project. Let's take, for example, the quick adjudication of a dispute between two people. That resolution sets the tone for the entire project team in several ways: It shows that honest technical disagreements are tolerable but holding grudges is not, that problem resolution should be approached early with an open mind, and that team play is valued.

The software project managers must always exhibit good leadership and set the proper tone. A recommended approach to dealing with situations requiring urgent action is described below:

1. Clearly state the problem.
2. Communicate the problem while working on the potential solutions to it.
3. Seek out the root cause of the problem and any relevant solutions.
4. Gain the necessary agreement for the chosen solution.
5. Act on the solution.
6. Communicate on the action.
7. Report on the status of the problem's resolution.

This set of steps, while obvious to many, is frequently not carried out on time or in full. Each of the steps will involve several substeps. Each one is almost a process that may require several methodologies. Step 1 is one of the most difficult. Often, the software project managers themselves will need to lead the questioning and thinking as the team attempts to clearly understand and state the problem in a concise way. Many times, in this process of defining the problem, the real root cause and the choices of solutions become apparent. After the problem is well understood, it should be communicated to the team while the underlying causes are being analyzed and solutions are being developed. This communication will provide constant feedback to the team and at the same time create a channel for those team members to suggest solutions.

Change Management

Once the solution is chosen, then the manager must ensure that all stakeholders agree on it. Implementing a particular solution may require acquiring more resources, changing assignments, changing direction, changing schedules, or scaling back features, for example. Almost any of these alternatives will call for the understanding and cooperation of the team members, peer managers, or upper-level managers before the actual solution can be put in place and acted on.

In some situations, the customers may be consulted. Consider the situation in which the software project is a customized project. Here, the sequence of delivery of the functions may need to be modified due to a change in demand from the customer. In this case, depending on the particular function, the change may or may not be easily honored. The software project team should meet with the customer and jointly work out the details of the change, taking into account the potential adjustments to schedule and cost required.

One key reason for acting on a problem with urgency is to "nip it in the bud" before major adjustments are required that might alarm customers or the organization's executives. If the solution necessarily involves dramatic changes to the project's schedule, functionality, or resources, however, then the project managers must consult both executives and customers as early as possible to win their support for the proposed solution.

Note that several potential solutions may be proposed before one is deemed acceptable. The actual solution must be "worked out" with all of the project's stakeholders. The initial exchange of information may be done by e-mail and other electronic means. The actual negotiation may take on different forms, depending on the situation. In spite of the availability of advanced electronic communications tools, some people still prefer face-to-face meetings. Each situation is slightly different, so project managers need to remain flexible and be able to adapt to each unique case.

In a sense, taking actions and making adjustments is similar to the more general topic of change management (discussed in more detail in Chapter 15). Change management must include the activities related to controlling changes and associating any solution to problems, but it may or may not include the actual solution discovery process.

Change management A set of activities directed toward controlling changes. These activities may include identifying changes, assessing and measuring changes, and tracking changes.

In both cases, one of the greatest obstacles to change can be the "people factor." Consider the list of potential targets for changes:

- The product's functional and nonfunctional attributes
- A process or methodology
- Schedule
- The customer's expectations
- Tools

In adjusting any or all of these items, people are inevitably affected. Small changes and adjustments are easily understood and may be implemented without causing too much alarm. In contrast, large changes and adjustments to those items may encounter a significant amount of resistance. Thus software project managers must be acutely aware of the importance of managing people's reactions to adjustments and changes. One of those reactions is often fear. Much of this fear of change derives from people not knowing what is changing. To deal with this issue, the project managers must communicate often and dispel the unknowns. For example, explaining the rationale behind the changes and proposed adjustments, the actual adjustments, and the details of the steps involved in the change process would alleviate the anxiety about the changes. This is not much different from the change management process discussed in the books cited in the "Suggested Reading" list at the end of this chapter.

The chosen solution must be immediately implemented. If the team sits on the solution for too long, then the original problem may be further exacerbated. Then the agreed-upon solution may need to be modified—most likely to a more expensive option. The team should be notified of the action taken, and the resolution should be tracked, in a similar manner in which product and project attributes are tracked during the monitoring phase of POMA, until the action is completed.

PLANNED ADJUSTMENTS

Any planned adjustments should be put together by all affected parties and presented to all stakeholders of the project, including the customers. The project should not be allowed to move forward if the agreed-upon adjustments and actions are not taken. Otherwise, the credibility of the software managers and other parties who recommended the adjustments will always be questioned.

The Planned Adjustment Decision-Making Process and Targets

The software project managers should regularly plan on making adjustments throughout the project cycle. As an example, consider the simple project process that develops a software component through the following set of activities:

- Requirements analysis
- Design
- Implementation and coding
- Testing
- Integration

The software management team may decide to have a planned adjustment at the end of each of these major activities. This approach of "anticipatory adjustment" should be built into the management monitoring/review process and must not come as a surprise to the project team or anyone else in the management group. The key metrics are always reviewed, and the software team should be made aware that there will be a discussion to review potential adjustments to the project. Inevitably, the review will center on the following areas:

- Functionality
- Resources
- Schedule

Although the topics of review should not be limited to just these three variables, the software managers do have a large amount of control over these areas and can readily take actions to modify them. As part of the exit criteria of each phase of the project, the software project managers should assess the status of the activity and conscientiously make adjustments, if necessary. For example, if attempts to meet the exit criteria for the requirements specification phase run into a schedule obstacle, the project managers might choose to review and modify the resources, functional content, or schedule plans for the downstream activities. The actual changes to the plan will depend on the reasons underlying the difficulties in meeting the exit criteria on time.

Notice that several notable areas—especially product quality and people productivity—were omitted from the preceding list of items to be reviewed. Their exclusion does not mean that quality and productivity are not important. Rather, for software project managers, the quality goal should be tracked continually and not become relegated to an "adjustable parameter." Productivity is something that is monitored, but it is not adjustable; one would instead adjust resources—for example, people, education, process, or tools—to influence the project productivity measure.

The regular review of the project status, complemented by constant small adjustments and changes, should have given the software project managers a good overall picture of the project. If regular, incremental adjustments to the project has ensured that everything was tracking to plan and moving along relatively smoothly, then the planned action would be simple: Stay the course. Conversely, if a large number of changes and variations from the plan resulted in a significant number of deviations during a particular project phase, then the software project managers should review the three key project parameters (functionality, resources, schedule). The question of how much change and how large an accumulative quantity of changes would constitute grounds for reexamination is a difficult one to answer. Indeed, the answer will depend on the type of project and a variety of parameters.

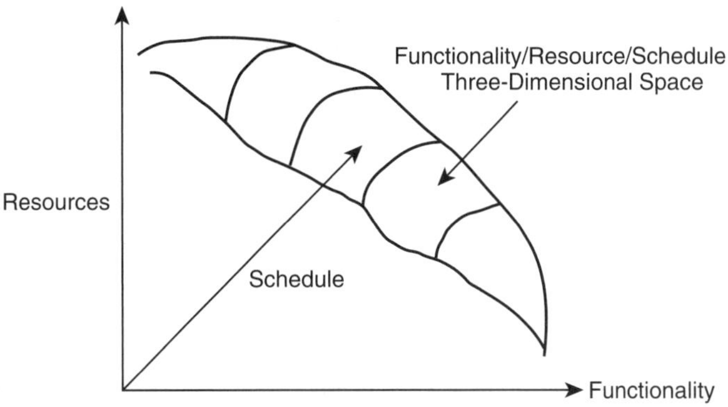

Figure 12.1 Three main project parameters

Making Planned Adjustments to Functionality, Resources, and Schedule

The decision-making process includes an assessment of whether adjustments are needed to all or some combination of the commitments made to the three areas of functionality, resources, and schedule. If one or more parameters need to be modified, then the degree of adjustment required must also be determined before the project continues on to the next phase. These three main parameters may be viewed as three variables affecting each other on a three-dimensional surface (see Figure 12.1). Rarely does one change without affecting the other two.

Project cost is an important parameter that may be varied. With software projects, the cost is folded into the resources parameter. As more resources are applied, the cost generally increases in tandem. In any project, it is crucial to understand the adjustment of the functionality parameter. Carefully identifying and agreeing to provide less functionality is not the same as providing less functionality by accident or providing nonperforming functionality. In the software industry, a planned reduction in functionality, for whatever reason, is usually acceptable if a follow-up release expects to restore the dropped functions. In contrast, an unplanned reduction in functionality that is unwittingly discovered by customers and users is usually met with a great amount of hostility and mistrust. Customers and users want to know whether the project is under control or out of control. Planned slippage, while not desirable, still portrays a certain degree of control. Similarly, planned delays in the schedule are very different from missing the schedule. The software project managers should look at all elements, including high-risk items (see Chapter 5), that may influence these three main parameters and decide on whether any preventive adjustments are warranted prior to undertaking the next phase of the project.

Sometimes the project functionality parameter is tracking to plan, the schedule parameter is tracking to plan, but the resources plan is failing to meet expectations. Perhaps the customer did not ask for any change in functionality or schedule, but the initial estimates of resources needed were nevertheless low. This problem sometimes arises in software consulting and service projects. In such a case, the software project managers may not be tracking to budget but the extra cost cannot be readily passed on to the customers. Even if the software project pricing is based on "time and expense," the customer should be alerted to the difference at the end of a project phase and should be presented with data on any anticipated growth in expenses in downstream activities.

Other projects operate on a fixed-fee basis; in theory, any extra costs cannot be passed on to the customer. For example, during the early 1990s, when various enterprise resource planning (ERP) software service businesses were still establishing themselves, many offered their services under fixed-fee terms. Even corporate giants, such as IBM, found the fixed-fee approach to be very difficult to manage due to the lack of experienced ERP resources. The time-and-expense approach relieved some of the cost overrun risks.

A hybrid approach of using time-and-expense billing for the requirements gathering and specifications phase but switching to a fixed-fee basis for the remaining phases is a compromise approach that is well accepted by many. Sophisticated customers and experienced project managers understand the risks of planning and estimating for a fixed-fee project without having a good understanding of the project requirements first. As a result, they will typically utilize a hybrid approach.

Whatever the pricing system, the software project manager must have a feel for what the customer is willing to pay for the consulting and services on software. Sometimes the software project manager may decide to simply "write off" the extra expense that he or she does not feel that the customer will be able or willing to bear. The project team and the manager would then need to ensure that the remaining tasks of the project are carried out within the budget—if this goal cannot be achieved, the project may generate a financial loss for the organization. Perhaps the project members can be asked to put in some extra time on their own clock, but without charging all the extra time to the project. In that case, the project manager essentially writes off some of the extra time, and the company's profit margin suffers. The team members also suffer financially because they are writing off some of their performed work. In effect, this strategy increases the resources available to the project without paying for them. Of course, this option cannot be exercised too many times or the software project managers will lose some of the members of their team.

A more preferable adjustment would be finding a more efficient methodology or tool for the next phase of the project. These adjustments may seem like planned adjustments, but they are really reactions to a negative set of information that was not handled promptly or was not detected during the regular project status meetings. If these situations persist, then they must definitely be acted upon at the planned end-of-a-phase review.

UNPLANNED ADJUSTMENTS

Unplanned activities usually come in response to unanticipated requests or incidents. Most of these unplanned requests and incidents involve high-priority or crisis-level problems. Perhaps a customer suddenly requests a tighter schedule or a key member of the project team leaves, causing direct changes to one of the three main parameters (functionality, resources, schedule). These changes will, in turn, affect the other two main parameters.

In software projects, the schedule is rarely allowed to expand. Rather, most requests call for condensing the schedule. Likewise, resources are rarely allowed to grow (at least, without some major justification). The loss of a key resource, whether voluntary or involuntary, may create a mini-panic. Both schedule and resource changes are relatively easy to recognize. In contrast, functionality can be a highly complex parameter, whether the request is for a greater number of functions, for modifications of existing features in functions, or for extensions to existing features in functions.

This section on unplanned adjustments has a recurring theme: Any change in one of the three main parameters of functionality, resources, or schedule should evoke a corresponding adjustment in one or both of the other two parameters. This adjustment should not be delayed, and the actions must be taken with urgency.

Functionality Changes

Defining changes in the functionality parameter takes more effort and time than defining changes in resources or schedule. Although each functionality change request may seem innocuous viewed on its own, the cumulative effect of these simple changes can topple an entire project. These unplanned, functionality-change requests must be accompanied by or result in appropriate adjustments to the resources or schedule parameter.

Functionality status should be discussed in terms of the amount of changes that occurred, rather than any sheer increase in the number of functions provided in the software artifact. A modification to an existing feature within a function can trigger a substantial set of activities that was not taken into account in the original project plan. Aside from each individual change, the cumulative effect of these changes is what the software project managers need to recognize.

It is well understood that changes made in earlier stages of software development require less effort and have smaller effects on the project schedule and resource costs. While there is no general metric that applies to all possible situations, Barry Boehm has stated that "finding and fixing a software problem after delivery costs 100 times more than finding and fixing the problem in early design phases" (see his article in the "Suggested Reading" list at the end of this chapter). For example, a functional change made in the requirements stage is not as costly as a change made during a later stage of the project life cycle, such as testing. This discrepancy arises because a problem found during testing may require multiple changes and rework in previously completed areas such as design, code, test cases, and test analysis. Similarly, changes made in response to some major defect found in the product during the system testing phase can create a crisis in the entire project. The schedule pressure on a software project is tremendous at the system testing stage or as the project approaches the product release date. In addition, the amount of wasted time from the earlier stages and repeated work is not only costly but also demoralizing to the software project team members.

If the number of functions or the number of modifications to functionality increases, then the software project managers must make corresponding adjustments to the resources, schedule, or both. Adjusting these parameters would certainly have implications for the budget. Recall that software projects are usually undertaken in businesses, where financial considerations are important. Too many software projects have failed due to this problem of ever-increasing functionality, which is widely known as "scope creep." Unfortunately, if resources and schedules are not adjustable, then quality often becomes the unintended victim of such functionality changes. Software project managers need to be especially sensitive to the quality issue when extra resources or time in the schedule is needed, but not provided to the project.

Scope creep Unsuspected, gradual increase in work units. The accumulated effect of these increases is often underestimated and potentially poses a high risk to the project.

Scope creep does not always result from customers' demands. Sometimes, the project team members will take it upon themselves to improve or expand the project functionality. Often these scope creep modifications are well intentioned. For example, software engineers might be enticed by some recent technology improvement, such as a shiny new device, and decide to include support for it without informing anyone. Because no one is aware of this addition, no test cases will ever be designed for it. Customers may not know about it and will never evoke it. Unfortunately, an implementation defect related to this kind of stealth improvement may be found by accident, usually in an untimely situation such as during a product demonstration when a sales person may inadvertently evoke the function. Another similar situation is one in which the well-intentioned support programmer inserts several related "fixes" under the umbrella of one documented customer problem report. The extra fixes sometimes are not completely tested and may cause surprises and adverse consequences to those who are unaware of their existence. These changes are subtle, and software project managers need to be constantly on the lookout for these internal, self-initiated scope creeps.

Asking for more resources or more time is difficult. If the functional scope of the project has increased, however, then the software project managers must ask for a corresponding increase in resources or a lengthening of the schedule. Many software projects are asked to somehow swallow the increases. On other occasions, the decision-making process for changing the resources or schedule may take so long that the project will begin a downward slide, sitting in an abeyance stage. The consequence—a deterioration in team morale and the earlier-mentioned decline in software quality. It is essential to make timely unplanned adjustments if the general product quality attribute and team morale attribute are to be maintained. In this case, the undesirable results that follow from not completing the functionality, not correcting all known functional defects, not following design or programming standards, not updating the project documentation, and so on, may all be the consequence of not increasing resources or expanding the schedule as needed.

Resource Changes

As you might expect, adjustments need to be made to the schedule or product functionality if a change in resources occurs. Suppose several key designers leave the project prior to the completion of the design and implementation activities. Software project managers must understand that they need to adjust either the functionality or the schedule unless the organization is lucky enough to have replacement talents in waiting—a highly unlikely scenario. Even if skilled replacements were readily available, it would take some time for them to familiarize themselves with the specific software project. Rarely will the software project be so standardized that a talented software engineer can be replaced without missing a beat. A software project team is not like a baseball, football, or soccer team, where a position player can be moved from team to team with relative ease. That movement is possible because the game itself does not need to be learned again when the player changes his or her team; it is the same game. In contrast, software projects are rarely the same. The more complex and unique the project, and the more interactions required among the team members, the more difficult it is for the team members to be treated as "replaceable" parts.

Besides human resources, changes to resources such as tools, processes, or the budget will require adjustments to either schedule or functionality. For example, a well-intentioned improvement to a tool or a process undertaken in the middle of a project may require additional training of team personnel. The timing of such changes may still require adjustments to the schedule of affected tasks while not affecting the project's final end date.

Note that the resource change is not always negative. Of course, this generosity usually comes at a price. Sometimes resources may be increased, but then either functionality must be increased or the schedule tightened. Increasing the amount of resources available without adjusting the other two parameters would make one question whether the original plan were correct or whether the increased resources will simply be squandered.

Schedule Changes

As stated earlier, the schedule of a software project is viewed as almost a sacred cow, rarely being considered as a candidate for change. Most of the time, the requested adjustment is to shorten the schedule for reasons such as marketplace competition, customer needs, or budget needs. Like the other areas typically targeted for adjustment, the schedule cannot be modified without the software project managers making corresponding resources or functionality adjustments.

A word of caution is in order about trying to shorten the schedule by applying additional resources. With certain software activities, adding resources in terms of people or tools simply will not improve the schedule.

Consider the work of design. This activity often takes special talent, so increasing the raw amount of resources will not necessarily improve the schedule. Running test scenarios, in contrast, may be greatly hastened by acquiring additional resources and tools.

A schedule can be shortened if there are subactivities that can be performed in parallel. However, if the activities are all serially gated, then putting in more resources will not improve the schedule. For example, programming algorithms must be designed before any coding of them can start. Applying additional resources (e.g., more designers and coders) usually will not improve the schedule, and it may even slow down the design activity because the original designer has to spend time bringing new people on board. (This phenomenon was mentioned in a quotation from Fred Brooks's book *The Mythical Man-Month* in Chapter 3, in the section titled "Interrelated Attributes.")

Another factor is whether any tool or methodology is available that will allow a specific subactivity to be completed faster than planned. If so, then employing that new tool or methodology resource will contribute to shortening the schedule. In some cases, a tool such as a configuration manager may even help in coordinating multiple, serialized activities and achieve something similar to parallelism.

In summary, software project managers who need to tighten a schedule should explore two types of resource-based adjustments:

- Look for parallel subactivities for assignment of more human resources.
- Look for specific activities that a new or different methodology or tool might help complete faster. (One must be aware of and balance the potential adverse effects of having to learn a new methodology or tool, taking into account such factors as time needed to be trained on a new tool.)

The software project managers' other immediate reaction to schedule shrinkage might be to seek to cut functionality. This kind of adjustment also needs to be made with care. Taking apart intricately designed software may not be as easy as just not doing something; it may actually require some redesigning to drop certain functionality that is already partially implemented. In particular, dependencies across components may need to be redesigned if one component of a multicomponent design is dropped. Suppose parameters are passed between two components to support a required function between these components. The passed parameters may have required a large amount of setup work and computation within these two components. If the required function is later dropped, the amount of work needed to take out the original setup code, computational code, and parameter-passing mechanism, along with the retesting required, can amount to as much or more work as needed for the initial implementation. In all cases, adjustments to functionality due to changes in schedule must be carefully considered.

KEY CONCEPTS

While the project is progressing and being monitored (as discussed in Part Three of this book), the software project managers should be prepared to make any adjustments deemed necessary. These actions must be undertaken with the support of a broad consensus and with a sense of urgency. If the adjustments are made in response to some detected problem, then the project managers need to take the following actions:

1. Clearly state the problem.
2. Communicate the problem while working on potential solutions to it.
3. Seek out the root cause of the problem and relevant solutions.
4. Gain the necessary agreement of all stakeholders on the chosen solution.
5. Act on the solution.
6. Communicate on the action.
7. Report on the status of the problem's resolution.

The software project managers must also be aware of the need to implement a change management process when the adjustments needed are large.

Both planned and unplanned adjustments are possible. Planned reviews for adjustments should be performed at the end of each software development or service activity. Even the best-planned projects will need to make midcourse adjustments, however. Such unplanned adjustments usually stem from unexpected crises. Either planned or unplanned adjustments normally require the software project managers to consider three main parameters:

- Functionality
- Resources
- Schedule

Any change to one of these parameters necessitates a proactive consideration of the other two parameters. Usually some adjustments must be made to one or both of the other two parameters; this "ripple effect" poses a challenge for software project managers, who must gain the support of the project's stakeholders on all subsequent adjustments.

EXERCISES

1. List some of the items that you consider to be major adjustments and actions, and discuss which ones might spur resistance from your team.
2. Why is a sense of urgency important in making adjustments, especially unplanned ones? Describe the steps a manager may put in place to ensure that an adjustment is put in place to solve a need.
3. Why is there any such thing as a "planned adjustment"? Under what circumstances might you decide to skip any reviews for planned adjustments?
4. Discuss the relationship or possible association between risk items and unplanned adjustments.
5. Describe how change management is related to making adjustments.
6. Discuss the potential impact that a schedule change may have on resources and on functionality.
7. Consider a situation in which your team has just finished the design phase and is about to start coding. Your key applications designer just walked in and handed you a resignation notice. Describe what actions you would take and in what sequence. How would your adjustment actions differ if the person were the lead tester?

SUGGESTED READING

B. Boehm, "Industrial Software Metrics Top 10 List," *IEEE Software,* September 1987, 84–85.

F. P. Brooks, Jr., *The Mythical Man-Month,* Addison-Wesley, 1995.

H. E. Chambers and R. Craft, *No Fear Management: Rebuilding Trust, Performance, and Commitment in the New American Workplace,* St. Lucie Press, 1998.

W. G. Dyer, R. H. Daines, and W. C. Giauque, *The Challenge of Management,* Harcourt Brace Jovanovich, 1990.

D. A. Level, Jr., and W. P. Galle, Jr., *Managerial Communications,* Business Communications, 1988.

R. A. Paton and J. McCalman, *Change Management, a Guide to Effective Implementation,* 2nd ed., SAGE Publications, 2000.

Chapter 13

Release Management Council

Chapter Objectives

This chapter discusses the following concepts:

- How adjustments are made and actions are taken using a team management approach
- How a Release Management Council is established
- How a Release Management Council operates

THE TEAM MANAGEMENT APPROACH

Software projects are becoming ever larger and more complex, which has led to a new way of developing projects: through cooperative teams. Although some evidence indicates that collocated software development results in higher productivity and better schedules, many times the team members are located physically apart from one another. There is very little reason for all aspects of software projects to be completely managed by only a single person—that is, the software project manager—especially when the project is sourced from physically distant areas. The decision-making process would be much better, easier, and faster if the project management activities and management actions were also conducted by using a team approach, in which the knowledge of as many of the organization members as possible can be utilized. Even for small software projects, involving only five or six people, the project managers should still solicit as much of the team members' inputs as possible without imposing too much extra work on them.

All the stakeholders of a software project need to be included in the definition of the software project "team." In undertaking a team management approach, one must also consider the software project organization as a whole, in which people are divided into different groups by tasks and expertise. In such an organizational structure, there are typically specialized subgroups, such as the design or testing teams, and each of these subgroups is headed by a team leader. These subgroup team leaders are equivalent to the "player-coaches" on sports teams. Their knowledge, opinions, and cooperation should definitely be sought by the software project team.

For projects to be team-managed, a special team management group, called a *Release Management Council,* needs to be created from the sponsoring organization (e.g., executive management) and the project stakeholders. The members of this group must understand two important complementary principles: responsibility and authority. The team management approach has very little chance of success if one person is given all the responsibility for the software project but is given no authority to impose decisions on the rest of the team. The reverse situation is also undesirable: A person who has all the authority but shoulders no responsibility would most likely abuse that power. Ideally, every member of the software project team will be given clear responsibility and authority:

- *Responsibility* relates to the team members' accountability for project success or failure. That is, the group members must view the success of the project as a team goal.
- *Authority* relates to the power to make or participate in the making of decisions so as to achieve the team goals. These decisions must lead to actions.

Thus, for any person to bear a certain amount of responsibility, that individual must be given commensurate authority to take actions based on the monitored project status. The people who are asked to participate in joint (team) management of projects will, therefore, need both the responsibility and the authority to make the necessary project adjustments (see Chapter 12).

FORMULATING A RELEASE MANAGEMENT COUNCIL

Release Management Council is just a name given to a team of people, including the software project manager, who are charged with setting goals and policy, shepherding the project, ensuring that the best decisions are made on a timely basis, and making appropriate adjustments as necessary. The Release Management Council provides the project manager an explicitly designated and recognized support mechanism. It allows the project manager to formally practice team management.

> **Release Management Council** A group of project-related people from all areas of software development and support, including the software project manager, who are given both the responsibility and the authority to set goals, make decisions, take actions, and generally guide the project to its successful completion and product release.

The members of the Release Management Council are picked from different parts of the organization that represent the major activities that need to be coordinated through the project cycle. The Release Management Council still needs a person who guides and leads the group, however; this person is usually a midlevel manager or an experienced project manager. Typically, the members of the council are team leaders who represent the following project activity areas (see Figure 13.1):

- Customer requirements
- Design and architecture
- Implementation, coding, and information development
- Tools, techniques, and equipment support
- Testing
- Library and configuration management
- Quality assurance and measurements
- Customer support
- Finance
- Personnel
- Purchasing

As shown by the dotted lines in Figure 13.1, the finance and human resources representatives do not need to be full-time participants in the Release Management Council, but they are an important part of the decision-making group in that both finance and human resources affect the project resources. Representatives from marketing/sales, education, purchasing, and even customers may be asked to directly participate in the council if there is some specific topic that pertains to their areas. With the popularity of component-based development, purchasing also plays a vital role in many projects. They are situated in the "outer ring" in Figure 13.1.

Another exception is the representative from customer support, who may join the council when the testing phase of the project begins. Some

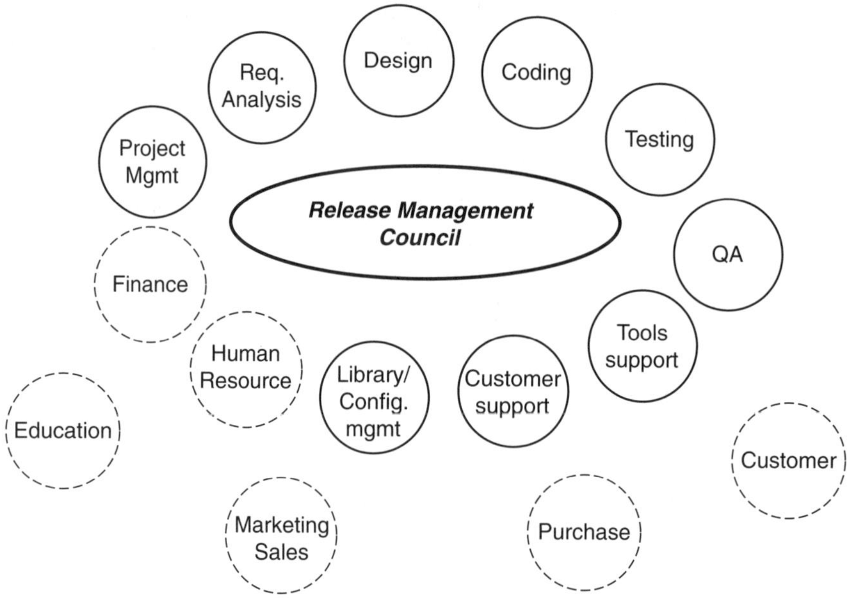

Figure 13.1 Team management through a Release Management Council

project managers have argued that the customer support representative should participate in the council from the project's inception so that they will be able to truly understand the customer requirements, the difficulties encountered in design and programming, and the results from testing.

The other members of the council should be full-time members who participate in the regular project status meetings. These individuals should not carry full-time development or other assignment workloads, because their duties on the Release Management Council will occupy a significant portion of their time. Occasionally, some of the council members may be involved in off-line meetings that deal with special-topic discussions and decision making. If the project is large enough, each Release Management Council member may be the team manager of each of the subgroups listed earlier. For smaller projects, one member may represent two or more groups, such as the tools support and configuration administration groups.

At the inception of a software project, if the team management concept is adopted, then the Release Management Council concept should be introduced as well. During the early stages of planning and organizing, representatives from the personnel and finance groups may play vital roles in the council. These individuals do not necessarily need to be their respective department managers. These departments are often organized in such a manner that the same individual participates in multiple projects. The person who is assigned to work on a particular project should also serve on the Release Management Council for that project.

The Release Management Council would then expand in size and in membership as the project enters the active performing phase and management enters the monitoring phase. The members need to be chosen carefully, and their task descriptions should be part of the members' normal personal performance plans. Because these individuals are asked to help in the broader project management decision making and coordination of the project, they must have a propensity for taking on issues beyond their own specialized fields of expertise or narrow departmental interests. They should also possess excellent communication and negotiation skills. If one needs help in obtaining these skills, many local and community colleges offer short, self-improvement courses in these topics.

THE RELEASE MANAGEMENT MODE OF OPERATION

As noted earlier, the mode of operation of a project utilizing the release management approach is that of shared responsibility and shared authority. As such, the Release Management Council members are also the stable and constant attendees of the regular project status meetings. They participate in all the following activities:

- Sharing the data and information
- Analyzing and evaluating the information
- Making decisions and resolving problems
- Communicating the information
- Coordinating their own groups' activities with other groups

Conducting the Release Management Council Meetings

For the regular project status meetings or any subsequent off-line meetings (which involve fewer people than the regular status meetings), the ideal situations are face-to-face, in physically collocated meetings. Of course, with today's virtual teams and remote locations, the Release Management Council members may very well be physically separated. If some of the council members start communicating with some other members without being 100%

inclusive of the entire group, then the software project managers need to be alert to the danger of formation of "subgroups" and cliques, especially if the subgroups and cliques form on the basis of physical locations. The Release Management Council meetings should be inclusive and mandatory for all members, with no substitutions allowed. In fact, where release management is practiced, the regular project status meetings should be similar to the Release Management Council meetings, according to the Release Management Council meeting agenda we discuss later. The Release Management Council covers more than just the status of the project, however; it is also involved in the planning, organizing, solution, and change decisions.

Minutes for each Release Management Council meeting should be promptly compiled and sent out to all council members. This document should summarize the project's current status and serve as a prompter to follow up on all open issues. These notes also provide an audit trail of the project status and the corresponding decision-making process.

The status of open issues from the past meeting should be one of the items reviewed at the beginning of each Release Management Council meeting. It is important not to let past items continue rolling unchecked. If the software project manager sees a particular item that is discussed repeatedly without any resolution, then it signals that the problem should be decomposed into smaller subproblems so that specific actions can be taken to resolve the subproblems. If the subproblems continue to be unresolved, then further division may be needed until resolution or progress toward resolution appears in the monitored data.

Release Management Council meetings should follow an agenda, preferably a fixed one. If the agenda is fixed, then it probably does not need to be circulated in advance. The agenda should include the following topics:

- The status of unresolved items
- The status of risk items
- New, but regular, tracking data collected for this period by attribute (such as schedule, functionality, quality, resources, and cost—the particular attributes targeted are predetermined each time the council meets)
- General inputs from the specialized areas represented by the various council members
- A short discussion and scheduling of any off-line meetings
- The generation of status and follow-up on open items

If the meetings follow the same pattern (i.e., a constant agenda) each time, then the speed with which they are conducted will pick up. The software project manager may choose to run the Release Management Council meetings or have a senior staff member conduct them. It is preferable to have the software project managers themselves run the meetings, with senior staff members performing the backup roles. That will also lend a certain amount of weight to the Release Management Council; accordingly, the meetings and the decisions, although jointly made, will be viewed with more respect and gain more acceptance by the project team as a whole.

Making Decisions about Product Release

One key role that the Release Management Council performs is to decide on the relative state of the product's or project's conclusion prior to the actual release of the software artifact to customers. This decision is a simple one if the project has been moving along and tracking close to the plan with a negligible number of adjustments. The decision becomes more difficult, however, when the project has been showing any of the following signs:

- Constant and erratic deviations from the plan, even though each problem is resolved
- Tracking to plan but with a continuous and widening deviation from the original plan, even though the deviation may still be within tolerable limits
- Tracking to plan all along, except for a sudden change just prior to release

The Release Management Council would have to make a final call prior to releasing the product to the customers. If there are reasons to believe that the product is not ready, then the council must hold the product release back. This can be a very painful decision because of its implications for the organization's revenues, costs, or reputation, as well as the council members' careers. The Release Management Council has several options that are available to it in this difficult situation; these options vary and include the following:

- Flat-out delay of the project with no release to customers
- Release parts of the product, delaying the problem areas until the problems are fixed
- Release the product to a small, controlled group of customers
- Release the product to everyone, but establish a superb customer support group

A flat-out delay means that the product is not ready and more time is needed for its development. All the negatives associated with a product release delay, such as customer fears about the product's quality and usability and competitors' innuendo about the lack of project control, should be expected. Software project managers should be prepared to tackle both the product problems, such as completing all the functions, and the associated problems, such as reestablishing customer support confidence in the product, created by the release delay.

The options of releasing only a portion of the product or releasing the product to only a controlled group of customers can lessen the brunt of the delay. There are many situations in which customers may be willing to take an imperfect release. Perhaps the problem areas may not be needed until later, when the problems will ideally be fixed in the final product. Alternatively, the customer may have planned an installation/training period prior to the actual usage of the software and be willing to take the not-so-perfect version first to get a head start. If a partial or controlled product release is planned, then the Release Management Council should always consult the sales and marketing groups—or even the customers directly. The council, which includes members of the organization's support group, must ensure that customer service representatives are aware of the conditions under which these customers are accepting the release, that the customer support group is properly and fully funded, and that the support resources are trained and on board for such situations.

Finally, some software project managers and the Release Management Council may choose to release the product anyway to the general customer set to establish a marketing presence for it if the problems in the product are deemed "non-life-threatening." In such a case, the organization must take anticipatory and preparatory actions to ensure that the customers will be properly supported. In particular, the funding of the support group will need to be substantial. Of course, there is always a risk of this strategy backfiring and creating an early image of low quality.

KEY CONCEPTS

Most software projects of significant size and complexity require the combined knowledge of the entire software project team. In those cases, team management is very much the preferred approach. For team management to succeed, the members of the software project team must exercise both of the following traits:

- Obtain authority to make decisions and take actions
- Accept responsibility for the outcome of the project

A management structure often utilized in software projects is the Release Management Council. The members of this group are chosen from the various stakeholders of the software project; customers may be represented on the council either directly or by personnel from the organization's requirements and support groups. The Release Management Council participates in monitoring the entire project, takes part in adjusting the project, and makes the final decision about releasing the product or project to customers. In situations where the established project goals are all met, the decision is a very easy one. When some of the goals are not met, however, it will require a concerted effort by the Release Management Council members to develop the potential options, assess the risks, make the adjustment decision, and take the necessary follow-up actions.

EXERCISES

1. Discuss the pros and cons of utilizing a team management approach versus a single project manager approach in a large, ill-defined software project versus a small, well-defined software project.
2. A Release Management Council may be formulated at various POMA stages of a software project. When would you establish such a group and why?
3. Imagine yourself as the leader of a Release Management Council. What words of guidance (in terms of responsibility and authority) would you say to the council members at the first meeting?
4. Discuss the various forms of release delays. Which one do you think is most costly and why?
5. If you had to limit the Release Management Council to only five members, which ones would you choose and why?
6. Consider a situation in which an irate customer calls in with a problem. Describe how software support personnel might usurp authority without being responsible.
7. How should you, as the software project manager, react to the situation stated in Exercise 6? Specifically, how would you explain the concepts of authority and responsibility to your team?

SUGGESTED READING

C. A. Bartlett and S. Ghoshal, "Building Competitive Advantage Through People," *MIT Sloan Management Review,* Winter 2002, 34–41.

M. E. Bays, *Software Release Methodology,* Prentice Hall, 1999.

A. V. Hoek and A. L. Wolf, "Software release management for component-based software," *Software–Practice & Experience,* vol. 33, issue 1, January 2003, 77–98.

R. Pressman, *A Manager's Guide to Software Engineering,* McGraw Hill, 1993.

S. D. Teasley, L. A. Covi, M. S. Krishnan, and J. S. Olson, "Rapid Software Development Through Team Collocation," *IEEE Transactions on Software Engineering,* July 2002, 671–683.

F. Tsui and L. Brooks, "Release Management of Non-Zero Defect Software," *Proceedings of the PSQT/PSTT South Conference,* March 2002.

Part Five

Additional Skills

Part Five discusses additional skills that are needed for effective project management. Some of these skills are generally applicable to all types of project management; others are more specific to the IT systems and software industry. The topics covered range from teamwork to early software effort estimation.

The information technology and software industry continues to be a growth industry. Part of its expansion involves the movement from being a product-oriented industry to being a more services-oriented industry. At the same time that this trend is occurring, a large amount of work is being outsourced. As noted earlier, some of this work is performed at physically remote locations—even in different countries. All of these trends have turned the task of managing teamwork into much more of a challenge.

Chapter 14 discusses software project teams as they pass through a three-stage life cycle—team formation, team development, and team maintenance. Although special software skills are undoubtedly needed in such a team, there are also some desirable personal traits for the team members to have, depending on the role each person is expected to play. This chapter may serve as an extension to Chapter 6 on Human Resources. It is a particularly important chapter for new project managers and project leaders. It is also a good review chapter for experienced managers.

As noted throughout this book, most projects inevitably go through some degree of change. The concept of change management in software projects is discussed in Chapter 15. Software is particularly likely to have requests for change because, as stated in the Introduction to this book, it is often thought of as just code. The control of all the software artifacts related to change requests needs to be managed successfully. Change management was briefly mentioned in Chapter 12. Chapter 15 may be viewed as a companion to Chapter 12 on Planned and Unplanned Adjustments and Actions.

Large software projects often have many complex prerequisite and corequisite relationships. The scheduling of a large number of such tasks may require a more organized effort than simply eyeballing the tasks. As a result, some scheduling techniques are a handy addition to the project management's bag of tools. Chapter 16 introduces the notion of a project's critical path and highlights different scheduling approaches focusing on early and late start times. By examining the "slack times" of the tasks on the noncritical path, project managers may be able to vary the scheduling of these tasks. Chapter 16 also provides definitions of PERT (a way to improve estimations) and the critical path method (a way to make trade-offs in reducing the critical path length). This chapter serves as a natural extension to Chapter 2 on Task Analysis.

The importance of understanding the requirements and implementing the Work Breakdown Structure (WBS) concept prior to putting together a plan and making commitments has been discussed earlier in this book. Because the software industry is still so young, however, many customers may not be experienced enough to appreciate the need for front-end work and, therefore, may demand an early rough estimate of the project effort. Naturally, such an estimate must be given with extreme care and plenty of caveats. Chapter 17 discusses ways to provide a general estimation of effort for software projects, along with an example from Barry Boehm's Constructive Cost Model (COCOMO) technique. The content of this chapter, effort estimation, may be viewed as an additional topic associated with Part One, the planning phase of POMA.

Project monitoring can be summarized as the management task of understanding the current project status and comparing it against the project plan. In Chapter 18, we present the Earned Value Management (EVM) technique, which is a well-defined way to collect, analyze, and express the status of a project. The EVM technique was originally introduced in U.S. government projects, but it is now employed by a much wider set of projects in various commercial industries. It provides a much-needed formality to project-status tracking.

Finally, Chapter 19 presents an introduction to the complex topic of purchasing and supply chain management. In today's systems and software projects, many resources are acquired externally. The tasks involved in purchasing these resources and managing the vendors and suppliers are explored in Chapter 19, which can be used as a companion to Chapter 4, where project resource planning is discussed.

Chapter 14

The Project Team

Chapter Objectives

This chapter discusses the following concepts:

- What the stages in the software project team life cycle are
- How a software project team is formed
- How a team can be developed so that it works effectively
- How a team is maintained

PROJECT TEAM LIFE CYCLE

In today's expansive technology world, very few software projects can be completed by individuals. This statement is especially relevant as the software industry grows to serve and cover more diversified areas. Although the life cycle of a team may be described in many ways, it typically goes through three stages:

1. Team formation
2. Team development
3. Team maintenance

It is important to recognize that a group of software specialists is just a group—not a real team. The group becomes a team through proactive efforts made by both the group members and the software project managers. Software project teams are not dramatically different from other project teams in that regard; all sorts of teams need forming, developing, and maintaining.

A variety of tasks are required of software project managers to form, develop, and maintain an effective software team. The amount of management attention needed differs at different stages of the team life cycle, as shown in Figure 14.1. In the initial stage, when the team is being formed, the software project managers will expend an ever-increasing amount of effort until the entire team is recruited.

As most of the team is brought on board, team building needs to start. Most of the team-building activities with which the team members are associated center on education and training in nontechnical areas such as:

- building trust
- negotiation skills
- listening skills
- accepting responsibilities
- responding to pressure

These are some of the most important characteristics that are needed for a "group" of people to function together and transform into a "team." The project managers must ensure that there is enough time in the project schedule reserved for this type of training.

Developing a new and growing team takes a relatively larger amount of energy and effort. Once the team is operational, effort is required for the continual nourishment and maintenance of the team until the project is completed; even a mature team requires ongoing maintenance. Thus the amount of effort is never zero.

TEAM FORMATION

Large, complex software projects require technology specialists, application subject area experts, customer support experts, and project management specialists, among other personnel. Obviously, one would like the software project

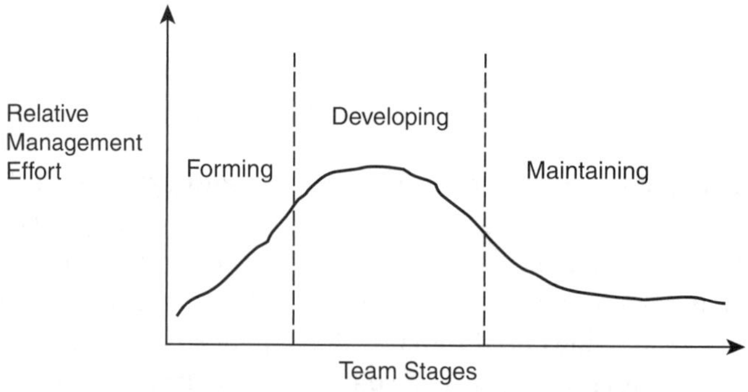

Figure 14.1 Management effort needed at various project team stages

team to include the best people from each of these areas. In reality, having "the best" from each area does not guarantee success for the project unless these experts work together effectively as a team.

A team is not created overnight. People cannot be just thrown together and then expected to quickly work out their differences by themselves. Sometimes one may get lucky and the people just fall into place and cooperate. Other projects might be delayed or fail utterly due to personnel conflicts. Each individual on the team may perform a specific software engineering task well. Because those tasks are interrelated, however, the software engineering specialists performing them are themselves interdependent. To work effectively, they must cooperate and follow a process that results in a synchronized team effort. It is the duty of the software project managers to provide the guidance and leadership needed to ensure that the team members share a common goal, follow an agreed-upon process, and uniformly work toward the successful completion of the project. Thus, a team is a group of people with complementing skills, operating with a high degree of interdependence and responsibilities, sharing a common set of goals, and working toward a well-defined set of objectives.

As described in Chapter 6, formation of the team—the human resources—is one of the first steps in planning and organizing a software project. The software project managers will first review the various tasks and decide on the skills required to complete those tasks. The candidates must initially possess these technical skills. In addition, the team members should possess several other behavioral characteristics, or "soft skills." It is important to state, at the outset, that no "perfect" person exists. Project managers should not be looking or waiting for such a mythical candidate.

Technical Software Skills

Let's look first at some of the technical skills required to carry out a software project.

> **Technical skill** A specialized skill in a subject that is needed to perform the activities in that subject domain. The skill usually requires in-depth knowledge and training in a scientific, engineering, or business discipline.

The following list identifies some general software development and support skills, one or more of which should be possessed by each of the team members. The skill areas include:

- Database design
- Detail design, programming, and debugging
- Network and telecommunications design

- Applications high-level design and architecture
- Requirements solicitation and specification
- Test design and test script writing
- Configuration and library control design and setup
- Tools setup and support
- Industry application subject matter design
- Customer problem analysis
- Customer problem resolution and follow-up

In addition to skills in these general areas, a complementary set of specific skills and experiences related to the tools that support these areas is needed. These particular technical skills focus on experience in vendor-specific programming-language compilers, debuggers, editors, configuration managers, code libraries, development platforms, and so on. The software project manager should be cognizant of the value of these tool-specific skills. The learning curve for highly complex tools may be prohibitively long for schedule-sensitive projects, so having a ready-made expert can be a major advantage.

Many times, a single person may possess several needed technical skills. When a person is brought on board, it should be clear what that person's role will be and which of that individual's skills will be primarily used in that role. On occasion, a person is brought on board to perform a particular role, such as that of the lead programmer, but he or she also possesses other useful skills, such as database design experience. Ideally, that person would be considered for a dual role and be willing to play the role of database design "backup." Unfortunately, many people with impressive skills come with impressive egos, too. The presence of two people who are highly skilled in the same area, such as database design, might very well turn out to be the source of great conflict and a detriment to the team. The software project manager must ensure that where skill overlap occurs, team members' responsibilities and roles are clear. He or she must continuously be on guard for any confusion among the team members. If any question about a responsibility or role crops up, it must be resolved immediately.

Soft Skills and Personal Traits

Aside from pure technical and applications skills directly related to the performance of the software project's tasks, managers should be looking for other characteristics, many of which are "soft skills," while forming the team. These personal traits might include the following:

- Personal ambition
- Level of commitment to the team concept and to team members

- Interpersonal communications skill
- Strongly held likes and dislikes or biases
- Amount of experience and type of experiences in working with others
- Attention to details
- Sense of urgency
- Energy level
- Major nonproject-related commitments
- Flexibility and maturity

Soft skill A nontechnical skill that can be utilized on multiple occasions and is not restricted to any specific domain. Examples of soft skills include listening and presentation skills.

These personal traits are often subtle, yet play a vital role in determining the success of a team. Traditionally, software project managers tended to focus on the technical skills and associated technical experiences of non-management personnel. As a result, these soft skills and personal characteristics were sometimes overlooked. Many successful managers have, at times, temporarily sacrificed team morale and put up with a team member who has some negative personal traits. Usually, this situation cannot continue very long without the project manager eventually taking some corrective action. A team member who places his or her personal ambition before the team's goal, for example, may very well kill a project. Similarly, a person who is more committed to his or her tennis game or to some other avocation than to the project and to his or her professional career may be a drag to the overall project.

Every team needs a mix of personalities–strong, ambitious leaders as well as less ambitious followers–for the team as a whole to work smoothly. This balance of skills and characters needs to be taken into account while the team is being formed. Throughout this process, however, the software project manager should bear in mind that the initial recruiting of the team members is based on a best "guess" and is no guarantee of later success. Even the best-planned team can go awry if the initial assessment of a seemingly "perfect" candidate turns out to be wrong. Also, the new member may have had some erroneous expectations of the organization, which can later cause disappointments and degradation in performance.

TEAM DEVELOPMENT

Once a team is put together, it should not be left in isolation to grow, change, and adapt to the changing environment in which the team must operate. The evolution of a group of people into a smoothly functioning team takes a long time. The natural process is often characterized by trial and error, with progress occurring in fits and starts. Such a slow process is often painful and sometimes unsuccessful. We need to clearly identify a path for team members to resolve their differences that don't seem resolvable among themselves. This provides:

- a defined way to address problems quickly
- a better understanding of the levels of authority that can be brought in to help

To smooth the way, the software project manager may need to intervene in the team's adjustment process. Necessary adjustments might even include the extreme actions of dismissing some participants and changing the team members. The following list identifies some key activities in which the project managers should be actively involved so as to help the team evolve gracefully. These items will require constant management attention through both formal and informal monitoring techniques discussed in Chapter 9. Many of the tasks will be conducted through informal conscientious socializing. The activities are not listed in any priority order, as they are all important.

- Ensuring that an ample amount of communication is taking place
- Ensuring that the members are treating one another with respect
- Ensuring that there is clear understanding of each person's assignment and role
- Ensuring that the team is not harboring a chronic laggard
- Ensuring that all team members understand and support the team and project goals
- Ensuring that the team members are following the agreed-upon process

To promote effective team building and development, the software project managers need to bring the members together and review these topics at the inception of the project and as new members come on board. One of the more popular methods that managers utilize to promote team building is to sponsor a one- or two-day, off-site meeting. Typically, a motivational speaker is brought in, team games such as softball are played, individual character tests are given to all team members, and all personnel attend lectures on character traits. Sometimes, the team is asked to jointly perform a potentially dangerous task, under the auspices of an expert, such as climbing a cliff. The sharing of a risky experience is meant to create a strong bond through trust, ensuring that the team members will later appreciate and understand the need for interdependence in their software project.

In addition, team members' behavior needs to be continuously monitored through the project. The software project managers should perform conscientious socializing with the team members and engage in informal data gathering to pick up any nascent signs of team harmony or disorder (see Chapter 9). Such a sign may be as simple as a nonreturned e-mail. Disharmony in communication usually signals that something is not working quite right. Perhaps a team member is just temporarily overwhelmed with his or her workload–or maybe the problem is more dire.

With the advent of remote and virtual software project teams, communication is emerging as a major source of team-related problems. If the simple courtesy of returning an e-mail or a phone call is not part of the individual's working etiquette, then that person may need management counseling on "respect for the other team members," "sense of urgency," or "communications skills." This counseling of employees is a key project management task that requires some experience on the part of the project managers. It must be guided by a single motive: to help the individual and, thereby, create a better-functioning team. The offending team member must always be given an opportunity to improve and change.

Repeated emphasis of team goals, team harmony, and clarification of the roles of the individual team members is a task that some may view as "nagging." All software project managers need to understand that some aspects of management do border on constant complaining. At the same time, this trait of continuous and tenacious focusing on details is one of software project managers' major assets.

Sometimes the notion of team cohesion and spirit is stretched excessively. Perhaps more capable members are carrying one or a small number of team members and performing their responsibilities. Several reactions to this situation are possible:

- The team does not seem to mind carrying the laggard(s).
- The team minds the situation but does not want any change.
- The team minds the situation and is waiting for management actions to fix it.

In all cases, the laggard needs to be counseled by the project manager. That person should be asked to pick up his or her part of the team's responsibility. In the case in which the team does mind the situation, the project manager must "fix" matters or risk having a demoralized team. This resolution may require further training of the team member, if a skill problem is involved. A change of assignment may be another possibility. Ultimately, the potential solution may include the dismissal of the offending team member if all efforts to improve the situation fail.

	Team members concerned	Team members not concerned
Existence of a personal trait problem	Manager must take immediate action	Manager must consider some future action
Nonexistence of personal trait problems	Manager must monitor continuously for problem	Manager may monitor intermittently

Figure 14.2 Problem–action handling matrix

The problem–action handling matrix in Figure 14.2 describes what the project manager should consider as potential actions when faced with some personal trait problem. Let's look at the matrix and the associated actions, starting with the upper-left corner and proceeding clockwise. As stated earlier, when there is a problem and team members are concerned, the situation must not be ignored. The specific action taken by the manager depends on the problem at hand. At a minimum, the manager must investigate and understand the problem, develop a solution for it, discuss the solution with the offender, explain the solution to the affected team members, and implement the solution.

In the second scenario, even if the team is not concerned with the problematic situation at the present time, the project manager must consider some future action to resolve it. Once again, the specific resolution of the problem depends on the type of problem. In extreme situations, it may include the dismissal of the employee from the next phase of the project. Such problems, if neglected for a long period, could eventually affect the morale of the other team members.

The last two cases, in which there is no problem, just requires continuous monitoring of different degrees. The project manager should always be perceptive to changes in the team, but not turn this monitoring into an obsession.

Continuous monitoring and adjustments are necessary to mold any group of skilled people into a smoothly functioning team. The team members themselves must diligently try to work out their differences. The project managers, in turn, must give the team members a certain amount of time for them to become acclimated with one another and with the team culture; if this step is omitted, every little problem could escalate into a large one and eventually wind up in the software project managers' offices. By working out some of the small differences by themselves, the team members will become bound together, resulting in a much stronger team.

All teams take effort and time to formulate and develop. Some project managers are so highly cognizant of the value of a harmonious team that they try to recruit the same group of people whenever they move on to a new project or to a new environment. This trend is evidenced in many corporate cultures where new CEOs and senior managers are chosen from within the company to preserve the existing team harmony and team culture. Of course, a contrary school of thought advocates bringing in new blood so that the team or the company will not become complacent and noncompetitive.

TEAM MAINTENANCE

Once the team is functioning, continual nourishing of it is still required. Effective software project managers are continuously involved in the following team maintenance activities:

- Reward
- Punishment
- Attrition
- Growth

Rewarding Team Members

When the project is progressing well and milestones are being met, the team members need to have positive feedback. Giving awards is one of the most pleasant tasks for managers, yet somewhat tricky. Although the project success is attributable to the team effort, it may also owe its success to a few individuals' extra effort. Recognizing those individuals is important, but the software project managers should always acknowledge the efforts of the team as a whole.

For example, prior to handing out any individual award, the significance of all the players should be emphasized and the interdependence of the team members should be brought out. The individual award should be stated as an acknowledgment of individual effort made above and beyond the team effort. Such a reward-giving event should be public, as any award handed out in private will always be viewed with suspicion of favoritism.

Punishing Team Members

Although it is important to bring the entire team into the reward spotlight, the reverse situation is a little different. When an individual's performance or behavior requires counseling, the software project manager should not bring the entire team together and speak vaguely about the concern. Rather, the project manager should bring the individual into the manager's office, be very clear about the problem, and offer the individual the opportunity to change and improve. In these counseling sessions, the project manager should stay focused on the individual's problem and not wander into discussions about the team. If multiple problems exist, it is best to address each negative issue separately. However, all problems need to be resolved as soon as possible.

For example, we often encounter problems of developers not responding promptly to problems discovered during testing. If someone is either deliberately being unresponsive or just being slow, that person needs to be brought in for counseling quickly, before the problem queue becomes so deep that it jeopardizes the test schedule. The resolution of the problem, depending on the cause, may range from a private warning, to a shift in the workload, to a change in assignment, to dismissal of the team member.

Handling Team Attrition

No matter how well a project is working and how happy an individual is, there is always the possibility of attrition. If a person has chosen to leave the project, for whatever reason, the project manager should offer him or her the opportunity of an exit interview with another manager (e.g., the human resources manager). This exit interview will allow the departing person to express more candidly the reasons for leaving. From the exit interview feedback, the software project manager may be able to gather some information relevant to improving the team. If there is truly some room for improvement of the team, the project manager will have to take the appropriate action.

Often, the departing employee's criticism relates to some perceived unfairness or favoritism. This type of feedback is crucial because other team members may feel the same way but not be willing to express their views openly. Most people conclude that favoritism is exactly that, and cannot be changed. The manager needs to first ascertain the truth of the "accusation." If the allegation is true, then he or she should change the situation starting with an apology. If it is not true, then the manager must decide how to prevent others from developing the same false impression and take appropriate preventive action.

In any event, the departure of a team member should always be shared with the rest of the team. In addition, any planned action to replace that person needs to be shared with the team. The team should never be left with a feeling of the unknown. Such a feeling will sometimes stimulate false fear, especially if the individual who left is a key team member. If the departure of a person emanated from some real problem, as long as it is nonpersonal, that problem should be shared with the team. In the same breath, the project manager must offer up how he or she is planning to handle the problem.

Team Member Growth

As new members are brought on board due to team growth or replacement, the software project manager must make a special effort to explain the team composition, the underlying dynamics, and the expected rules of behavior, along with the formal process and procedures followed by the team. One potential way to acclimate the new member to the team is to tag the new member to an existing member. This mentoring arrangement often will accelerate the new member's introduction to the project and to the team. For this mentoring mechanism to work effectively, the aforementioned tagging of each new employee to an existing team member should be done in a formal manner. That is, the mentor needs to be trained in the skills of mentoring, the workload of the mentor should be reduced, and the mentoring period should be specified. The new member should also be formally informed of the role of the mentor and the expectations for the new employee during the mentoring period should be outlined explicitly.

As a part of efforts to grow the team, the senior members of the team should continuously be given leadership roles such as the mentoring of new and less experienced team members. Other methods of developing and cultivating the team members may include providing special assignments to help other projects, short-term assignments as assistants to senior management, and sabbaticals to train in new technology or new processes.

■ KEY CONCEPTS

Project managers play a key role in the formation, development, and maintenance of a project team. The relative effort expended by the manager is skewed toward the periods involving the formulation and the development of a project team.

The group of individuals assigned to a project becomes a team through proactive efforts made by both the group members and the software project manager. In the formation phase, team members are selected on the basis of both technical skills and behavioral qualifications ("soft skills").

Once a team is put together, it needs time to evolve into a smoothly functioning unit. Along the way, the software project manager may need to intervene in the team's adjustment process and definitely needs to monitor its performance. The important activities of monitoring and adjusting can be translated into a more general problem–action handling matrix, which can help the project manager decide which actions to take.

Maintenance of the project is essential to ensure that the team continues to function smoothly. Team maintenance activities include those focused on doling out rewards, meting out punishments, handling attrition, and providing for team members' growth.

EXERCISES

1. From the soft skills and personal traits list, pick three traits that you believe are especially important for teamwork and explain why you think they are more important than the other choices. Would your list be different if you were only concerned with individual performance?
2. Discuss how much time you, as a project manager, would be willing to spend discussing (1) the departure of a team member and (2) the addition of a new team member. List the items that you would discuss in each occasion.
3. Refer to the problem–action handling matrix (Figure 14.2); what are some of the "immediate" actions that you might take if a problem arises and the team members are concerned? For the case in which the team members are not concerned, what are some future actions that you might consider taking?
4. Briefly describe the three stages in the project team lifestyle and discuss one item in each stage that may present difficulties to a project manager.
5. Consider the situation in which the project team is jointly performing coding and testing. Describe a situation in which you believe an individual member deserves an award and a situation where an individual deserves a punishment.
6. Give an example where team members are not treating each other with respect. What are some of the choices of action for management?
7. What is the difference between a group of professional software engineers and a team of software engineers? (Review the list of actions that managers must ensure during the team development period.)

SUGGESTED READING

A. T. Cobb, *Leading Project Teams: An Introduction to the Basics of Project Management and Project Team Leadership,* Sage Publications, 2006.

R. Cross, W. Baker, and A. Parker, "What Creates Energy in Organizations?" *MIT Sloan Management Review,* Summer 2003, 51–56.

W. S. Humphrey, *Introduction to the Team Software Process,* Addison-Wesley, 2000.

W. Humphrey, *The Team Software Process,* Technical Report CMU/SEI-2000-TR-023, November 2000.

R. B. Hyman, "Creative Chaos in High Performance Teams: An Experience Report," *Communications of the ACM,* October 1993, 57–60.

D. Phillips, *The Software Project Manager's Handbook,* IEEE Computer Society, 2000.

K. A. Smith, *Project Management and Teamwork,* McGraw Hill, 2000.

S. D. Teasley, L. A. Covi, M. S. Krishnan, and J. S. Olson, "Rapid Software Development Through Team Collocation," *IEEE Transactions on Software Engineering,* July 2002, 671–683.

Chapter 15

Change Control

Chapter Objectives

This chapter discusses the following concepts:

- How the changes that characterize all software processes can be managed
- What impact analysis is
- Which techniques are used to decide on change request denial or acceptance
- How the cumulative effects of changes can be handled effectively

It is well recognized that software projects are particularly prone to changes, in large part because there is a general belief that software can be easily modified. This maleability is in fact both a strength and a weakness: Changes may be made in software, but must be implemented with care. The worst situation occurs when changes are allowed without proper control. To prevent this type of "change control chaos," the software project team should develop and follow a change control process.

Change control process A set of information and a sequence of activities used in the tracking and managing of a change request from its inception to its closure.

The processes, methodologies, and tools needed to manage change requests must be designed ahead of time. The process and people resources needed as part of the management of change requests, described in this chapter, should also be set aside, trained, and properly included in the project plan and budget.

AN EXAMPLE CHANGE REQUEST PROCESS

Every change to the product or to the process should start with a baseline, which represents the first, formally defined version of a product or process, and go through a change control process. The product change control process depicted in Figure 15.1 will be used in this chapter as the basis for discussing the different factors that influence how changes are managed within an organization.

The change request may come from anywhere, but it needs to be formalized so that it can be traced back to its source, if that step becomes necessary. A change request form, which represents a formal method for submitting a change request, may be a paper-based form or part of an online system. At a minimum, it should include the following items:

- The requester's name
- Date of the request
- Request description
- Reason for the request
- Priority of the request
- Preferred date of completion

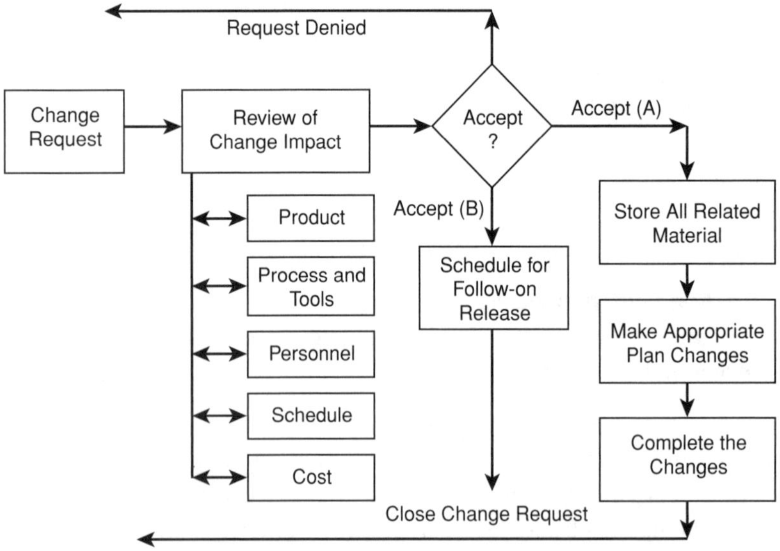

Figure 15.1 Product change control process

- Funding source for the request
- Areas known to be affected by the requested change

Once the request form is filled out, it should be submitted to a "catcher." The catcher is a handler who may be on-line or off-line, but in any event is someone who should be designated to formally take charge of the request. This handler might be the software project manager, the Release Management Council, or a special change request administrator.

Upon its submission, the change request needs to be reviewed and assessed in terms of its implications for other parts of the software project. The change impact analysis (discussed in detail in the next section) will list and describe the items that are affected, including the following areas of consideration:

- Schedule
- Cost
- Human resources
- Processes and tools
- Product content and size
- Product marketing strategy

Although Figure 15.1 does not show this particular situation, sometimes the change control process also needs to take into account how a change request affects the customers' work flow and work environment. For example, suppose a change request for a data entry screen asks for the inclusion of a new input field. Imagine that this new input field requires the person who keys in the data to look up some information if the default data defined for that field do not apply. Then an additional procedure explaining where to look up information and how to pick the information to enter needs to be defined and made available to the users of the modified data entry screen. Thus this change request to the software requires an associated modification in the users' work procedure that must be defined, documented, and disseminated.

CHANGE IMPACT ANALYSIS

Software impact analysis identifies the effects of a software change request. As noted earlier, these effects may manifest themselves in a variety of areas. Each impact needs to be somehow quantified and prioritized. That is, a measurement scheme must be designed such that each change request may be gauged in relation to other change requests. Examples of quantifying some of the impacted areas follow:

- A *schedule impact* may be designated with values ranging from 1 to 4, where 1 means a schedule impact of one to two days, 2 means an impact of one to two weeks, 3 means an impact of one to two months, and 4 means an impact exceeding two months.
- A *personnel impact* may also be designated with values ranging from 1 to 4, where 1 means a slight assignment change to one person, 2 means two to three people are involved in the change, 3 means one-fourth of all team members are involved in the change, and 4 means half or more of the team members are involved in the change effort.
- A *cost impact* is very key to the decision process and may be directly quantified, by using the schedule impact, the personnel impact, and the conversion of those impacts into dollars. For example, a schedule impact of 1 and a personnel impact of 2 would convert to (2 days $\times$ 3 people) = 6 people-days of impact. This value may be further converted to (6 people-days $\times$ z \$/person-day) = 6z dollar of cost impact. The computation of cost impact with a change request that has a personnel impact value of 3 would be a little more complex in that the term "one-fourth of all team members" needs to be converted to a numerical figure first.

In the above examples, note that the assigned numerical values all increase as the impact to the project is perceived to increase. This uniformity makes the computation and the decision process for acceptance a little easier. The actual measurement scheme may be designed differently, with the particular metrics depending on the type of software project at hand. After each impacted area is quantified, the change requests can be compared by area and possibly ordered.

Furthermore, each impacted area may be assigned a numerical weight. The aggregate or the weighted average of the impacted areas may serve as a single index to represent the change request. Then a cut-off criterion needs to be defined, and all those requests that fall within the cut-off criterion may be accepted. The definition of a cut-off criterion may be as simple as "the requests with the top five indices." Such a prioritization scheme makes the decision-making process for accepting (or rejecting) a change request more objective and organized. The actual cut-off criteria would depend on many parameters, including the past history of the project team and the project managers' experiences.

CHANGE REQUEST DENIAL OR ACCEPTANCE

Based on the impact analysis and the review of the results, the project managers must decide whether to accept the change request or to deny it. In the event that the request is denied, that fact must be communicated back to the requestor, along with a reason for the rejection. The denied change request itself may or may not be stored and kept for future usage.

If the change request is accepted through the Accept (A) path shown in Figure 15.1, then all of the affected items need to be marked and assembled. In addition, a plan for performing the change must be formulated. The actual change activity is then scheduled, performed, and tracked to completion. Upon completion, the change request is closed and the requestor is notified of the new status. A typical accepted change request that goes through this path might be a customer requirement change to an input field size or format caused by a change in the customer's business. For example, in the merger of two companies, often the product codes of the merged companies would need to be expanded. This will prompt a change request related to the input field size or input format for the order processing software, and this change request will have to be immediately accepted, quickly worked on, and brought to closure. Such a change request, which has a high business impact, will definitely be under tight change control.

It is also possible to accept a change request, but not be able to accommodate it within the current release date or budget. In that case, the Accept (B) path in Figure 15.1 is taken and the change request is held for scheduling into a future release. The requestor is informed of the decision and given a probable time frame for the earliest release that may contain the requested change. An example of an accepted change request that is held for a future release is the case in which a small number of influential customers request an extension to an existing function. This type of change request will usually be delayed and put into a plan for implementation with a set of change requests that affect the same software areas (e.g., design and code).

The complete change management may be performed via an on-line work-flow tool—usually a proprietary system built with some collaborative processing tool such as IBM's Lotus Workflow—that moves the work order from one area to another, from one status to another, and from inception to end. If such an on-line tool does not exist, then the organization must maintain a "paper trail" for the change from inception to closure. This information should be placed into a file so that it can serve as a repository for consultation and analysis of future change requests. Alternatively, a configuration management tool such as Merant's PVCS or Atria Software's Clear Case may be used to help manage the changes. (Clear Case was later acquired by Rational, which in turn was acquired by IBM.) A configuration management process tool, as mentioned in Chapters 4 and 7, allows the tracking and managing of all pieces of the software artifacts. As such, it can readily be applied to change request control.

CUMULATIVE EFFECTS OF CHANGES

A small change in a software artifact can have huge ramifications for both the end product and the work effort required to develop that product. A typical small change in a database field, for example, might generate the following changes:

- Design and code changes to all areas that utilize that field
- Modifications to all affected help scripts and user documentation materials
- Reviews of all changes
- Development of new test scenarios and test scripts
- Running of new test scripts and re-running the old test scripts
- Fixes for any related problems from the tests
- Updates to the library and change control tools
- Locking and promotion of the successfully changed material
- Communication of the completed change to all interested parties

Even experienced software engineers are often surprised by how much effort is required to complete a seemingly simple change. The complications come not necessarily from the initial change itself, but from the "ripple effect"—the effect of related work that can dramatically affect both schedules and costs. It has been said that a change request may lead to one line of altered code but result in one week of effort to complete that change request. Imagine the cost of that one line of modified code—and how incredible it would sound to the original requestor. The software service support personnel and quality assurance personnel will be painfully familiar with the similar way in which costs can balloon when a small fix needs to be introduced into the product.

How Hard Can It Be to Make a Simple Change?

The author's personal experience as a manager for IBM's JES3 product offers a good example of how an apparently simple change can lead to unexpected complications. JES3 was the I/O component of IBM's MVS operating system. A change request that required modification of about six lines of code ended up taking approximately two months of work. The changes spanned several modules, and they affected the interfaces to both the database product and the network product. This multiple-product effect necessitated performing regression tests over both the database and the network products. The two months of work across three product organizations meant that a change request that required only six lines of code change cost approximately $50,000! Interestingly enough, this lesson seems to get relearned with every new generation of software engineers and project managers.

Although the time and effort spent in analyzing an individual change and its consequences may not be a problem, the cumulative effects of a continuum of change requests can be staggering, evolving into a full-time job for a small group of people. Furthermore, to fully and accurately assess the change request impact, the team managing the change process must have good knowledge of the product and all items associated with it. Most software projects are not well equipped to handle the extra workload required to even assess these requests. The required work for change management is similar to that involved in requirements management, another process whose complexity is often underestimated. It takes a very disciplined software project management team to insist on proper change management. And insist they must.

Another important aspect of change requests that the software project managers need to be aware of is the requests' psychological effect on the team. If there is a cyclical and flip-flopping chain of change requests made, the project team may decide not to perform any changes until the requestor can make up his or her mind. Even when the changes are not flip-flopping but seem to be concentrated in some specific functional area, the feeling of instability will sometimes cause the project team to feel helpless and demoralized. This kind of vacillation occurs often when the team is developing software artifacts that will enter a new or unfamiliar marketplace that both the customers and the requirements analysts are still exploring.

In this type of situation, the software project manager must step outside of the normal change management process (i.e., outside the process depicted in Figure 15.1) and ask for a review of the reasons for such a large number of change requests. Such a review may be undertaken by the Release Management Council (discussed in Chapter 13) or, if it is requirements-related, by the Software Product Management Board (discussed in Chapter 2). It is the software project manager's responsibility to shield some of these change request activities from the mainstream project that is under development. This step, which is not part of the normal change control, is performed at the project manager's discretion.

KEY CONCEPTS

Software projects are particularly prone to changes, in large part because there is a general belief that software can be easily modified. In reality, changes may be made in software, but must be implemented with care. To prevent change requests from wreaking havoc on the software project team, all change requests should be managed through a change control process.

The following impacts of a change must be considered when one is making the acceptance or rejection decision:

- Schedule
- Cost
- Human resources
- Processes and tools
- Product content and size
- Product marketing strategy

Furthermore, the project managers must consider the cumulative effects of multiple changes that result from one change request. The complications come not necessarily from the initial change itself, but from the "ripple effect"—the effect of the related work that can dramatically affect both schedules and costs.

EXERCISES

1. How could the product strategy and market share impact be folded into the impact analysis of a change request? Devise a metric that could be included in the cost.

2. Assess the resource implications of an organization that receives 50 to 100 change requests per month versus that of an organization that receives 5 to 10 change requests per month. Discuss what types of adjustments a software project manager would have to make as the software change requests vary so dramatically.
3. Design a change request form and explain the relevance of each field on the form.
4. Consider the change request form designed for Exercise 3 and designate those fields that represent key areas that should be included as criteria for an acceptance or rejection decision. Discuss why you chose those fields as part of the decision criteria.
5. Using the change request form designed for Exercise 3, trace a request through the product change control process diagram (Figure 15.1). Indicate how the form may be used to track the work flow through the change control process, modifying it as necessary.
6. Consider the situation where your team has just completed the design of a small on-line purchasing application, much like a book-ordering application from amazon.com. The marketing organization has decided to expand into Central and South America and is requesting that there be a Spanish version of this software. Discuss all the items that your team needs to consider and simulate an impact analysis for this request.

SUGGESTED READING

M. E. Bays, *Software Release Methodology,* Prentice Hall, 1999.

R. T. By, "Organizational Change Management: A Critical Review," Journal of Change Management, Vol. 5, Issue 4, December 2005, 369–380.

E. H. Bersoff, "Elements of Software Configuration Management," *IEEE Transactions on Software Engineering,* January 1984, 79–87.

S. A. Bohner, "Impact Analysis in the Software Change Process: A Year 2000 Perspective," *International Conference on Software Maintenance Proceedings,* IEEE Computer Society Press, 1996, 42–51.

Clear Case User Manual, Atria Software, 1992.

PVCS tool, www.merant.com.

Chapter 16

Task Scheduling

Chapter Objectives

This chapter discusses the following concepts:

- How tasks are represented in tabular and graphical formats
- What critical and noncritical paths are
- How forward- and backward-pass scheduling methods—both early start/early finish and late start/late finish—are used
- How total slack time and free slack time are computed
- How the Program Evaluation and Review Technique (PERT) can improve estimation
- What the critical path method (CPM) is
- How a calendar schedule for the project can be created

Chapter 16 should be viewed as introducing a set of techniques that may be applied to and enhance task analysis, a topic that was discussed in detail in Chapter 2.

TASK SEQUENCE AND EFFORT REPRESENTATION

Software projects are composed of multiple, differing tasks that require different skills to complete. Nevertheless, all tasks share at least two basic characteristics:

- Required effort in terms of some unit, such as person-days, needed to complete each task
- A specified order for processing the tasks

Table 16.1 Task Sequence/Effort Table

Tasks	Immediate prerequisite tasks	Effort (Person-days)
A	None	9
B	A	5
C	A	7
D	B,C	11
E	D	8

Some person or a group of people must perform each task. In software activity scheduling, the tasks should initially be broken down to a level where each task may be assigned to one person. This strategy allows the effort to be measured in terms of person-days or person-months. The tasks are also ordered in that some tasks will have prerequisite tasks that must be completed prior to their initiation. Tasks sometimes may be carried out in parallel. In that case, the parallel tasks are independent of each other and thus may be performed simultaneously.

The project tasks may be represented in a simple table like Table 16.1.

The project represented in Table 16.1 is composed of five tasks: A, B, C, D, and E. There is a sequential order of tasks starting with A. Tasks B and C may be performed in parallel after the completion of A. However, Task D cannot start until both B and C are completed. The last task, E, cannot start until D is completed.

The total effort required is 40 person-days. If each task is assigned to one person and performed without any parallelism, then this project would take a total of 40 elapsed days. In project management, of course, one is always looking to minimize the schedule. Thus Tasks B and C may be assigned to two different people and performed in parallel. This strategy will shrink the total time for the project to 35 days, because Task C still takes 7 days even though it overlaps with the 5 days required for Task B.

This tabular representation of tasks may be easily converted into a graphical task network representation. A graph is commonly defined as a set of nodes and edges where an edge connects two nodes. Our graphical network representation of tasks here may be viewed as a directed graph. For deeper mathematical discussions on graphs, ordering, and algorithms, please consult Donald Knuth's book listed in the "Suggested Reading" section of this chapter. There are really two paths if one were to represent the project in

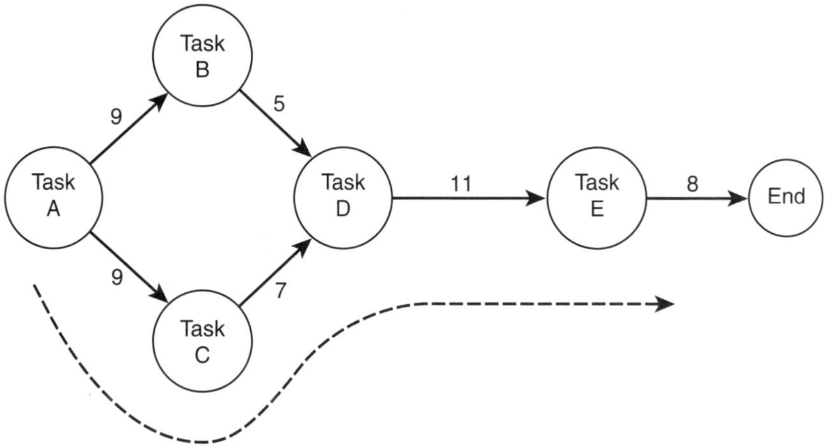

Figure 16.1 Graphical representation of tasks from Table 16-1

a graphical task network form as in Figure 16.1. This diagram assumes that Tasks B and C are carried out in parallel, and the task network representation depicts the task ordering a little more clearly. The tasks are labeled inside the nodes, and the effort required to complete each task is placed on the arrow after that task. Thus the 9 days on the arrow leading from Task A to Task B represents the 9 person-days effort required to complete Task A. A special node, End, is included to accommodate the task effort arrow of Task E.

CRITICAL VERSUS NONCRITICAL PATHS

The dotted line in Figure 16.1 shows the longer of the two paths–that is, the maximum-length path for this particular project. The maximum-length path in a task network is also called the critical path. The critical path is defined as the path that takes the most time units to complete.

Critical path The path that takes the most time units to complete.

As an example, consider the tasks in Figure 16.1 as program modules that must be coded and unit-tested prior to the beginning of functional testing. Although modules A, B, C, D, and E must all be completed before the functional testing starts, the path that includes program modules A, C, D, and E is the critical path because it is the longer of the two paths. Any delay in completing module A, C, D, or E will delay the start of functional testing. In contrast, a small delay in completing module B (not more than two units) will not delay the start of the functional testing.

The required total elapsed time for the project may be estimated by adding together the effort estimates of all tasks lying on the critical path. This summation answers the question, "How long will the project take?" In the case represented by Figure 16.1, the dotted-line path requires 35 days, so the project will require 35 elapsed time units at minimum.

The tasks that reside on the critical path are called critical activities or critical tasks. For the project managers to reduce the total elapsed time for the project, at least one of the critical tasks must be completed in less time. Similarly, any delay to or lengthening of a critical task's time of completion will elongate the critical path, thereby delaying the project's completion.

Critical task (critical activity) A task that resides on the critical path.

There may be more than one path that is the longest path—that is, there may be several "longest" paths that are equal in terms of required elapsed time. Thus the project may have multiple critical paths. In the case of multiple critical paths, a delay of a critical activity on any one of the multiple critical paths will delay the entire project. If the elongated critical task is unique to one of the multiple critical paths, then the result of that task elongation is the creation of a new unique critical path.

A noncritical path is shorter than the critical path in that the sum of the efforts of all activities on a noncritical path is less than the total effort for the critical path. In Figure 16.1, the only noncritical activity is Task B, because it is the only activity that resides on a noncritical path and does not simultaneously reside on a critical path.

Noncritical path Any path that is not a critical path and thus takes less effort (e.g., time) to complete than the critical path.

Noncritical task (noncritical activity) Any activity that resides on a noncritical path, which may accept some delay in completion, but does not also reside on a critical path. Note that a task that resides on both a critical path and a noncritical path is a *critical* task.

Thus the activities residing on a noncritical path are defined as noncritical tasks. These noncritical activities may be delayed somewhat without affecting the actual project completion time. Consider the noncritical Task B in Figure 16.1. Its completion may be delayed up to two days without affect-

Table 16.2 Early Start/Early Finish Scheduling

Tasks	Task precedence	Task length	Earliest possible start time (ES)	Earliest possible finish time (EF)
A	None	9	0	9
B	A	5	9	14*
C	A	7	9	16
D	B,C	11	16	27
E	D	8	27	35

ing the project completion time. In scheduling the complete set of project tasks, there is usually some room for setting the start and end times of these noncritical tasks without affecting the project as a whole.

FORWARD- AND BACKWARD-PASS SCHEDULING OF TASKS

There are two major ways to schedule activities:

- Early start (ES) and early finish (EF)
- Late start (LS) and late finish (LF)

Consider Table 16.2, which is a continuation of the previous example. The tasks are now shown with their earliest possible start time (ES) and corresponding earliest possible finish time (EF), while preserving the existing precedence and order relationships.

In early start/early finish scheduling, a forward pass is taken through the project tasks. All tasks are started as early as possible and thus all end as early as possible. Table 16.2 begins by scheduling Task A, which takes 9 time units to complete. Note that while Task B is actually completed at time unit 14 (shown with an asterisk in Table 16.2), the beginning of Task D must wait for the completion of Task C, which is not finished until time unit 16. Thus starting Task B later does not affect the project as a whole. Delaying Task B's completion by two or fewer time units will not affect this project's overall schedule.

The same project may be scheduled with the late start/late finish approach, as shown in Table 16.3.

Table 16.3 Late Start/Late Finish Scheduling

Tasks	Task precedence	Task length	Late start time (LS)	Late finish time (LF)
A	None	9	0	9
B	A	5	11*	16
C	A	7	9	16
D	B,C	11	16	27
E	D	8	27	35

The late finish and late start times are established by taking a backward pass through the tasks of the project. From Table 16.2, it can be seen that the last task, E, ends at time unit 35. One may also look at the critical path of the project and determine the total project time; the total project time units can also be used as the end time of the project. Working backward from that end point, 35, Task E must start at time unit 27 because it takes 8 time units to complete. Task D, which precedes E, thus must end at time unit 27 and start at time unit 16. Tasks B and C must both end at time unit 16. Continuing the backward tracing of the task network, Task B does not need to start until time unit 11 (shown with an asterisk in Table 16.3), while Task C must start at time unit 9. Finally, to start Task C at time unit 9, Task A must finish at time unit 9 and start at time unit 0. Task A, for its LF time, chose the earliest LS times of its successors. That is, when choosing between LS time unit 9 of Task C or LS time unit 11 of Task B, Task A should pick 9. In late start/late finish scheduling, any task faced with multiple choices for its late finish time should pick the earliest of the late start times of its successors.

Using late start/late finish scheduling, Task B, which is the noncritical activity in this project, may start as late as time unit 11 and not affect the overall project schedule. Compare the start time of Task B in this case, which is at time unit 11, to that in Table 16.2, which is at time unit 9. There are two units of time difference—the same two time units of delay discussed earlier.

SLACK TIMES

Total Slack Time

In our example, Task B has two time units of freedom. This period is called its total slack time. The total slack time of an activity is defined as the difference in start time between a noncritical task's LS time and its ES time. It is the difference between the latest time at which a noncritical task can start and the earliest time at which it can start. Note that total slack time is only applicable to noncritical activities, because there cannot be any difference in start times for critical tasks.

The slack time of a task is defined as follows:

$$\textit{Total slack time of a task} = LS - ES$$

or

$$\textit{Total slack time of a task} = LF - EF$$

Total slack time of an activity The difference in start time between a noncritical task's late start time and its early start time or its late finish time and early finish time.

Total slack time The maximum allowable delay that can occur for all noncritical activities.

The difference between the LS and ES for a noncritical task is the same as that between its LF and EF. In the current example, the only noncritical activity is Task B. The total slack time of activity B is either LS – ES (11 – 9) or LF – EF (16 –14). In either case, the difference is two time units.

In project scheduling, the total slack times of the various noncritical tasks provide a certain degree of freedom in starting and completing those tasks. Once its total slack time is used up, however, a noncritical activity will turn into a critical activity.

Free Slack Time

Sometimes software project managers need to know whether a noncritical task with a nonzero total slack time can actually be delayed without affecting the start time of its immediate successors. Consider the case of a noncritical path that contains several tasks, whose individual total slack times are all nonzero. Delaying a task that has a total slack time of x by x amount of time may delay the start time of some immediate successor task, which may in turn negate any total slack time that was available for that successor task. Conversely, if using up the total slack time of a task by delaying that task, does not affect the start times of its immediate successor activities, then that total slack time is considered free slack time.

Free slack time of an activity Amount of time that an activity can be delayed without affecting the start times of any of its successor activities.

To see how this works, let's return to our example. The total slack time of Task B is two time units. Delaying Task B by two or fewer units will not affect the early start time of any of its successors. In this example, Task D is the only successor, and Task D's early start time will not be affected by B's two-unit delay. Thus the two time units may be considered the free slack time for Task B.

The free slack time of a task is defined as follows:

Given a noncritical task X,
Free slack time of X = *ES (of the earliest successor of X) – EF of X*

The definition of free slack time of a task X requires one to pick the earliest ES time from the ES times of all of the immediate successors to X. If X had only one successor activity, then the ES time of that task would be used in the computation of free slack time.

In the task network of Figure 16.2, the critical path includes three activities: A, C, and F. Those activities require a total of 30 time units. The two other paths, A–B–D–F and A–B–E–F, have total times of 23 time units and 25 time units, respectively. Only Tasks B, D, and E are noncritical tasks and may have any total slack time or free slack time.

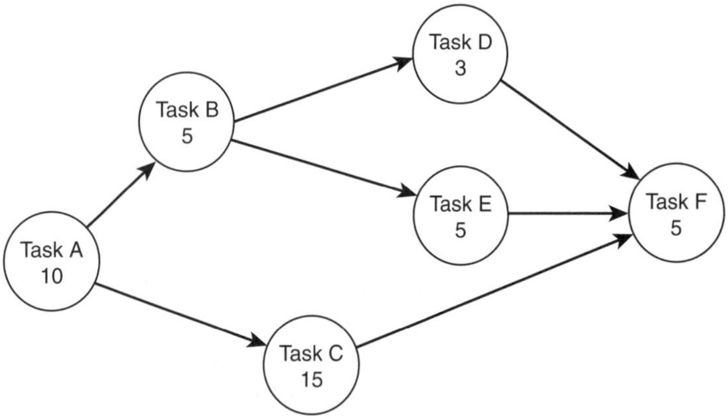

Note: The task completion time units appear inside each circle shown in Figure 16.2.

Figure 16.2 Task network

Table 16.4
Early Start/Early Finish and Late Start/Late Finish Data
Corresponding to Figure 16.2

Tasks	Task precedence	Task length	ES	EF	LS	LF
A	None	10	0	10	0	10
B	A	5	10	15	15	20
C	A	15	10	25	10	25
D	B	3	15	18	22	25
E	B	5	15	20	20	25
F	C, D, E	5	25	30	25	30

We can convert Figure 16.2 to a tabular form to show both the ES-EF and LS-LF data. Such a table will make the computation of total slack time and free slack time easier to comprehend.

The three noncritical tasks of B, D, and E may all have total slack time and free slack time. Following are the computations for each of these non-critical tasks.

For Task B:

Total slack time = LS – ES = 15 – 10 = 5
Free slack time = earliest successor ES – EF of Task B = ES of Task D – EF of Task B
= 15 – 15 = 0

For Task D:

Total slack time = LS – ES = 22 – 15 = 7
Free slack time = earliest successor ES – EF of Task D
= ES of Task F – EF of Task D = 25 – 18 = 7

For Task E:

Total slack time = LS – ES = 20 – 15 = 5
Free slack time = earliest successor ES – EF of Task E
= ES of Task F – EF of Task E = 25 – 20 = 5

Task B has two successor tasks, D and E. In this case, both D and E have the same ES, which is 15. Thus either Task D or Task E may be used in the preceding computation of Task B's free slack time; Task D's ES was used. If the ES of Task D and the ES of Task E differed, then the earlier of the two ESs would have been chosen. For Task B, even though the total slack time is 5 time units, there is no free slack time. Delaying the completion of Task B will affect the early start time of its earliest start successor, which, in this case, includes both Task D and Task E. Thus delaying Task B may not be a good idea until the effects on its successor tasks are assessed.

Consider the situation in which Task B is completing a key module, Task D is conducting a performance test, and Task E is conducting a user interface test. Without getting into the exact time units and scheduling, one can see that the effect of a delay to user interface testing, Task E, will be larger because it usually involves a longer and more complex testing effort.

Task D has a total slack time of 7 time units and a free slack time of 7 time units. Thus delaying task D's completion by 7 or fewer time units will not delay any of its successors' early start times. Similarly, Task E has a total slack time of 5 time units and a free slack time of 5 time units. Delaying the completion of Task E by no more than 5 time units will not delay any successor's early start time. When the total slack time of a noncritical task is the same as its free slack time, that activity may be delayed by the total slack time units without further considering the effect on its successors. In this example, both D and E have their total slack times equal to their free slack times, so these tasks' completion times may be delayed by their respective free slack times.

IMPROVING ESTIMATIONS: THE PROGRAM EVALUATION AND REVIEW TECHNIQUE

Each task's estimated effort plays a crucial role in the overall task network and scheduling. The computations of start and finish times, slack time, and free slack time all heavily depend on the initial estimation of the effort (time units) required to complete the tasks. The more accurate the estimation, the more meaningful the task scheduling.

There are many ways to improve these kinds of estimates. For instance, one can create a range of estimates for each task and then take the average of the range estimates. This technique of averaging the ranges eliminates some of the variability of the estimates.

For example, our estimates for a Task X may be obtained by consulting three experts. Suppose these experts give us the following three estimates: 6 time units, 9 time units, and 3 time units. Which estimate should we use? We can choose the middle one to minimize our risk. One way to choose the "middle" one is to take the average of the three estimates: (3 + 6 + 9)/3, or 6 time units.

One specific averaging method is called the Program Evaluation and Review Technique (PERT). PERT was developed as part of a U.S. government program associated with the U.S. Navy's Project Office in the 1950s. This technique utilizes three estimates for a task: the most optimistic estimate, the most pessimistic estimate, and the most likely estimate of the task. These three estimates are then manipulated to provide an expected estimate of a task as follows:

$$\text{Expected estimate} = [O + P + (4 \times A)]/6$$

where

O = most optimistic estimate
P = most pessimistic estimate
A = most likely to happen estimate

Program Evaluation and Review Technique (PERT) An estimating technique that assumes each activity duration is subject to a range of estimates and uses a weighted averaging method to arrive at a specific duration figure.

Using the expected estimates of all critical path tasks, PERT will provide the expected project time as the sum of the expected estimates of the critical tasks:

$$\text{Expected project time} = SUM\ (EE \text{ of critical task})$$

where

SUM = summation function
EE = expected estimate value of the task effort unit

Software project managers should keep in mind that all three of the estimates used with the PERT methodology are just that—estimates. That is, they are only as good as the Work Breakdown Structure activity performed during the project planning phase. The final expected estimate is just a weighted average of these component estimates.

REDUCING SCHEDULES: THE CRITICAL PATH METHOD

Once the project schedule is estimated, the software project manager may be faced with an unacceptable project end date. Because the critical path determines the project schedule, it makes sense to review the critical tasks to determine whether any one of them might have its required time units reduced. With software project tasks, the most popular time reduction method is to apply more human resources to a task to trim its schedule. It is also possible that one will not find any critical task whose task length can be reduced.

> **A Word of Caution**
>
> Software project managers must always heed the age-old warning: Do not blindly increase human resources in software projects. More often than not, the introduction of new people into an ongoing software project will actually extend the project time. As Fred Brooks has pointed out in his book *The Mythical Man-Month,* the addition of new resources to an already-delayed software project must be undertaken with care. New personnel will often require education and information updates from the very people whose time is most critical to the project. To reduce the schedule for a particular activity by applying more people to it, that task must have independent portions that may be broken out and assigned to multiple people. In a sense, that task must be decomposable into several independent subtasks.

Assume that there are several critical tasks whose schedules might be shortened without incurring many negative effects to the project as a whole. Now the software manager faces a choice: Which one should he or she pick as a target? One strategy is to consider the cost required to reduce the task length. Specifically, the critical path method (CPM) reviews all critical tasks whose schedules may be reduced by comparing the cost-to-effort ratios of those tasks.

Critical path method (CPM) A procedure for estimating the trade-offs between project duration or schedule and project cost.

The effort will be expressed in terms of time units here. This ratio is expressed in the form of a cost slope, which is defined for each critical task as follows:

$$\text{Cost slope for Task J} = |C_J - C_J'| \;/\; |T_J - T_J'|$$

where

C_J = cost of the resource to perform Task J
C_J' = cost of the resources to perform Task J with "improved" time
T_J = time required to complete Task J
T_J' = "improved" time required to complete Task J

Here the absolute value is used so that the negative slopes will be converted to positive values.

In Figure 16.3, a critical task J has its task time reduced from T_J to T_J', and there is a corresponding increase in cost from C_J to C_J'. The cost slope for Task J is depicted by the relative increase in cost, $(C_J - C_J')$, divided by the relative decrease in time or effort, $(T_J - T_J')$. To avoid the use of negative numbers, one may use the absolute values.

The cost–time or cost–effort relationship for all critical tasks should be investigated if the goal is to trim the project's schedule. The CPM technique assesses these critical tasks and attempts to improve the overall project schedule by following these steps:

1. Compute the cost slope for each critical task whose time needed for completion may be reduced.
2. Pick the critical task with the lowest cost slope, as it will be the most cost-effective to trim, and apply the necessary resources.
3. Remove the critical task picked in Step 2 from consideration as a future pick.

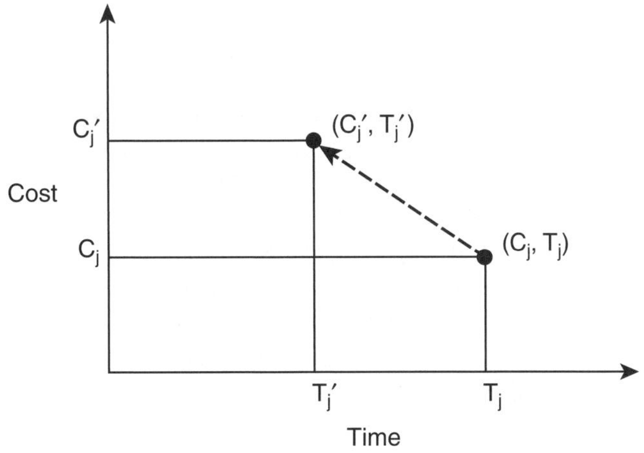

Figure 16.3 Cost–time network

4. Ask whether the desired project schedule is achieved with the application of additional resources to the just-picked critical task.
5. If the desired project schedule is achieved, then stop. Otherwise, repeat Steps 1–4 until the desired result is reached or until all critical tasks are exhausted.

In applying the CPM, the software project manager might potentially find a way to break a critical task down into a series of subtasks that may be performed by multiple personnel. This change—breaking a critical task into multiple tasks—can, in turn, cause another path to become the critical path.

CREATING A CALENDAR SCHEDULE

The tasks and the project schedule need to be ultimately converted into a calendar format. This calendar schedule, which will show weekends, holidays, and other pertinent dates, will be the preferred form from which the software project managers will conduct their monitoring and adjustment of the schedule. Once the tasks are laid out in calendar form, the managers may decide to adjust the schedule even further. For example, they might decide that implementation of some tasks may overlap. Of course, this adjustment must be done with a careful review and understanding of the details of each particular task.

There are many automated calendar/schedule tools—for example, Microsoft's MS Project, Primavera's SureTrak Project Manager, ProChain Solutions' ProChain Project Scheduling, and Smartdraw's business and charting software—that software project managers may use to facilitate creation and manipulation of the schedule. Currently, MS Project is still the most popular software tool in project management.

Each manager needs to decide how much effort he or she wants to put into choosing/using tools and how much effort he or she wants to put into analyzing the schedule. The analysis of the schedule is a critically important aspect of management. The actual manipulations of databases and figures in a timeline or calendar tool may be relegated to some administrative support personnel, however. Certainly, the schedule adjustment process is made much easier with an automated tool. At the same time, because these tools facilitate making changes, software project managers must be extra careful and thoroughly think through all consequences before tweaking the schedule.

Table 16.5 A Calendar Schedule

Activity	Team member	Days of Week																		
		M	T	W	Th	F	S	S	M	T	W	Th	F	S	S	M	T	W	Th	F
A	Tom	■	■	■	■	■														
B	Sally				■	■			■	■	■	■	■							
C	Jill		■	■	■	■			■	■	■	■				■	■	■		
D	Tom								■	■	■	■	■							
E	Sally															■	■	■	■	■

Table 16.5 shows an example of a calendar schedule. It illustrates the assignments of tasks, people to their tasks, and planned task lengths given in days.

The calendar schedule is expressed down to the specific day of the week. Weekends are not included as work days in the schedule. Also, any known personal vacation day, such as the second Friday for Jill in Table 16.5, is noted in the schedule. After looking at the people assignments, the software project managers may further adjust the initial task length estimate to better fit the productivity rate of each person. The supposedly "final" schedule may still need adjustments when viewed in the calendar form, so the software project managers should demand that the tabular and network graphical representations of the tasks schedule be converted to this form.

■ KEY CONCEPTS

The result of the Work Breakdown Structure activity is a project task network, which may be depicted in either a tabular or graphical representation. The graphical representation allows for easier viewing and spotting of different task paths, including critical paths. The tabular representation allows for easier representation of scheduling results.

Both forward- and backward-pass scheduling methods are employed with software projects. Two approaches are possible, based on the task start and end times:

- Early start and early finish
- Late start and late finish

A critical path is the path–the series of tasks–that takes the most time units to complete. A noncritical path is necessarily shorter than the critical path. For noncritical tasks, the possibilities of schedule delay or slippage can be examined by computing two measurements: total slack time and free slack time. A task that has free slack time may be delayed without causing any delays to its successor activities.

In an attempt to improve the estimation of effort for each task, the Program Evaluation and Review Technique (PERT) was developed in the 1950s. With PERT, one takes a weighted average of the most optimistic estimate, the most pessimistic estimate, and the most likely estimate to develop the expected estimate of the effort needed to complete the project as a whole.

Another technique seeks to improve the overall schedule by assigning more resources to shorten the time required to complete critical tasks. The critical path method (CPM) assesses the potential cost of trimming the schedules for the various critical tasks (by improving the cost slope of each critical task), enabling software project managers to pick the best option. This process continues until the desired project schedule is reached.

The project schedule should be placed into a graphical bar chart form so that it is easier to view and any further adjustments may be easily made.

EXERCISES

1. Can a noncritical path include a critical task? Show an example.
2. Can a critical path include a noncritical task? Show an example.
3. For the task network shown in the diagram below, perform the following:
   a. Identify the critical path.
   b. Develop a table that shows the early start, early finish, late start, and late finish for all tasks.

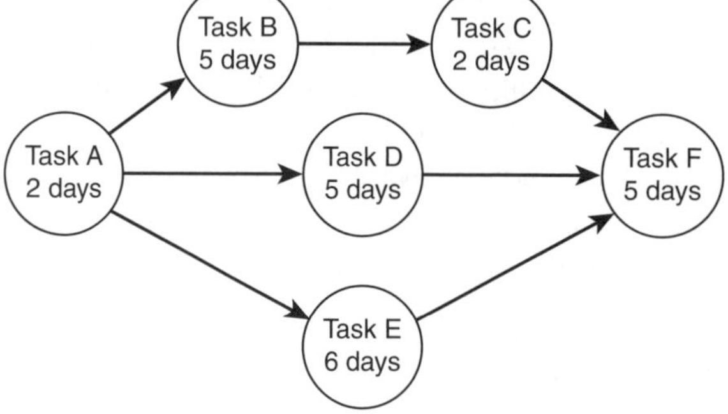

4. Using the diagram in Exercise 3, compute the total slack time and free slack time for the following:
   a. Task D
   b. Task B
   c. Explain your answers.
5. Explain how the PERT method reduces the risk in estimation.
6. Suppose that the cost of reducing 1 day of effort from each of the tasks in the diagram in Exercise 3 is represented as follows:
   Task A–$1,000, Task B–$1,200, Task C–$900, Task D–$500, Task E–$850, Task F–$1,800.
   Based on the CPM methodology, which task will be a candidate for the first round of schedule reduction?
7. Transform the task diagram in Exercise 3 to a calendar schedule similar to that in Table 16.5 (include weekends) based on the following Task–People assignments:
   Task A–Jill, Task B–Tom, Task C–Jill, Task D–Sam, Task E–Susan, Task F–Ken
   a. Assuming that the people can be interchanged in the performance of tasks, do you need to employ all these people?
   b. Rework the calendar schedule to use the minimum number of employees without elongating the schedule.
   c. If Task B were a special task that only Tom could perform, then what would your calendar schedule look like?

SUGGESTED READING

F. P. Brooks, Jr., *The Mythical Man-Month,* Addison-Wesley, 1975.

K. A. Cori, "Fundamentals of Master Scheduling for the Project Managers," in R. H. Thayer, ed., *Software Engineering Project Management,* 2nd ed., IEEE Computer Society, 1997, 171–182.

C. F. Gray and E. W. Larson, *Project Management: The Management Process,* Irwin McGraw Hill, 2000.

D. E. Knuth, *The Art of Computer Programming, Volume 1: Fundamental Algorithms,* 3rd edition, Addison Wesley Longman, 1997.

J. M. Nichols, *Project Management for Business and Technology: Principles and Practice,* Prentice Hall, 2001.

K. A. Smith, *Project Management and Teamwork,* McGraw Hill, 2000.

Chapter 17

Effort Estimation

Chapter Objectives

This chapter discusses the following concepts:

- How informal effort estimation techniques are used
- How a general estimation model works
- How the original COCOMO estimation technique fits within the context of the general estimation model

INFORMAL EFFORT ESTIMATION

Effort estimation is an essential part of all project planning. In Chapter 16 we introduced PERT as a method to obtain a weighted estimate of estimates of a task. Estimation of any kind of work that involves some amount of design is more of an art than a science, however, because so many parameters affect the actual estimation that it is almost impossible to have considered all cases. The first question is, "What are the relevant parameters that affect the work being estimated?" Even if all possible parameters are considered, still more questions may remain unresolved, including the following:

- How much does each parameter contribute to the total effort estimation?
- How can the amount of each parameter's contribution be converted into some numerical form?
- How do the parameters affect one another?
- How would these effects be combined?

The software industry and software project managers face this same set of questions, all of which point to the lack of good metric definitions related to estimations. Historically, software project managers have based many of their estimates on some form of "consulting the expert":

- Consult other peer managers who have past experience in the work
- Engage consultants who have experience in similar work
- Draw analogies to past projects that seem to have similar characteristics
- Break the project down into its various components and ask the component owners to provide estimates based on their experience and knowledge of their own specific work area; then combine their estimates into an overall project estimate

For many software project managers, this practice of consulting the experts and using past experience has worked well. These managers are fortunate, because in many other cases the software project lacks any clear precedence. Also, many of the experts or people with extensive past experience are not always available to the software project managers. Experienced managers—and especially those who are able to retain their key team players from project to project—will continue to draw upon their past experience and utilize this informal approach to effort estimation.

A more precarious situation arises when a particular target goal is "handed" to the project team. This goal may come from the customers, from the organization's executives, or from the marketing organization. Examples of goals include the following:

- The project must be completed by a certain date.
- The project must be completed within a certain budget.

When these types of goals are "mandated," they often do not include much detail. For example, the goals may not necessarily allow for variations in the expected functionality. Thus they may be distorted forms of informal estimations of effort that are simply handed to the software project teams. When this happens, the result is almost predictable: The project usually misses the goal. Alternatively, the mandated goal may be met, but the product functionality or product quality target may be missed. In addition, some negative project attributes, such as exhausted employees and a demoralized team, may creep in and turn into a sudden outburst of mass team resistance. (Readers who are interested in additional examples and deeper analysis should refer to the Standish Group report mentioned in the Introduction or

Capers Jones's book, *Patterns of Software Systems Failure and Success,* listed in the "Suggested Reading" section at the end of this chapter.)

GENERAL ESTIMATION MODEL

It is important to have as accurate an estimation of effort as possible. The effort estimate is used as the input for estimating other key project parameters, such as schedule and resources. These estimates all play a vital part in the project planning phase of POMA.

In software estimation, several models have been developed to push and improve the state of the art. That is, several groups of software researchers have constructed effort and cost estimation models. To date, these models have produced mixed results and encountered mixed receptions.

> **Software effort estimation model** A set of information and relationships organized for the purpose of estimating the effort needed to complete a software project. The information and the values assigned to the information may vary from project to project. Similarly, the relationships may be organized into a mathematical equation, which may vary from project to project.

Most of the models use the following general form, or its derivative, to estimate effort:

$$\text{Effort} = (a + [b \times (\text{Size}^{c})]) \times \text{PROD}(f\text{'s})$$

where
a, b, c = statistically derived coefficients or best approximations
Size = estimated size of the project
f's = factors that influence the project estimates
PROD(f's) = the product of arithmetically multiplying those factors

Many software engineers and researchers have studied a variety of projects from different disciplines in an attempt to find the best estimation model. The coefficients a, b, and c were derived by fitting the best curve against known data for the Effort and Size parameters for those projects. Effort is usually the amount of person-months expended on a project. Size is usually the number of lines of code created as part of the project.

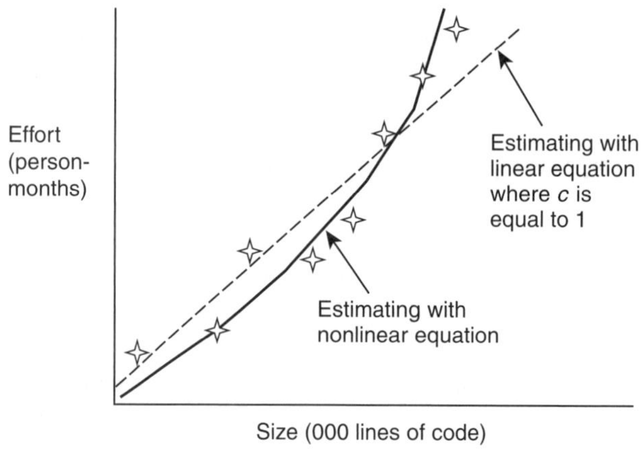

Figure 17.1 Effort estimation

Figure 17.1 shows two cases with the same set of data points. In one situation, the coefficient c is estimated as 1, and the estimation equation becomes a linear one. In the second situation, c is estimated to be larger than 1, and the estimation equation becomes nonlinear.

The relationship between the Size and Effort parameters was first established without a clear understanding of the other factors that affect the effort required to complete a project. In the early days, experienced managers would estimate the project size from past experiences and then do a mental calculation of effort required, based on that particular team's productivity history. This "mental calculation" took into account the various factors that affect the productivity (f's) and the a, b, and c coefficients that determine the shape of the curve.

The Size Factor

The estimation of project size starts the process of effort estimation. This factor provides a feel for the magnitude of the product as well as the project. Unfortunately, the size estimate continues to be a source of contention, for several reasons.

First, the Size metric itself is a problem. If it is measured in terms of "lines of code," there must be a clear definition of and agreement on what a line of code is. This topic has generated debate within the software community for years and certainly has introduced everyone to the variations possible in the definition of a line of code.

How Do You Define Lines of Code?

Although "lines of code" as a metric for software size has spurred many debates, it continues to be used by many software project managers. This metric is also the one with the longest history, despite the objections raised to it.

One objection focuses on whether a line of code should include only executable code. If so, how do we handle comments included in the code for clarity and documentation purposes? Certainly, some work is required to write meaningful in-line documentation, and that effort should be part of the effort estimation.

Another area of controversy centers on the programming language. Is a line of code written in the assembler language the same as a line of code written in C++ or JavaScript? The effort required to develop a function with assembler language versus a high-level language is surely different. How do we account for that difference in a line of assembler language code and a line of code in high-level language? Is there a convenient and acceptable conversion table?

A third debate considers whether a line of code is a physical line, like a line of text in a book, or a logical line, where the end of the line is determined by the specific end-of-line delimiter defined by that language.

These debates have prompted software engineers to seek "better" metrics for software Size.

More recently, function points have been introduced as a possible alternative for the Size parameter. The reference materials listed at the end of this chapter offer further discussions of lines of code and function points as metrics for software development effort.

How Do You Define a Function Point?

A "function point" is a metric for measuring the size of software, proposed as an alternative to the lines-of-code metric. First proposed by Allan Albrecht, it estimates the amount of functionality, as opposed to the number of lines of code used, in the software.

Briefly, the value of a function point is estimated by following this set of guidelines:

1. A value is assigned to each of five attributes–inputs, outputs, inquiries, master files, and interfaces–in the software. These five attributes represent the five functional components of a software, and each is assigned a weight. The value assigned to each attribute is then multiplied by the respective attribute weight. The weighted attributes are summed to give an initial estimate of function points, called the unadjusted function point.

2. Fourteen factors related to the software are used to adjust the initial estimate. These factors include considerations such as portability, reusability, performance criteria, and distributed data needs. Each factor is assigned a value ranging from 0 to 5. The sum of the values of these factors multiplied by 0.01 plus a constant value of 0.65 is used to adjust the initial estimate (i.e., the unadjusted function point). This sum, which is called the *total complexity factor,* may range from 0.65 to 1.35. The lowest value, 0.65, is the result of all 14 factors taking on the value of 0: total complexity factor = $0.65 + [0.01 \times (0 \times 14)]$. The highest value, 1.35, is the result of all 14 factors taking on the value of 5: total complexity factor = $0.65 + [0.01 \times (5 \times 14)]$.

3. The function point is computed by multiplying the unadjusted function point and the total complexity factors. One may view the function point estimate of a software as the unadjusted function point estimate that has experienced a 14-factor adjustment. The unadjusted function point may go through as much as a 35% up or down swing as a result of multiplying it by a value between 0.65 and 1.35.

To promote and ensure that the function-point estimates, and especially the 14 factors, are performed with consistency and accuracy, a nonprofit organization called International Function Point Users Group (IFPUG) provides education about and certification of function-point estimators. Consult the IFPUG Web site (www.ifpug.org) for further information.

Aside from reaching agreement on how to define Size and which metric to use, software project managers must recognize that estimating project size is no easy task. If the project size estimation will be performed with just a high-level set of requirements, most software project managers will utilize the "consult the expert" approach or depend on their own past experiences. Most of the effort estimation takes place during the planning phase, long before any code is actually written. Sometimes code prototypes may be created for a small portion of the project solely for the purpose of estimating the size of the final product. Thus estimating the size of the project for the Size parameter in the general effort estimation equation can start to look as difficult as estimating the effort itself.

Other Factors Affecting Project Effort

In addition to the project size factor, the effort required to accomplish a project depends on the conditions under which the project is being undertaken. For example, many software project managers know from experience that programmer productivity is a key factor but can be highly variable. Thus the team's membership is a critical criteria. The software development and support processes will also affect the effort. For example, a process that includes three levels of testing (e.g., functional, component, and system testing) will require more work, and therefore more effort, than a process that includes only functional and system testing. The maturity of the organization, as measured in terms of its working with an established process, is another important factor. The type and amount of tools used for the project may significantly influence the team's productivity as well. Certainly, the attributes of the end product, besides its size, are important. For example, if a certain new technology must be part of the end product, then much more risk—and possibly more effort—is involved.

All of the preceding factors—the *f*'s in the general effort estimation equation—affect the project, and thus they must be considered when the software project managers are estimating the effort required to complete that project. Having a standard list of factors to be considered for estimation would generally help them in this endeavor for two reasons:

- A list will serve as a reminder.
- A list will bring some consistency to what the software project managers consider.

Once the list of factors is established, the next issue is to assign values to these factors. Unfortunately, a parameter that one manager considers to be highly relevant may not be seen in the same way by another manager. A particular tool may be viewed as extremely important by one manager, while a second project manager may consider the key personnel issue to be more important. Thus the team needs a methodical way to interpret each situation and assign values to these factors in a consistent manner.

The influencing factors (f's) may also be interrelated. The question of how to account for the combined effects of all of these factors continues to pose a perplexing challenge. Depending how we want to combine the effects, we may assign values to the factors differently. In the general effort estimation equation, the arithmetic multiplication operation is used as the integration mechanism to combine the relevant factors. If a factor is given a value of 1 when it is considered to have only a nominal effect on the project, given a value greater than 1 when it results in more effort, and given a positive fractional value when it saves effort, then "multiplying" the factor values may be the correct operation. Conversely, if one assigns the value 0 as the nominal case, some positive value when the factor affects the project negatively (more effort), and some negative value when the factor affects the project positively (less effort), then "adding" the factor values may be the better operation. If the multiplication operation was utilized for this second case, then there is a chance of getting a result of zero for the effort when only one factor is zero. That is, the combined effect of all the factors will be deemed "nominal," even though that most likely is not the case. The integration operation of the multiple factors and the assignment of values to these factors must be carefully considered for one to adopt and adapt the general effort estimation equation for a specific project.

Most of the estimation formulas follow the general equation given earlier, in which the factors are multiplied. The nominal situation where the factor is considered to be nonessential is given the value 1. The multiplicative product of all influencing factors will be greater than 1 when the cumulative effects of all factors are negative (more effort). In such a case, the estimated project effort will exceed the effort in the situation in which only the size of the project is considered. Conversely, when these factors are a positive influence on the project, the multiplicative product of the factors should be less than 1. In this case, the total estimated project effort, after multiplying by a fraction, will be less than the effort in the situation in which only the size of the project is considered.

THE COCOMO EFFORT ESTIMATION MODEL

One specific example of the general effort estimation equation and methodology is Barry Boehm's estimation technique, called the Constructive Cost Model (COCOMO), which Boehm developed and initially tested with more than 60 projects at TRW. COCOMO has been used by a number of software project managers, especially those in the aerospace industry and those working on government projects. Boehm's first model was introduced in the early 1980s, and it has since gone through several versions. The basic concept has not changed, however, and the variations on the original model still follow the same general formula. In this chapter, the original model will be discussed to demonstrate how it conceptually works.

COCOMO includes three levels of models: a macro estimation model, an intermediate-level model, and a more detailed, micro estimation model. The intermediate-level model is used as an example here.

The general process of using COCOMO is as follows:

1. Pick an estimate of what would be considered the "nominal" development effort of the project. The "nominal" effort may be viewed as the "typical" mode of development. Three nominal project modes are defined: Organic, Semidetached, and Embedded. These three project mode names were given by Boehm and are further defined and explained in the next section and in Table 17.1.
2. Pick an estimate of the size of the project to use for the Size parameter.
3. Review the factors that influence the project, called cost drivers, and estimate the appropriate amount of influence that each factor will have on the chosen "nominal" case.
4. Determine the effort for the software project by inserting the estimated values into the Effort formula.

Identify the Nominal Mode of Development

The three nominal modes of development (Organic, Semidetached, and Embedded) are used to initially determine the type of project that is under consideration. The following key project characteristics are used to differentiate between the modes:

A: The team's understanding of the project objective
B: The team's experience with similar or related projects

C: The project's need to conform with the established requirements
D: The project's need to conform with established external interfaces
E: The need to develop the project concurrently with new systems and new operational procedures
F: The project's need for new and innovative technology, architecture, or other constraints
G: The project's need to meet or beat the schedule
H: The project's size range

One of the three modes of development is picked as the "typical" case based on how the project matches up against this set of key characteristics. Table 17.1 provides a guideline.

The Organic mode consists of projects that are fairly easy and familiar to the software development team. The Semidetached mode involves projects that are medium-sized and somewhat familiar to the software development team. The Embedded mode consists of complex projects that may be unfamiliar to the project team. One must be cautious when using these summary statements, however; they should serve as only a starting point in the decision process when choosing the most appropriate mode for the project estimate. Table 17.1 provides the actual definitions for these three project

Table 17.1
Modes of Development Used in COCOMO

Key project characteristic	Organic mode	Semidetached mode	Embedded mode
A	Detailed degree	Considerable degree	Only general degree
B	Extensive amount	Some amount	None to modest amount
C	Only the basic ones	Considerably more than the basic ones	All and full conformance
D	Only the basic ones	Considerably more than the basic ones	All and full conformance
E	Little to some	Moderate amount	Extensive amount
F	None to minimal	Some	Considerable
G	Low	Medium	Must
H	Less than 50,000 delivered lines of code	50,000 to 300,000 delivered lines of code	All sizes

modes, and it should be consulted so that project managers do not just "guess" at the project modes.

An untrained software project manager might not be able to easily pick the correct mode. Very few projects' characteristics will all fall neatly within any one of the mode categories. Instead, most projects will have key characteristics that will fit within different columns in Table 17.1. The software project manager would have to do his or her best in estimating the mode of the project, possibly by picking the column that has the most number of key project characteristics.

A software organization or a corporation would need to establish a consistent methodology for choosing what it considers the typical mode of the project. Each key project characteristic must be interpreted in a consistent way, and what is considered to be the minimal, moderate, or extensive level for each characteristic needs a more detailed explanation. After a certain amount of experience in using the definitions, the organization will generally settle into a consistent usage pattern.

For each of the three modes, a different formula is used for estimating the Effort:

Organic: Effort (in person-months) = $3.2 \times (\text{Size})^{1.05}$
Semidetached: Effort = $3.0 \times (\text{Size})^{1.12}$
Embedded: Effort = $2.8 \times (\text{Size})^{1.20}$

where Size is expressed in lines of code (loc).

One of the three formulae will be used to perform the preliminary estimate of the effort in person-months. The formula employed will depend on which mode was chosen as the typical case for the project.

Estimate the Size of the Project

The next step is to estimate the size of the project. This size has traditionally been expressed in the form of delivered lines of code. As discussed earlier, the metric of "lines of code" has a long history and has inspired its share of controversy. Nevertheless, it continues to be used by many software managers.

Other managers have adopted function points as a metric. With this metric, the coefficients used in the formula need to be modified. There is much less history with the coefficients in the case of function points, however, because most of the COCOMO estimates have utilized lines of code.

Nevertheless, an appropriate time to use function points as the size estimate is when the project is at an early stage and estimating lines of code is much more difficult.

One potential source of guidance for estimating with function points is the new COCOMO II model, which is mentioned later in this chapter. COCOMO II offers an estimation equation in the following form:

$$\text{Effort} = 2.45 \times (\text{Size})^m \ \text{PROD}(f\text{'s})$$

Here, the Size estimate may be in either function points or lines of code. PROD(f's) is a product of several factors that influence the project, and the exponent m varies in value depending on the project situation. If the project is large and there is a lot of communications and integration overhead, then $m > 1$. If the project has a high potential for savings due to better tools, better processes, or better people, then $m < 1$. If the project has neither great overhead nor great savings, then $m = 1$.

Review and Assign Values to the Cost Drivers

As mentioned earlier, in the original COCOMO model, a set of 15 factors—known as cost drivers—influences the project. These factors are assigned a range of values, but then each specific factor needs to be assessed and assigned a specific value. These 15 factors are listed here by category:

Product Attributes

1. RELY: Required software reliability
2. DATA: Database size
3. CPLX: Product complexity

Computer Attributes

4. TIME: Execution time constraint
5. STOR: Main memory constraint
6. VIRT: Virtual machine complexity
7. TURN: Computer turnaround time

Personnel Attributes

8. ACAP: Analyst capability
9. AEXP: Applications experience

10. PCAP: Programmer capability
11. VEXP: Virtual machine experience
12. LEXP: Programming language experience

Project Attributes
13. MODP: Use of modern programming practices
14. TOOL: Use of software tools
15. SCED: Required development schedule

These four categories of factors are considered to be vital factors that influence the estimation of the efforts required to complete a project. Some interesting factors, such as virtual machine complexity (VIRT), may have been important when the COCOMO technique was first introduced but are less important today.

> **Cost drivers** A set of influential factors used in the cost estimation or effort estimation of software projects. These factors are usually attributes that characterize the project team's expertise and experience; the project environment such as the process and tools utilized in the project; and product characteristics such as complexity.

Once the 15 factors are reviewed, there remains the task of assigning a value to each one of them. The value assignment is based on what type of influence and how much influence the software project estimator believes each factor will exert in the typical project case. For example, if the factor is believed to be neutral, the value assignment is 1. If the factor is believed to increase the effort required, the value assignment is greater than 1. If the factor is believed to lessen the effort required, the assigned value is less than 1. Table 17.2 shows the value assignments for the 15 factors, as made by Boehm.

The ranges of potential values are different for different factors. Likewise, the gradations of values are not constant from Very Low to Extra High. Note that the Nominal column is filled with the value 1. Consider the reliability factor (RELY). If the reliability requirement is Very Low, then it lessens the effort. Thus the Very Low value for RELY is 0.75. It may be viewed as 75% of the nominal case. Conversely, if the reliability requirement were High, then that factor would increase the needed effort, so it has a value assignment of 1.15. This value means that the nominal-case effort would be increased by 15%. The key point is that assignments of values to the 15 factors must be consistent within an organization.

Table 17.2
Value Assignments for the 15 COCOMO Factors

Factor	Range of values					
	Very low	Low	Nominal	High	Very high	Extra high
RELY	0.75	0.98	1.0	1.15	1.40	—
DATA	—	0.94	1.0	1.08	1.16	—
CPLX	0.70	0.85	1.0	1.15	1.30	1.65
TIME	—	—	1.0	1.11	1.30	1.66
STOR	—	—	1.0	1.06	1.21	1.56
VIRT	—	0.87	1.0	1.15	1.30	—
TURN	—	0.87	1.0	1.07	1.15	—
ACAP	1.46	1.19	1.0	0.86	0.71	—
AEXP	1.29	1.13	1.0	0.91	0.82	—
PCAP	1.42	1.17	1.0	0.86	0.70	—
VEXP	1.21	1.10	1.0	0.90	—	—
LEXP	1.14	1.07	1.0	0.95	—	—
MODP	1.24	1.10	1.0	0.91	0.82	—
TOOL	1.24	1.10	1.0	0.91	0.83	—
SCED	1.23	1.08	1.0	1.04	1.10	—

Calculate the Effort Estimate

After considering all 15 factors and assigning them the appropriate values, the factors are multiplied together and then multiplied by the initial Effort estimate, whether it is Organic, Semidetached, or Embedded. The intermediate-level COCOMO formula is expressed as follows for the three modes, where PROD(f's) is the product of the 15 factors:

Organic: Effort = $[3.2 \times (\text{Size})^{1.05}] \times \text{PROD}(f\text{'s})$
Semidetached: Effort = $[3.0 \times (\text{Size})^{1.12}] \times \text{PROD}(f\text{'s})$
Embedded: Effort = $[2.0 \times (\text{Size})^{1.20}] \times \text{PROD}(f\text{'s})$

After some experience with using the COCOMO formula and comparing its results with real data, the software project managers may decide to adjust their valuation techniques to improve the accuracy of their estimates.

Experts who have used the COCOMO formulas found the effort estimates to be less than 90% accurate at times. It is also known that the estimate may be improved as we re-estimate the project with better project knowledge at later stages of the project. Project estimates that are the outcome of the COCOMO formula should never be used without some further management buffering, because once an estimate is given, it is difficult to change it—especially if the change involves asking for more time or resources.

The Continuing Evolution of COCOMO

As noted earlier, COCOMO has evolved significantly since its introduction in the early 1980s. One newer version, called COCOMO II, is targeted at the software engineering practices of the 1990s and 2000s. During this time, the development process moved from the traditional waterfall process to a more iterative process, the development technology moved from structured programming to object-oriented programming, and the user operational environment moved from transactional to Web-based. To keep pace with these trends, the development tools have improved to become toolkits of integrated tools, which combine application programming logic, database, communications middleware, and screen development.

COCOMO II recognizes that the estimation model itself should take these factors into account. For this reason, it includes three models: one for creating early estimates during the prototyping stage, one for making estimates during the project design stage, and one for developing post-architectural estimates after the design is set and development has commenced. A different set of cost drivers, or PROD(*f*'s), is used for each model, reflecting the new software development environment and the new software technologies.

Despite the introduction of shiny new models, the fundamental concept underlying project effort estimation remains valid. Future software project managers simply need to realize that change is inevitable in the software industry and, therefore, that critical cost drivers for software projects must be modified to respond to these changes. The value assignment process will also change as technology continues to improve and as software engineers gain more and broader experience with various types of projects. What was once considered difficult may not seem very hard in the future. What was once considered highly reliable may evolve into a standard expectation. In the future, software project managers will be asked to be more accurate in their planning. The effort estimation equation represents just a starting point for achieving more accurate planning of efforts and cost.

KEY CONCEPTS

Software effort estimation has traditionally depended on the past experiences of managers and team members, with planning taking advantage of their expertise through an informal estimation strategy. Today, as part of an attempt to both formalize and improve the effort or cost estimation for software projects, a variety of new estimation techniques, involving several factors and drivers, have emerged. One such general formula is as follows:

$$\text{Effort} = (a + [b \times (\text{Size}^{c})]) \times \text{PROD}(f\text{'s})$$

where a, b, and c are statistically derived coefficients or best approximations; Size is the estimated size of the project; f's comprise factors that influence the project estimates; and PROD(f's) is the product of arithmetically multiplying those factors. This general equation still requires the project manager to estimate the project size and the key factors influencing the project.

Barry Boehm's COCOMO technique is one specific example of a general effort estimation model. It involves four steps:

1. Estimate the nominal development effort of the project.
2. Estimate the size of the project.
3. Review the factors that influence the project and assign values to them.
4. Calculate the effort for the software project by inserting the estimated values into the effort estimation formula.

Since COCOMO was introduced in the early 1980s, there have been numerous changes to the software industry and software engineering disciplines. The newer COCOMO II model reflects those trends to improve the effort estimation process.

EXERCISES

1. Explain the PROD function in the general effort estimation equation. What other integration or aggregation operator may be employed instead of PROD? Explain how.
2. We are often asked to provide a "quick" effort estimate in planning. If we were to use any of the effort estimation formulae discussed in this chapter, what element do we need to estimate first? How accurate is that estimate, and how do we obtain such an estimate?

3. Discuss the pros and cons of consulting an experienced "expert" in estimating project efforts.
4. Are there factors that you would include today that are not among the 15 original COCOMO factors? (Note: You may want to consult the literature on COCOMO II in the "Suggested Reading" section.)
5. Take a small program that you have completed. Count the lines of code. Generate the effort estimate by assuming the Organic mode. Use the COCOMO estimation technique without the 15 factors and compare this estimate with your actual effort. Include the 15 factors and recalculate the estimate. Compare the new estimate with your actual effort.
6. Compare and contrast lines of code and function points as metrics and describe what attribute, you believe, they measure. What would you use the metrics lines of code and function points for?

SUGGESTED READING

A. J. Albrecht and J. Gaffney, "Software Function, Source Lines of Code, and Development Effort Prediction: A Software Science Validation," *IEEE Transactions on Software Engineering,* November 1983, 639–648.

J. Baik, B. Boehm, and B. Steece, "Disaggregating and Calibrating the CASE Tool Variable in COCOMO II," *IEEE Transactions on Software Engineering,* November 2002, 1009–1022.

B. Boehm, *Software Engineering Economics,* Prentice Hall, 1981.

B. Boehm, C. Abts, A. W. Brown, S. Chulani, B. K. Clark, E. Horowits, R. Madachy, D. Reifer, and B. Steece, *Software Cost Estimation with COCOMO II,* Prentice Hall, 2000.

C. Jones, *Applied Software Measurement,* McGraw Hill, 1996.

C. Jones, *Patterns of Software Systems Failure and Success,* International Thompson Computer Press, 1996.

C. F. Kemerer, *Software Project Management Readings and Cases,* Irwin McGraw Hill, 1997.

M. Morisio, D. Romano, and I. Stamelos, "Quality, Productivity, and Learning in Framework-Based Development: An Exploratory Case Study," *IEEE Transactions on Software Engineering,* September 2002, 876–888.

C. Stevenson, *Software Engineering Productivity,* Chapman & Hall, 1995.

Chapter 18

Earned Value Management

Chapter Objectives

This chapter discusses the following concepts:

- What principle the Earned Value Management is based on
- What the definitions are for different planned and completed project task efforts
- What the earned value metrics are
- How to use earned value metrics

A PROJECT-MONITORING TECHNIQUE: COMPARING ACTUAL VERSUS PLANNED

Earned Value Management (EVM) is a project-monitoring technique that emerged in the 1960s in U.S. government projects. In its early days, EVM was used by a small number of experts in manufacturing and in procurement in various government defense contracts. Quickly expanded beyond the defense industry, today it is used by NASA, the U.S. Department of Energy, the U.S. Office of Management and Budget, and other federal agencies. The integration of EVM technique into general project management practices accelerated in the 1990s. Now, EVM is being used not only for government-related contract and subcontract projects, but also for many commercial projects in a wide range of industries.

The fundamental principle of project monitoring is comparing planned versus actual. In the project-monitoring phase of EVM, the major activity is to assess the status of a project by reviewing what was planned and expected against what is really occurring. This does not mean that the plan is always correct. Sometimes we have to make adjustments to a plan based on the information gathered during the monitoring phase. A graphical example in Figure 18.1 shows the accumulative planned project cost through time and the accumulative actual cost of the project through time. The analysis of the differences and the subsequent actions that are taken should be the focus of the project managers. EVM is a tool, or a methodology, that allows the project managers to first track the planned against the actual project status and then to perform the analysis of that information.

Figure 18.1 shows that the actual accumulative project cost exceeded the planned accumulative project cost several times during the project's duration. Based on this figure, you may believe the project to be over cost and that it may not be completed on schedule. If, at time unit 5, the cost of the project has already reached the total planned cost but the project has accomplished only 80% of the tasks, then clearly this project is headed to cost overrun and a missed schedule. However, it is possible that the project has completed all of the tasks ahead of schedule at time unit 5, and that the total cost is exactly what was planned. If so, we would be celebrating a successful project. What is missing from Figure 18.1 is the information of how much of the work has been accomplished. EVM uses task-effort units as cost in conjunction with a set of defined measurement units that will allow us to analyze both the cost variance and the schedule variance.

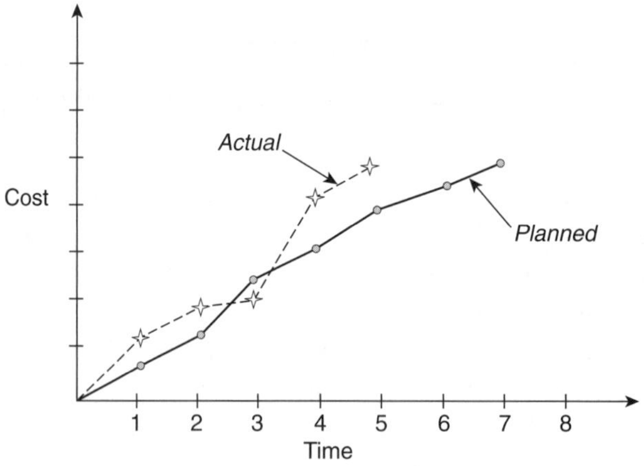

Figure 18.1 Tracking of planned versus actual

Work Effort and Related Key Definitions

We will first provide some fundamental definitions and then illustrate EVM technique through a simple example. Three very important activities must be performed in advance of carrying out EVM:

- The tasks for the project must be well defined,
- The effort required for each task must be well estimated, and
- The effort expended on each task must be tracked.

Task effort is a central unit used for measuring project cost. Task effort may be in person-hours, person-days, or some similar unit. The following are the key definitions of EVM that depend on the notion of task effort:

- Budgeted Cost of Work (BCW): Estimated work effort for each task defined in the project.
- Budgeted Cost of Work Scheduled (BCWS): The sum of the estimated work effort for all the tasks that were *scheduled* to be completed by a specified time. (This is the sum of only those BCWs that were planned or scheduled to be completed by that specific date of interest.)
- Budget at Completion (BAC): The estimate of the total project effort that will be expended at the end of the project. (This is the sum of all the BCWs for the entire project.)
- Planned Value (PV): The percentage of the total estimated effort that is assigned to the particular task, *j*, or (BCW of *j*)/BAC.
- Budgeted Cost of Work Performed (BCWP): The sum of the estimated effort of the tasks that have actually been accomplished by the specified time.
- Actual Cost of Work Performed (ACWP): The sum of the actual efforts expended for the tasks that have been completed by the specified time.

A few subtleties in the definitions need to be pointed out. BCWS includes the estimated effort of the tasks that were planned to be completed at some time of interest. Thus, this number is not the sum of actually completed tasks at that time of interest. This number varies by the actual time when the measurement is taken. While both BCWP and ACWP sum the efforts of the completed tasks, BCWP is the sum of the planned effort number of the completed tasks and ACWP is the sum of the actual effort number of the completed tasks. Consider Figure 18.2, which depicts the tasks of a project with the estimated effort and the actual effort expended.

Date: 4/5/2011

Work tasks	Estimated effort in person-days	Actual effort spent so far in person-days	Estimated completion date	Actual completion date
1	10	10	2/5/2011	2/5/2011
2	25	25	3/15/2011	3/25/2011
3	30	9	4/25/2011	
4	25	20	5/5/2011	4/1/2011
5	15	6	5/25/2011	
6	20	5	6/10/2011	

Figure 18.2 Example of estimated and actual task effort on April 5, 2011

Note that, in Figure 18.2, not all tasks are actually completed on the planned date. The expended effort to complete a task does not always match the planned amount of effort. Also, note that at the time of interest—in this case 4/5/2011—some projects are partially complete. For the project status on 4/5/2011 depicted by Figure 18.2, the measurements for the key EVM definitions are shown as follows:

- BCW for task 3 is 30 person-days.
- BCWS is the sum of the estimated efforts that are scheduled to be completed by 4/5/2011. These comprise tasks 1 and 2, and the estimated efforts are (10 + 15) = 25 person-days.
- BAC is the sum of the estimated efforts, or (10 + 15 + 30 + 25 + 15 + 20) = 115 person-days.
- PV of task 3 is 30/115 = .26, or 26%.
- BCWP is the sum of the estimated effort of those tasks that are actually completed by 4/5/2011 (tasks 1, 2, and 4). The respective estimated efforts for tasks 1, 2, and 4 are 10, 15, and 25. Thus BCWP = (10 + 15 + 25) = 50 person-days.
- ACWP is the sum of the real expended effort of those tasks that are actually completed by 4/5/2011. Those are the same three tasks as BCWP, but we sum the number of days of actual effort spent, which are 10, 25, and 20. Thus ACWP = (10 + 25 + 20) = 55 person-days.

Earned Value Metrics

From the earlier concepts and definitions of tasks planned and completed, we now define Earned Value as follows:

> **Earned Value**, or EV, is an indicator of how much of the total project is completed at a specific time of interest. More specifically, EV = BCWP/BAC.

Thus for the project described in Figure 18.2, tasks 1, 2, and 4 are completed on 4/5/2011. The estimated effort for each of these three tasks is 10, 15, and 25 person-days respectively, and the estimated effort for all the tasks is 115 person days. Therefore, EV = 50/115. The project is estimated to be approximately 43% complete on 4/5/2011. Note that for EV, the actual number of person-days expended is not used.

There are two indices that may provide an even better indicator. One is the Schedule Performance Index (SPI), which is an indicator of schedule. It is defined as follows:

$$SPI = BCWP/BCWS$$

This formula defines the estimated effort of all those tasks *actually completed* by a specific date as compared to the estimated effort of all those tasks that were *estimated to be completed* by that specific date. Thus when SPI = 1, the project is on schedule. If SPI > 1, then the estimated effort of all those tasks actually completed is larger than the estimated effort of all those tasks planned to be completed, and the project is ahead of schedule. If SPI < 1, then the project is behind schedule. In our example, SPI = 50/25 (and this is greater than 1) on 4/5/2011, so the project is ahead of schedule. Again, note that we are comparing estimated effort of the tasks and have not used the actual expended effort.

The other index is the Cost Performance Index (CPI), which is a cost indicator. It is defined as follows:

$$CPI = BCWP/ACWP$$

CPI compares the *estimated* effort of all those tasks actually completed by a specific date against the *actual* effort spent for all those same tasks that were completed. Again, if CPI = 1, then the project is on target. If CPI > 1, then the estimated effort is greater than what was actually expended. Thus CPI > 1 indicates that the project is running under budget. On the other hand, when CPI < 1, the actual effort spent is larger than the estimated effort. Thus

CPI < 1, shows that the project is running over budget. For our example, the actual expanded effort for each of the tasks completed is 10, 25, and 20 person hours, and so the CPI = 50/55. Thus the project is running slightly over the budget on 4/5/2011.

The status taken on 4/5/2011 shows that we are approximately 43% complete of the estimated sample project. The project SPI is 2; thus it is ahead of schedule. The CPI for the project is .91; thus the project is running a bit over budget. The project is slightly over budget because it is ahead of schedule and has expended more person-days of effort than planned for 4/5/2011. Thus SPI and CPI provide more complete status information for project tracking than EV alone.

SPI and CPI indices may also be viewed through a different perspective using variances. Instead of SPI, the project schedule variance can be used. The schedule variance, SV, is defined as follows:

$$SV = BCWP - BCWS$$

When SV is greater than 0, the estimated effort of all the *actually completed* tasks is more than the *estimated effort* of all the tasks that were planned to be completed on that specific date. For our example, SV = 50 − 25, or 25 person-days ahead of schedule on 4/5/2011.

Similarly, instead of using CPI, a cost variance (CV) may be used. The cost variance is defined as follows:

$$CV = BCWP - ACWP$$

When CV is greater than 0, the *estimated* effort of all the actually completed tasks is greater than the *actual* effort spent for all those same completed tasks. Thus CV > 0 would indicate that we are running under budget. For our example, CV = 50 − 55, or −5, which shows that we are actually 5 person days over the budget on 4/5/2011.

The two variance indicators serve the same purpose as the two indices, but the variance indicators provide a more specific number in terms of units of effort. One may choose to use EV and both sets of SPI and CPI indices along with the SV and CV variance indicators. The earned value management methodology provides a specific way to gauge the project status by comparing the actual versus the planned. This provides a much more concrete status measurement for monitoring projects.

Graphically, one can also see in Figure 18.3 that the project on 4/5/2011 is ahead of schedule (BCWP is higher than BCWS on 4/5/2011), but a bit over the budget (ACWP is higher than BCWP on 4/5/2011).

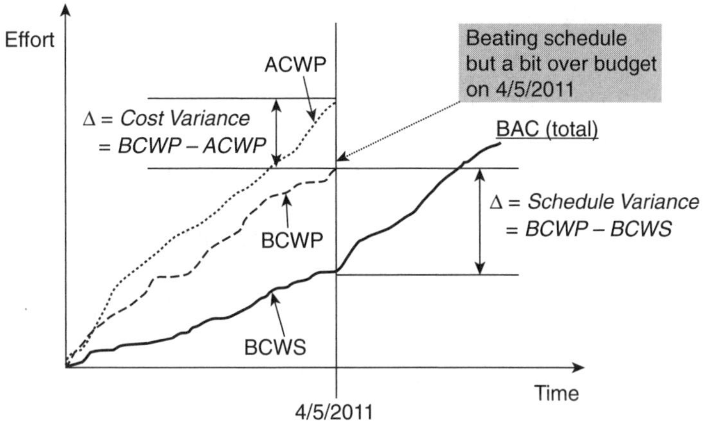

Figure 18.3 Graphical representation of SV and CV

KEY CONCEPTS

Earned Value Management is a project-monitoring and control technique based on the concept of comparing what was planned with what was actually accomplished. Each major task is broken down to subtasks whose effort is estimated via some technique, such as the Work Breakdown Structure defined in Chapter 2. Each estimated task effort is the Budgeted Cost of Work, or BCW. By the end of the project, the total amount of estimated effort expended will be the sum of all the BCWs, called the Budget at Completion, or BAC.

On any specific status date, the estimated effort for all the tasks that are *planned* to be completed is defined as the Budgeted Cost of Work Scheduled, or BCWS. On the other hand, on that same specific status date, the total estimated effort for all those tasks that are *actually* completed is called the Budgeted Cost of Work Performed, or BCWP. Lastly, on that same status date, the total *actual* effort expended for those *actually* completed tasks is called the Actual Cost of Work Performed, or ACWP. Earned Value, or EV, is defined as BCWP/BAC. EV provides a sense of how much of the total project is completed on a specific day in the schedule.

With these fundamental definitions of different estimated and actual completed tasks, we use a pair of indices, Schedule Performance Index (SPI) and Cost Performance Index (CPI), to monitor and assess the project's status. A similar pair of indicators is the Schedule Variance and Cost Variance. These indices, together with EV, give us a way to assess the project status.

EXERCISES

1. What is the fundamental principle behind project monitoring? In other words, what is being assessed?
2. Explain how Earned Value Management helps in monitoring a project's status.
3. When SV is a positive number, does that indicate that a project is ahead of schedule? Why or why not?
4. When CPI is greater than 0, does that mean that a project is over budget? Why or why not?
5. Is EV, as a single indicator, enough to monitor a project, and why do we need the other indices? Explain.

SUGGESTED READING

M. J. Christensen and R. H. Thayer, Chapter 12 in *Project Manager's Guide to Software Engineering's Best Practices*, IEEE Computer Society Press, 2001.

A. Cukr, "Dispelling Some Myths about Earned Value Management (EVM)," *Software Tech News*, September 2009, Vol. 12, No. 3, 5–7.

P. J. Solomon, "Agile Earned Value and the Technical Baseline," *Software Tech News*, September 2009, Vol. 12, No. 3, 9–14.

Chapter 19

Procurement and Acquisition

Chapter Objectives

This chapter discusses the following key concepts:

- What the main procurement management activities are
- What the general procurement planning concerns are
- What basic procurement process steps are
- What needs to be considered in supplier selection
- What needs to be done after the supplier is selected, in terms of monitoring and controlling the procurement-related activities of both the supplier and the receiver

PROCUREMENT MANAGEMENT

All management is concerned with increasing productivity and lowering costs. These business drivers forced manufacturing and other industries to seriously improve their procurement and supply chain management. Managers of software systems and IT projects also need to focus on productivity and cost. When both software systems and IT projects were conducted and completed on site with all in-house or in-sourcing development, improving in house-defined processes and techniques with "permanent" personnel was the key to productivity gain and cost reduction. The notion of permanency in employment with a single enterprise through a person's lifetime is a dream of the past. Today's competition is much more global in nature. New technology is introduced at an increasingly faster pace. The current landscape has dramatically changed for all enterprises, and thus for all projects.

Many systems and IT projects are increasingly dependent on incorporating existing and purchasable components, both software and hardware. Many projects are also outsourced. Thus for today's projects, human resources, technical components, and subsystems are often purchased. New tools and development platforms are constantly introduced at an astonishing rate. In addition, the Internet has introduced e-commerce and a new paradigm that provides "instantaneous" flow of information among suppliers, providers, and customers. Going forward, managers of these large, complex projects will often need to include a hefty amount of procurement and supply-chain management skills as part of their project management tool set.

Not all organizations perform acquisition in the same manner. A well-established, experienced, and large organization usually has a formal procurement department with a formal process. Even then, project managers still need to estimate when and what needs to be purchased and be able to put together a procurement plan that folds into the master project management plan. A formal liaison and interface to the procurement department needs to be established. As the project proceeds, the established procurement process steps need to be followed. The awarding of the contract, managing the schedule, and receiving and acceptance of the delivery of product all require careful monitoring. Project managers should also be ready to make adjustments should there be any schedule change, product content change, or requirements change. In short, procurement management goes through the same Plan–Organize–Monitor–Adjust (POMA) set of activities as described in the Introduction of this book. Figure 19.1 depicts the four major activities related to procurement management. There are times, though, when the existing procurement process may not suffice. In those cases, the "organize and perform procurement process steps" box in Figure 19.1 needs

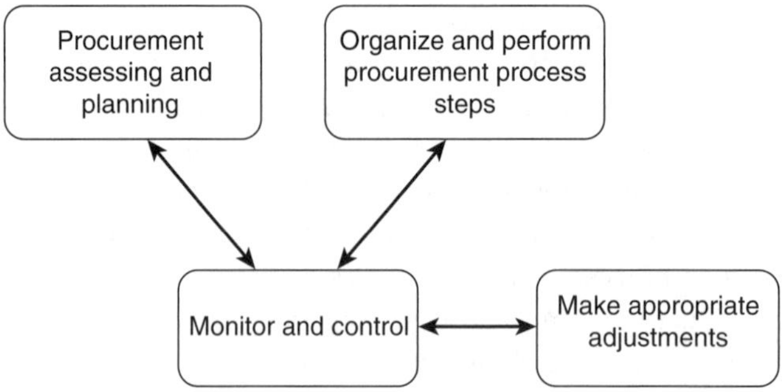

Figure 19.1 Procurement management activities

to be expanded to include "redefining" and "modifying" the procurement process. As the project proceeds, further adjustments to the original plan or process may be necessary. The procurement management activities need to be an integral part of the overall project management.

In smaller organizations where systems and IT projects are not supported by a professional procurement department, the project manager needs to have the appropriate personnel and process in place to perform the necessary contracting and purchasing activities. The "organize and perform procurement process steps" box in Figure 19.1 may include the establishment of a small procurement group. Certainly, such a group must be properly educated on procurement and acquisition processes and methodologies. Where a large portion of the project is dependent upon resource outsourcing or on purchasing technical components, a procurement-related set of management activities will need some extra attention. When outsourcing, and later offshore outsourcing, first became economically popular, many projects failed because the project managers mistakenly underestimated the amount of preparations needed and the amount of risk involved. Contract tracking and control was not done, and projects often suffered in the form of missing milestones, missing product requirements, or exceeding budget. Unfortunately, the blame often was erroneously placed on the contracting vendors rather than on poor procurement management.

PROCUREMENT PLANNING

Procurement planning is composed of two sets of planning activities:

- General business assessments, and
- Specific resource assessments

These topics will be discussed separately.

General Business Assessments

The planning stage of procurement begins with the consideration of general business implications. In large, established organizations that have a purchasing department, the business considerations may have already been established. However, with the ever-changing world, we still need to review the following business-related areas from time, to time even with a well organized procurement policy:

- Core competency and business strategy
- Cost benefits
- Technology trend and strategic alliance

Here we are discussing the purchasing of items directly related to our project, rather than the purchasing of general items such as those related to overhead, which all businesses need to address. Before we purchase or outsource something, it is important to first ask how that decision affects the core business and the business strategy. Before outsourcing the service or the production of some item, it is crucial to assess the impact to the current business, in both the short term and further out. For example, a key technology or a key competency may be compromised if the development of some system involving that key knowledge is outsourced. The friendly vendor who outsourced the activity today may be a future competitor. There needs to be an assessment of business alliance and partnership, both short term and long term, before a supplier is brought into the project. An example from the author's personal experience is a case where systems support activities in a Latin America country were outsourced to a local country vendor. After a few years of good service, the vendor learned the system, gained local customer confidence, and started to develop add-on subsystems. This eventually lead to the local vendor developing a competing system, ultimately turning it into a competitor. Similar cases have occurred in many other outsourcing situations. In large enterprises with well-established procurement departments, some of the general business planning and business alliances are thoroughly explored and considered; thus, individual project teams may not need to repeat the broad business assessment activity.

Cost–benefit analysis is always a crucial activity. The key is to include all the costs and compare them against purchasing the same services or materials from a vendor. Both the direct and indirect costs need to be included. As part of the cost analysis, most large enterprises look to multiple engagements with a vendor to receive deeply discounted bulk rates. Thus purchase orders from multiple projects are often aggregated into one large order. There also are risks in both purchasing and *not* purchasing services. One needs to include the cost of risk containment and risk mitigation (discussed in Chapter 5) for each situation.

Technology trends and strategic alliances are uniquely important for software systems and IT projects due to the significance of technology's impact on these projects. Often, projects involving old technology are outsourced because of their perceived insignificance to the future, and those projects and tools involving new technology are developed internally. However, project management should view this assessment in terms of core competency and business alliance. New technology may be attractive, but if it is not part of the core competency that the business enterprise wants to keep, then establishing a technology alliance with an outside vendor may be a better solution, especially if that vendor already has an established reputation with the new technology.

General business assessment and planning needs to be performed before any individual project commits to the purchasing of a service, a resource, or materials. For many projects, the business side of the enterprise may have already completed the general purchasing planning, a formal purchasing department exists, and many of the purchasing policies are preestablished. However, many smaller establishments do not have a well-organized procurement group, have not thought through all the business implications, and thus should engage in business assessment and planning.

Specific Resource Assessments

The identification of all potential acquisitions is a necessary first step. This identification can be divided into three major parts: (1) the human resources, (2) the service resources, and (3) material resources.

The needs of human resources for a project are part of the up-front planning. During this phase, a portion of the plan should include identifying the necessary personnel. Today's organization is made up of many categories of people: full-time employees, part-time employees, and temporary and contract personnel. Full- and part-time staff members are managed with one set of rules because they are employees of the organization. Temporary and contract personnel require a separate set of rules. While these temporary and contract personnel are folded into the project team, they have to be managed differently from both a cost and a personnel perspective. Most of the time these people are paid at an hourly rate and qualify for overtime pay. They should come with the required skill set. They are just a resource and will not necessarily be afforded any long-term career planning. From a project management perspective, we are procuring temporary resources and special skills. In many cases, project managers must identify a list of special skills that are needed only for a specific period of time rather than for the duration of the project or for maintaining and supporting the project. For these projects, there may be a need for a temporary surge of a large number of programmers or testers. To accommodate a temporary surge in the schedule, a number of skilled temporary and contract personnel must be brought in. The project plan must include the procurement of the number of, and type of, skilled contract personnel. In some situations, the temporary human resources make up the complete team for the duration of the project. The plan should include the schedule and duration of those needs. These resources must be estimated and their cost included in the budget.

Services may need to be procured. Sometimes the procurement service itself is purchased. During the project-planning phase a specific task or service, such as software programming and test environment tools support, may be identified as something that can be purchased. The project plan must list the needed tools and the required accompanying services. The level of service also needs to be clearly specified. For example, requirements such as the 24 × 7 availability of programming and test environment and tools need to be part of the procurement criteria. The vendor, version levels, and acceptable performance level of the tools must be identified. If the service is offshored, the need for proper and adequate support of the service in terms of language, working cultural style, and availability due to time-zone differences should be specified. The costing of procuring an entire service should still include some amount of in-house interfacing with the outsourced service provider. The entire service cost should be budgeted for the estimated duration of the required services.

Many systems and IT projects require the purchasing of existing components off-the-shelf, or COTS. The type of components, the number of these components, and the schedule of when they are needed should be part of the plan. The planning of these off-the-shelf components may be a bit tricky. At the project planning time, the design has not started in earnest yet. Thus there is a high probability of some changes. At the same time, the vendors of the components themselves may create newer and better ones while making the existing components obsolete. There are constant changes and multiple moving parts. Nevertheless, we need to list the specific component required, the number of them required, and when they are needed in the project. Again, the pricing of the components and the budgeting must still be performed during planning, and, if appropriate, the previously mentioned bulk-rate discount across multiple projects should be sought.

One important concern in the procurement of software, hardware, or tools is that they must properly interface with existing components. In the case of software, the task of ensuring proper fit is even more difficult. Consider the example where the procured software uses one set of terminology and the existing software uses another set. This difference in terminology alone will make checking whether the two software components will properly interface with each other a complex endeavor, thereby making the procurement task more than just a matter of finding the lowest cost provider.

Regardless of the type of resources needed, the basic planning steps for resource acquisitions are listed below:

- Identify and describe all potential types of resources and the amount needed
- Incorporate the timing of acquisition into the general project schedule
- Determine the total cost and incorporate it into the overall project budget

In addition, depending on the complexity and size of the project, there may be a need to identify someone to be a permanent procurement interface or liaison to help administer, monitor, and control the procured resources. This level of extensive planning is recommended for large, complex systems projects.

Procurement Process Steps

Once the plan is set, the preparation and organization of the tasks related to procurement still need to occur. The required purchase will need to be clearly written in the form of a Request-for-Price (RFP) and sent out to potential vendors and suppliers. The RFP document is essentially a requirements document for purchasing the needed resources, whether it is COTS, services, or human resources. The responses to the RFP must then be evaluated, potentially followed by face-to-face meetings with a short list of the providers who are chosen after the first round of evaluation. The vetting of the vendors is a time-consuming effort that requires the participation of management, procurement personnel, the contract lawyer or legal administrator, and any necessary technical experts. A set of selection criteria needs to be developed. This set of criteria may be different for each project depending on the goals of the project. For some projects, vendor reputation and sustainability are important, whereas for others, cost may be a significant contributing factor. Some of the common criteria include the following:

- The history, reputation, and reliability of the vendor/supplier
- Past experience with the vendor/provider
- The price of the resources
- The quality of resources and availability of resources
- The degree of fit and completeness of the solution
- Conformance to government or industry standards

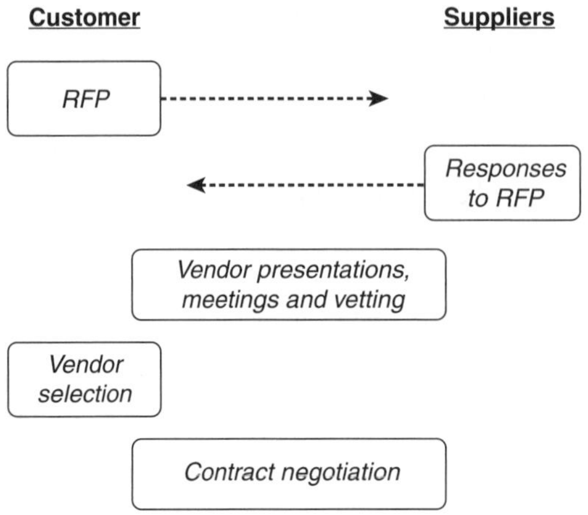

Figure 19.2 Major procurement process steps

Once the provider is chosen, a formal contract needs to be put in place. The formal contract should include a clear description of the level of service, often known as Service Level Agreement, or SLA. This often requires the service of a lawyer, especially for large and complex transactions. Although the formal contract must be reviewed and approved by all interested parties, it also is essential that the project is not delayed or adversely affected by formal and lengthy procedures. Once the procurement contract is signed, the actual administration of the contract through the project may be performed by the procurement liaison. These major steps of administration are depicted in Figure 19.2. As Figure 19.2 shows, some activities, such as the RFP, are completely within the domain of one party. Other activities, such as contract negotiation, span both the customer and the supplier.

Contract and Procurement Monitoring and Control

As with general project management, procurement activities do not stop with the signing of the contract; they must also be monitored and adjusted as the project moves along. To ensure that the resources that are scheduled for delivery do in fact get delivered on time, the procurement liaison needs to monitor the delivery schedule. The quality of the delivered resources must

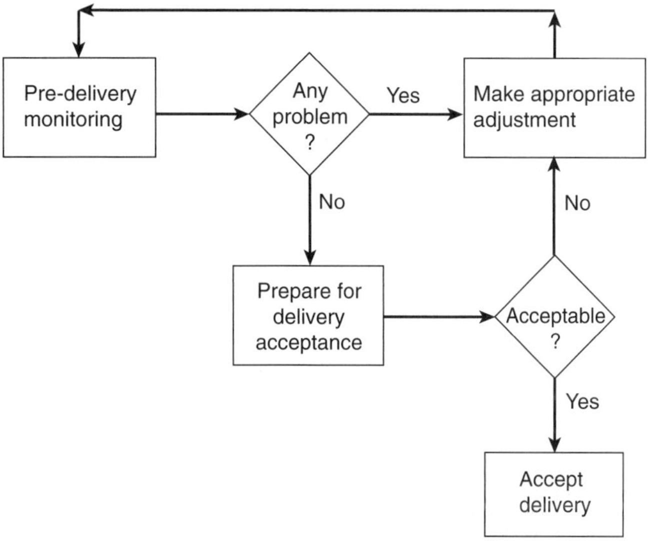

Figure 19.3 Pre-delivery procurement control

also meet the acceptance criteria. Thus the procurement liaison and the project team must be prepared to inspect the delivered product prior to acceptance. If there is any problem, then the impact of the problem must be assessed. Based on the impact analysis and the procurement contract, an appropriate course of action must be drawn and executed. The predelivery procurement control is depicted in Figure 19.3.

Adjustments

In the event that delivered resources are below the contractual level of quality specified in the SLA, one may need to make adjustments to the project schedule and insist on delivery of the needed quality level. In a drastic situation, a change in vendor may be required. The combination of monitoring and making adjustments is depicted in Figures 19.3 and 19.4

After the acceptance of the supplier's delivery, the project still needs to be monitored and controlled to ensure that all tasks are completed to the required target level. Thus post-delivery monitoring and adjustments are still necessary, as depicted in Figure 19.4.

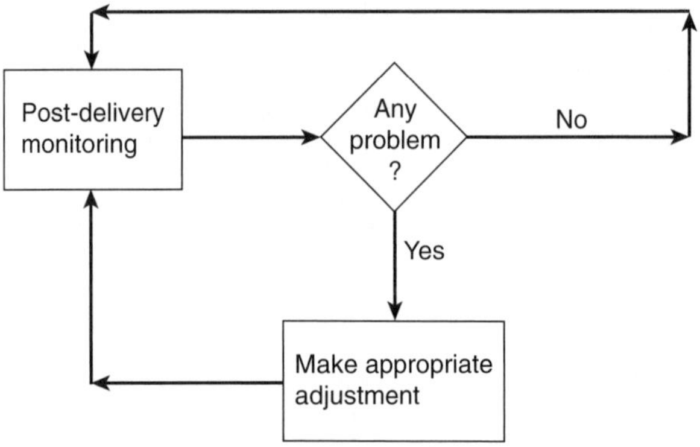

Figure 19.4 Post-delivery procurement control

KEY CONCEPTS

Procurement is a vital component of project management. For project managers, the activities involved in purchasing and procurement do not differ from the main activities of general management. That is, the following four main areas are very similar:

- Procurement planning
- Organizing and performing procurement process steps
- Monitoring pre- and post-deliveries of the purchased resources
- Making appropriate adjustments

Procurement planning is an essential set of activities that should not be short-changed for schedule or cost. The two main components of planning are (1) general business assessments, and (2) specific resource assessments.

The organizing and processing of procurement steps, as depicted in Figure 19.2, begins with the development of a well-thought-out requirements document called the RFP. The responses from the vendors and suppliers are then evaluated, based on a previously determined set of criteria. The vetting and choosing of the final supplier is then conducted, and the winning vendor is chosen. The actual contractual work, and the preparation of the contract document itself, may require the services of a lawyer.

The procured services or products must be monitored prior to delivery to ensure that the schedule, quality level, completeness, and other necessary attributes are met before formal acceptance. After the acceptance from the vendor, the project monitoring must still continue. In both cases, any deviation from the project plan and project requirements must be assessed and appropriate adjustments, if necessary, must be made.

EXERCISES

1. List and describe the main procurement management activities.
2. What are the three types of resources that may be purchased?
3. What is an RFP?
4. List the items that you would write into an RFP for software testers needed for your project.
5. List and discuss three criteria that may be used for supplier selection.
6. Why is it necessary to monitor the vendor before the acceptance of purchased resources?

SUGGESTED READING

R. Adams and S. Eslinger, *Best Practices for the Acquisition of COTS-Based Software Systems (CBBS): Experiences from the Space System Domain*, The Aerospace Corporation Report Presented at the Ground Systems Architecture Workshop (GSAW 2004), Manhattan Beach, CA, March 2004, http://csse.usc.edu/gsaw/gsaw2004/s12/adams_eslinger.pdf, accessed March 2010.

T. Bernard, B. Gallagher, R. Bate, and H. Wilson, *CMMI Acquisition Module (CMMI-AM) Version 1.0*, CMU/SEI-2004-TR-001, February 2004.

M. W. Berry, "Simulating Procurement in the Classroom," *ACM SIGCSE Bulletin*, December 1992, Vol. 24, No. 4, 15–19.

C. Drew, "Gates Tries to Get F-35 Program Back on Course," *The New York Times*, February 2, 2010.

D. R. Kraus, S. Vachon, and R. D. Klassen, "Special Topic Forum on Sustainable Supply Chain Management: Introduction and Reflections on the Role of Purchasing Management," *Journal of Supply Chain Management*, October 2009, Vol. 45, Issue 4, 18–25.

J. Mogilensky, "Future Approaches to Software Procurement," *Proceedings of the TRI-ADA '90 Conference*, Baltimore, MD, 1990, 543–550.

R. Monczka, R. Trent, and R. Handfield, *Purchasing and Supply Chain Management,* 2nd Edition, South-Western Thomson Learning, 2002.

Index